Being Well
When We're Ill

Being Well When We're Ill

Wholeness and Hope in Spite of Infirmity

Marva J. Dawn

Augsburg Books

Minneapolis

BEING WELL WHEN WE'RE ILL
Wholeness and Hope in Spite of Infirmity

Cover design: Brad Norr
Cover image: DAJ, Getty Images.
Book design: Jill Carroll Lafferty

Library of Congress Cataloging-in-Publication Data

Dawn, Marva J.
    Being well when we're ill : wholeness and hope in spite of infirmity / Marva J. Dawn.
        p. cm. — (Living well series)
    Includes bibliographical references.
    ISBN 978-0-8066-8038-5 (alk. paper)
    1. Sick—Religious life. I. Title.

BV4910.D33 2008
248.8'61—dc22

2007040025

Manufactured in the U.S.A.

12   11   10   09   08   2   3   4   5   6   7   8   9   10

*This book is dedicated
to my mother,
Louise Bayer Gersmehl,
who has cared intensely for several people
chronically ill and disabled
with amazing grace and faith*

*and to my husband,
Myron Sandberg,
who has kept me alive
with gentleness and generosity beyond imagining.*

*In memory of Duane L. Vahsholtz (1933–2007),
whose life with cancer inspired my writing,
who died before I could give him the book as thanks,
whose life and death gave glory to God.*

Soli Deo Gloria

Contents

1.　Loss and Finds

Incline your ear, O LORD, and answer me,
　　for I am poor and needy.
Preserve my life, for I am devoted to you;
　　save your servant who trusts in you.
You are my God; be gracious to me, O Lord,
　　for to you do I cry all day long.
Gladden the soul of your servant,
　　for to you, O Lord, I lift up my soul.
For you, O Lord, are good and forgiving,
　　abounding in steadfast love to all who call
　　on you.
Give ear, O LORD, to my prayer;
　　listen to my cry of supplication.
In the day of my trouble I call on you,
　　for you will answer me.

Psalm 86:1-7

When we use the phrase *lost and found*, we are usually referring to an item that we have misplaced, forgotten, or left behind and then recovered, often with the help of a "Lost and Found" agent. We usually experience great gladness when the item comes into our possession again.

This is a book, however, about losses that cannot be recovered. When severe or chronic illness or disability invades, we might lose our sight, our hearing, our physical strength or mobility, our mind. This book is not about those instances when these physical gifts can be restored by surgery or exercise. The losses might be delayed or somewhat softened, but there is no total cure. As my kidney transplant team often stressed, even a transplant is not a cure; it's a treatment. I'll be tied to immuno-suppressants for the rest of my life, and these medicines themselves cause all sorts of damage.

Out of my own experiences of various handicaps and debilitations, I write with the wish that these reflections on physical loss might be helpful to others grieving their own devastations, as well as to those who care for suffering people. May we all learn to cry out to God, as does the psalmist cited above. May we all grow to see the workings of the Triune God in and through our infirmities.

These pages will also deal with spiritual, social, or emotional losses, like the tamping down of emotions caused by my immuno-suppressants. What we lose perhaps cannot be restored in the same forms those elements of our lives once took, but we can experience diverse patterns of powerful healing that take us into wholeness and into new relationships with ourselves, others, and God.

That is why this chapter is entitled "Loss and Finds," for the possibilities for new sources of social and intellectual, psychological and spiritual wellness are as boundless as God's grace. The processes of moving toward and discovering these possibilities, however, require careful attention on our part. Let us engage in these processes together and see what we can encounter for our transformation.

Grief and Hope

These processes always involve at least two parts, which may circle around each other for the rest of our lives. We must acknowledge and lament the griefs of our losses, lest we turn our despair inward and drown in depression. But we are also freed to face our griefs boldly by the assurance of hope given to us through our faith in the Triune God.

That is *much* easier said than done!

Each chapter in this book, therefore, will wrestle with sorrows. People who are not suffering from any difficulties might think that to do so is a "downer," but actually the opposite is true. Genuine lament is good for the soul. For several reasons it helps us if we cry out our anguish.

One is that we realize that we are not alone, that others have struggled with the same sorts of feelings (or lack of feelings!) that we are experiencing. Another reason is that when our distress is brought into the light of day it does not fester in darkness and turn in on itself into such a self-centered focus that we hem ourselves into gloom. Still another is that we move away from any pretending that our society might force on us because other people "need" us to answer "fine" when they ask us how we are. The apostle Paul exhorted us to "weep with those who weep" (Rom. 12:15), so we will do that together in these pages.

But we will not wallow in collective self-pity. For we will also be exploring truths of the Christian faith that lift us up from despair into spiritual well-being. We will discover resources together and find practical activities that can help us deal with our woes. We will examine the Christian hope that "does not disappoint us" (Rom. 5:5).

We will not, however, give glib answers. People with disabilities or chronic illness are certainly offered plenty of those by unwitting people, many of whom love us deeply, but simply don't understand the depths of our sorrows and sufferings.

Instead, these pages will suggest some finds that might be helpful, will struggle with you to get past blockages, will remind you of truths that you no doubt already know, will point repeatedly to the amazing grace that undergirds us all.

My goal is that we all—including me as I continue to grapple with profound losses I have not yet resolved—may be surprised by some finds that we least expected or can't imagine now or never would have thought possible or effective. Some of our best finds might even break out of our worst complaining.

I think, for example, of the Israelites, who griped that the LORD had brought them out of Egypt only to let them starve in the wilderness. Exodus 16:13-15 records what God did in response:

> In the evening quails came up and covered the camp; and in the morning there was a layer of dew around the camp. When the layer of dew lifted, there on the surface of the wilderness was a fine flaky substance, as fine as frost on the ground. When the Israelites saw it, they said to one another, "What is it?" For they did not know what it was. Moses said to them, "It is the bread that the LORD has given you to eat."

In Hebrew the question "What is it?" is the word *manna*. Just as the Israelites were initially bewildered by the LORD's provision of manna (though we should be warned that they soon returned to grumbling), we might be dumbfounded by the bread which God gives us to eat to satisfy the hungers stirred up by our illnesses. It is truly astonishing what spiritual, emotional, and intellectual food might nurture us. Psalm 78:25 even calls manna the "bread of angels"!

One bite of intellectual food that will nourish us when we contemplate texts from the First Testament[1] in this book is the name *LORD*. It will be very important to recognize always that the customary biblical practice of capitalizing the initial *L* and using reduced capitals for *ORD* in that name means that the Hebrew word being translated is *YHWH*, which is often vocalized as *Yahweh* (formerly as *Jehovah*). That is the name by which the LORD revealed Himself* to Moses at the burning

---

*Rightful objections to masculine pronouns for God that oppress women are given more weight since we stopped capitalizing the pronouns and thereby lost the

bush in Exodus 3:14-15. It is a term that distinguishes the God of Abraham and Sarah from all the neighboring, false deities. This is not just any god, but the One alone who is the faithful covenant God, the great "I AM." We need to recover the promise of the name LORD in our times of suffering, to learn the glory of the LORD's constant faithfulness to His covenant and God's effective deliverance of His people from all their sorrows.

The Character of the LORD

For example, the poet of the psalm section cited at the beginning of this chapter calls God "LORD" both times that he asks God to listen to his prayers and supplications. In his neediness, he knows that the covenant God will heed his cries. The name LORD emphasizes promised intimacy. This God who chose Israel to be His own will always keep His promises to His people and, therefore, can be trusted to hear us when we call.

The psalmist also uses the term Lord (the way our Bibles render the Hebrew *adonai*), which highlights the Deity's sovereign power and his own humble submission to the God to whom he turns. By using both the covenant name LORD and the reverent term Lord the poet underscores the fullness of God's character on our behalf.

---

mystery of God's transcendence, which is non-gendered but still can also be personal. Though I try to avoid pronouns for the first and third persons of the Trinity (when it is possible without violating speakable English), we can certainly use them for Jesus, who had to become incarnate particularly as a man in order to offer His countercultural model of servanthood. However, I have returned to capitalizing pronouns for God to emphasize that they are meant to signify not gender, but surprising relational intimacy. Thus, the capitalized words *He, Him, His,* and *Himself* do not signify God's maleness, but carry a sense of the ineffable, the secret yet revealed wonder of the Trinity's immanence. I previously elaborated this idea in a book noted in the appendix ("Other Works by Marva Dawn"). Other ideas in this book which are expanded in other works of mine will be marked with a plus (+), and the works will be listed in the appendix.

The portion of Psalm 86 that heads this chapter was chosen because it illustrates, as will each chapter title in this book, the two sides of "loss" and "finds" that we will examine together. It is not the purpose of this book to look at biblical texts in scholarly depth, but as we ponder the psalm section above we notice a few grieving expressions of loss mixed in together with confident verbalizations of various finds about God that give us hope.

The poet asks the LORD to incline His ear and answer him, for he is "poor and needy" (v. 1) and yearns for his life to be preserved (2). He begs the Lord for graciousness because he cries to God "all day long" (3). He calls "in the day of [his] trouble" (7).

At the same time, the psalmist names the Lord's character as "good and forgiving, abounding in steadfast love to all who call" (5). With assurance he can bring his prayer and cry of supplication (6), for he knows that the LORD will answer him (7). He trusts that the Lord will "gladden the soul of [His] servant," for he lifts up his soul to God (4).

Notice that the poet's statements of struggle are intertwined with expressions of hope. The same is often true in our lives—we alternate between anguish because of our afflictions and affirmations of trust and faith because we are confident of God's care.

But for many individuals the gloomy side seems stronger. Perhaps a person has escalating handicaps, and she cannot see beyond the anxiety over what will go wrong next. What will bring her hope?

Or perhaps a patient was just given the diagnosis of terminal illness. What will ease her fears and intense grief?

These pages will enter into many kinds of struggles as these are encountered by people with severe or chronic illnesses and disabilities. Each chapter will discuss one particular kind of loss (though many of them converge) simply so that we can focus on it more intentionally. Each chapter will also explore one or more specific kinds of finds that are especially appropriate to the loss of the chapter, even though all the spiritual treasures contemplated in this book support and enlarge each other. (To avoid awkwardness, the word *find* will most often be used as a noun to indicate some gifts that help us. I will not use the word for anything else.) The titles in the table of contents suggest the specific losses and finds of the chapters, in case a particular subject is of more interest to you first.

Being Well When We're Ill

The title of this book was carefully chosen. It does not claim that we can *feel* well when we are ill or disabled. It does not even claim that we can *do* well, for we might presently be in a state which prevents us from being able to do much of anything. Nonetheless, it is possible for us to BE well by the grace of God, for spiritual wellness is sheer divine gift. We will, though, receive the gift of wholeness more easily if we know about and are open to its treasures.

We can understand this more deeply through differentiating between care and cure. Our severe, chronic, or terminal illnesses and impairments probably can't be cured, but in the midst of them we can be cared for well by others and can care for ourselves well to the best of our abilities and by God's grace.

Emotional, intellectual, and spiritual wholeness don't require physical wellness. One of the most whole people I know is a woman with Down syndrome who has multiple physical limitations. But she has an eternal Joy (see below) that radiates delight to all who are around her, and her unconditional love for others is the deepest I think I have ever experienced from a friend.

Her secret is her bedrock confidence in the grace and love of God. It is an invaluable "find" that she is more than willing to share with others.

I use the term *find* throughout this book because the word suggests not only the delight of discovery, but also the immense value of what is found. Since statistics show that 45 percent of U.S. citizens have some sort of chronic illness or condition, more than 135,000,000 people are looking for resources to help them cope. I believe that the spiritual resources given to us through faith in the Triune God are the best treasures available. All kinds of finds await us for our well-being because the Trinity has found us first.

Sources and Healers

Many resources have come together to make this book possible. I have read dozens of books on suffering out of my own need for comfort and to prepare for a course that I teach periodically at Regent College in Vancouver, British Columbia, "A Theology of Weakness: Thinking Biblically about Suffering."+ Very few of these books will be quoted specifically, but "Resources on Suffering, Evil, and Healing" in the appendix offers a list of some of the finest. Especially notice the entry for Kathryn Greene-McCreight's book, *Darkness Is My Only Companion.* This is the best (perhaps the only) book I have found that deals with spirituality and mental illness, a topic that will not be considered in these pages because Kathryn deals with it so well from her own experience and theological training.

For almost 30 years I have been working as a freelance theologian, traveling extensively to lead conferences primarily for Christians, but occasionally for interfaith groups. At many of these conferences people recognize my handicaps and come to talk about their own struggles with illness and disabilities. This book includes what I have learned from their stories and experiences, though their names are not linked to specific infirmities to protect their privacy.

Also, many doctors, nurses, and other medical personnel have given me information or examples or personal care. Specifically for these pages and for my present state of health, I am indebted to many professionals who work for Kaiser Permanente NorthWest. There are far too many to name without missing a few, but chiefly Marilee Donovan, supervisor for the pain clinic at Kaiser, and Jeannine Gilkeson, who serves in the Depression Care Management Program, gave tremendous assistance for chapters 10 and 18, respectively.

One of the best gifts to me has been the practice of praying through the book of Psalms every seven weeks, according to the pattern given by the Anglican/Episcopal *Book of Common Prayer*. I confess that I don't always pay attention very well when I am engaged in this practice, but those psalms which are used in this book were generally brought to my awareness through it.[2]

Similarly, these pages have been profoundly impacted because I began writing this book in earnest during Holy Week—and a Holy Week in which my husband and I were extensively engaged in worship because of my commitment to give a Good Friday noon meditation and by our involvement in both an octet that sang special music for Good Friday evening and the Saturday evening Easter vigil and also a choir that sang on Maundy Thursday and Easter morning. We also participated in a contemplative Eucharist service on Monday evening, a Tenebrae service on Tuesday, and a service of Eucharist and healing prayers on Wednesday. Such a daily worship schedule has not been available to me in the past (though since an infant I have always participated in the opportunities offered especially during Holy Week), so I am grateful to the Church of the Good Shepherd (Episcopal) in

Vancouver, Washington, for the influence these worship services had on this book and the remembrances of other Holy
Weeks that these services brought to my mind.

Other sources for this book will be noted in the following
chapters, but these five have been so pervasive that it seemed
essential to name them at the beginning and save extensive
annotation in the rest of the volume. As always, I am astonished that God brings memories, stories, texts, and truths to
our minds just when we need them, so I want to make explicit
what the previous five paragraphs have merely suggested: the
greatest source from which this book comes—as does anything good in our lives—is the grace of the Triune God, the
LORD who always keeps covenant promises to hear us and
answer, to be gracious and faithfully abounding in steadfast
love.

A Text with Which to Proceed

Psalm 126 is one of the "Songs of Ascents" (Psalms 120–
134),[3] which were sung by pilgrims as they journeyed up to
the Temple in Jerusalem for high festivals. The poem includes
the same mixture of rejoicing with hope and lamenting with
loss that this book emphasizes.

> *When the LORD restored the fortunes of Zion,*
>   *we were like those who dream.*
> *Then our mouth was filled with laughter,*
>   *and our tongue with shouts of joy;*
> *then it was said among the nations,*
>   *"The LORD has done great things for them."*
> *The LORD has done great things for us,*
>   *and we rejoiced.*
>
>   Psalm 126:1-3

These first three verses display the great delight of the
people who came back to Jerusalem from the Babylonian

Captivity. They laughed and shouted ecstatically, for the LORD had kept His covenant and returned them to their land.

When I was preaching for a Presbyterian church in Pennsylvania a few weeks ago, the choir sang a wonderful setting of this psalm by Abbie Betinis, whose brilliant composing led each section of the choir to laugh melodically in turn and then collectively. May there be such moments of laughter as we work through this book together—times when flashes of insight cause us to burst with heavenly Joy.

As is my usual custom, I capitalize the word *Joy* so that you will remember that it does not mean a simple exuberance, happiness, or excitement caused by circumstances. I use the word only when I want to signify that deep, abiding confidence, gratitude, and trust that are ours when our lives are transformed by the truths of the Christian metanarrative, especially the Resurrection of Jesus Christ. Just as the returning Israelites shouted with Joy because their LORD had "restored [their] fortunes" and brought them home, so may we find moments of Joy when we come home to the Triune God, whose grace embraces us and enables us to surmount our sorrows.

However, things were not easy for the returning Israelites. They encountered opposition from all sides as they sought to rebuild the Temple and the city walls of Jerusalem (see the prophets Ezra, Nehemiah, and Haggai especially). Consequently, the pilgrim song Psalm 126 also contains verses in which the people turn again to their covenant God for help. (These verses would have been especially poignant in Jesus' time to festival pilgrims who sang on their way to the Temple under Roman oppression.)

> *Restore our fortunes, O LORD,*
> *like the watercourses in the Negeb.*
> *May those who sow in tears*
> *reap with shouts of joy.*

Those who go out weeping,
bearing the seed for sowing,
shall come home with shouts of joy,
carrying their sheaves.

Psalm 126:4-6

When we turn to the LORD again and again in our times of sorrow and suffering, as we will in this book, we will find that the Trinity continually meets us at our point of need and sends us away from it carrying a harvest of comfort. Though we will grieve in our anguish, may we increasingly know that eternal Joy is our present possession. Our call is to be faithful in the sowing and reaping. May we engage in that together in the following chapters.

Each chapter in this book will end with a prayerful hymn or a prayer by a denomination or a faithful saint in the Church.[4] We will use the ancient ritual of the Church in order that we might remember that we are part of the whole Body of Christ's followers. (For the importance of rituals, see chapter 13.)

In the book of Ruth, Boaz goes to the harvest field and says to the reapers, "The LORD be with you," and they answer, "The LORD bless you" (Ruth 2:4). That exchange emphasizes that the covenant God is in our midst to care for us faithfully. What is especially important is that these sentences are not merely church talk, but street talk—or, in this case, barley field talk. In our churches we now say, "The LORD be with you" "and also with you," but let us not lose sight that the exchange is for more than public worship. It can be used in daily life to remind us that the LORD is here and that we belong to a great community, the people of God.

Especially when we use it in this book, may the clauses remind you that we are together in that Body—sharing each other's losses and griefs and also our finds and wellness. You are not alone! You are part of a large company of people who similarly deal with the struggles of chronic infirmity, and the Triune God is in our midst to gift us with wholeness and hope.

 The LORD be with you. [And also with you.] Let us pray:

Almighty and everlasting God, the comfort of the sad, the strength of them that suffer: Let the prayers of thy children who cry out of any tribulation come unto thee; and unto every soul that is distressed grant thou mercy, grant relief, grant refreshment; through Jesus Christ, our Lord. Amen.[5]

2. Loss of Dreams — God's Larger Story

Save me, O God,
*   for the waters have come up to my neck.*
I sink in deep mire,
*   where there is no foothold;*
I have come into deep waters,
*   and the flood sweeps over me.*
I am weary with my crying;
*   my throat is parched.*
My eyes grow dim
*   with waiting for my God.*

Psalm 69:1-3

When chronic illness or disabilities invade our lives, we lose our dreams of well-being, of how we expected to feel each day, of what we anticipated doing in our later years, of what we intended to accomplish with our lives. Some of our dreams are replaced by better ones, as we shall see later in this chapter and in future chapters, but some of our losses leave us inconsolable.

We experience the same sensations of sinking as did the psalmist quoted above, for, as we grieve our losses, we don't see any way out of the flood of our tears. Each realization of another dream lost pushes us more deeply into the mire, and we cannot find a foothold.

Countless people have told me that their life's story has not turned out the way they had wished. Some suffer serious emotional setbacks when all the travel they had wanted to enjoy during their retirement is rendered unachievable because of the onset of cancer or other severe illnesses. Others have had to change jobs because handicaps made their previous work impossible.

The most striking example to me of the latter was Englishwoman Jacqueline Du Pré (1945–1987), who was internationally acclaimed as a cellist already when she was in her teens and whose marriage in 1967 to Daniel Barenboim, an Israeli pianist and conductor, led to even greater triumphs as they performed together. But her career was cut short early in the 1970s when she had to quit playing because of her multiple sclerosis.

Physical losses nullify many other kinds of dreams. Many people are prevented by various problems from having children. For some, life without children is more difficult to take because they grieve deeply that there is no one to whom they can pass on their dreams. In my case, endometriosis necessitated a hysterectomy, and the state of my health together with our ages when my husband and I married later in life deterred us from seeking to adopt.

When I use personal examples in this book, please know that I name them not at all to beg for pity—for the illustrations come from issues on which God and I have been working for many years, and the Trinity's grace has been powerfully given to see me through them. But I will frequently offer my own particular manifestations of loss so that you can know that to a small extent I share your sorrows as you wrestle with your own damaged dreams because of physical limitations. I don't claim that I understand all your sufferings, of course, but it is my prayer that the processes in this book will give insight to you and eventually lead to comfort and a greater sense of well-being in spite of whatever afflictions you endure.

One important process that this book is endeavoring to follow is to name our afflictions specifically. It is really good if we can deliberately lament those devastations (see more on lament in chapter 5). Sometimes if we have not consciously grieved a particular physical loss, it lurks beneath the surface as a dull ache that deepens the mire into which we are sinking. Like the psalmist, we can't find a foothold to dig ourselves out of the bog.

As a guide to lamenting, let the psalm section at the head of this chapter suggest questions to ask yourself for the sake of working through your lost dreams. (Keep remembering that we are just beginning these processes of lamenting our losses and rejoicing in what we find to comfort us. We are not going to break through into unfailing gladness in this one chapter, but we will certainly make some progress.)

Questions to Help Us Name Our Losses

The psalmist's lament shows a progression, from "waters [coming] up to my neck" to "deep waters" and a "flood [that] sweeps over" the poet. How has the amount of your own losses grown?

Try to list the development of your physical limitations or illnesses. Perhaps you were able to handle the first few losses with some (maybe even minor) adjustments. At what stage did it seem that you began to "sink in deep mire"? What were the points at which you felt there was "no foothold"?

For me, that point arrived with a diagnosis of breast cancer just after I'd recovered from two other traumas. After seven months of nearly total blindness because my seeing eye had hemorrhaged, surgery to remove the blood succeeded (though it had failed twice in my permanently blind eye). At the same time an injury to my good foot (the other leg is crippled) had put me in a wheelchair for an extended period of time—but now that wound had healed, and I was rejoicing both to see and to walk again. The cancer verdict seemed to be the straw that broke the camel's back.

Suddenly I found it hard to trust God—and that remains a constant struggle. The deep waters of the psalmist seemed now to have swept over me in a flood. Too many dreams were now dashed. I had to give up long-awaited speaking engagements to undergo chemotherapy after a mastectomy. Writing was made almost impossible by the severe effects of chemotherapy.

Where was God? I was "weary with my crying" of that question.

What dreams have been dashed for you in the accumulation of your physical struggles? Crying over what has worn you out? What has happened to your relationship with God in your weeping? Have your previous notions about God also been dreams that were blighted?

New Dreams to Replace the Old

Cellist Jacqueline Du Pré dealt with the fracturing of her dreams by constructing a new career, even though she spent her last 14 years in a wheelchair. Perhaps her ability to do so was due to her attitude that her former career had been sufficiently satisfying. Once, before airing a recording of her powerful interpretation of Sir Edward Elgar's cello concerto, perhaps the piece for which she is best known, a radio host also provided an interview with her in which she said that she was satisfied not to perform on her cello anymore because she had played every piece that she had ever wanted to play. I wondered in hearing this how long it had taken her to find such contentment.

She did continue with her teaching as before, but also added a new role working as a spokesperson for those suffering from multiple sclerosis. She substituted new dreams for those that were lost.

In another case, a woman whose osteoarthritis made it impossible for her to do the carving that she had loved for years discovered a deeper fondness for playing with fabrics. She told me that she had "fallen in love with color" and enjoyed

immensely using swatches of cloth to make baby blankets and
lap robes that were then sent to shelters and hospitals and
such. Her new dream, like Du Pré's, has a wide impact in serving others.

In both cases, these women compensated for their losses
by finding new dreams, a different story. How have you seen
that happen in your own life?

These new possibilities are good remedies for our suffering, but this chapter is primarily interested in an even better
antidote, in a larger story, the biggest vision of all that enables
us to deal with the loss of our dreams even when they can't be
replaced.

Finding Hope in a Larger Story

The psalm section at the beginning of this chapter turns us in
the right direction, for the poet, whose eyes were growing dim
"with waiting for [his] God," still calls the Lord "my" God.
He still claimed his covenant relationship with God.

What can that relationship offer to us that will ease our
sorrow at the loss of our dreams?

Primarily in our relationship with the Trinity we are
given a larger story than the small one in which we usually
understand our particular lives. The idea to use this concept
of a larger narrative for this chapter was suggested to me by a
new book, John Wright's *Telling God's Story*.[1]

Dr. Wright's book is particularly concerned with preaching, but he analyzes extremely well the critical problem in
North American Christianity that splits believers between
those whose dominant concern is personal salvation and those
who are more interested in social action. He shows how this
division arose and emphasizes that both sides possess too
small a story. Instead, our faith should be rooted in the entire
Christian meta-narrative, the overarching story of who the

Trinity is and what the Triune God has done and is doing for the cosmos.

It is impossible to summarize even briefly the entire meta-narrative of God's good news to us—it takes the entire Bible and all theological discourse throughout history to present it all. A tiny sketch, however, might be sufficient for our purposes here.+

The God who created everything—all the universes that exist—grieved, of course, when human beings fell into sin. But in creating us with free will the Trinity knew from eternity that there was a strong likelihood we would rebel against Him. Therefore, the LORD had to decide to forgive us even before creating us.

For that reason, God had a plan from before time to rescue us—and the rest of the cosmos—from our fallenness. The LORD chose a particular people to be His own and to participate in His work of redemption. Though they were given God's own instructions, the Torah, they failed to be the people He had called them to be. Still, the LORD rescued them again and again from the bondages into which they fell because of their iniquitous ways.

Ultimately they were the people from whom God's own Messiah would come. God became incarnate in Jesus of Nazareth, who was born in suffering and poverty, lived in affliction and persecution, taught while constantly being misunderstood and harassed, was arrested dishonestly and tortured mercilessly, died in the loneliest agony possible, was raised in triumph, and ascended in glory. All of this travail and tribulation was not only to model enduring adversities within God's hands, but also to bear our sinfulness, remove our transgressions and failures, and thereby eventually restore the entire cosmos to its original creation design.

The risen and ascended Lord of all creation then sent His Holy Spirit, who continues to form a people to participate in

God's work of reconciling the cosmos to Himself. Someday Christ will come again, and at that time all sorrow and suffering will be ended forever, as all the powers of evil will be ultimately defeated. All the tears of the poet in Psalm 69 and of all of us will be dried forever as the Trinity accomplishes the recapitulation of the entire cosmos.

I love that word *recapitulation*; it means literally to put the Head back on. All creation will one day be put into subjection to Christ, our Head, and then there will be Joy for aeons upon aeons!

This is the grand culmination of the larger story in which we are a part. Because we are participants in working out God's big dream for all creatures and constellations, we discover that the loss of our smaller dreams is not so tragic as we usually think.

Even the poet of Psalm 69 who felt that he was drowning in the flood of tears sweeping over him later found comfort in the larger story of his Lord. Verses 32 and 33 of the psalm say this about what God has done and the praise and thanksgiving that result:

> *Let the oppressed see it and be glad;*
> *   you who seek God, let your hearts revive*
> *For the* Lord *hears the needy,*
> *   and does not despise his own that are in bonds.*
>
> Psalm 69:32-33

The Lord does not despise our neediness, for Jesus has entered into every kind of suffering we will ever undergo (see Heb. 4:14-16; 5:7-10; and 6:19-20). Even as Christ's story is much larger than His suffering, so our participation in that story frees us from focusing too minutely on our own sorrows. Since Christ "for the sake of the joy that was set before him endured the cross disregarding its shame, and has taken his seat at the right hand of the throne of God" (Heb. 12:2), so we can endure our losses because of the eternal Joy set before us! Meanwhile, "Consider him who endured such hostility against himself from sinners, so that you may not grow weary or lose heart" (Heb. 12:3).

Not only does God's larger story give us hope for eternal Joy, but in the meanwhile it gives us courage for living through our physical limitations and the losses of our lesser dreams.

The Mystery of Our Participation in God's Larger Story

All we can do is stand in wonder and adoration at the mystery of it all. As the writer to the Ephesians concludes the magnificent prayer that asks for their full knowledge of God's love and their strengthening in faith (see chapter 3),

> *Now to him who by the power at work within us is able to accomplish abundantly far more than all we can ask or imagine, to him be glory in the church and in Christ Jesus to all generations, forever and ever. Amen.*

Ephesians 3:20-21

We do not understand how God accomplishes using even our brokennesses for the fulfillment of the Trinity's purposes for the cosmos, but I am convinced that the Holy Spirit does. Just one little example will suggest much wider possibilities than we could ever imagine.

Before embarking on one trip for a speaking engagement, I was complaining to my husband because a problem with my feet had put me in a wheelchair. I did not use this specific vocabulary, but basically groaned that my "dream" of ease while fulfilling my obligations for that particular assignment was "shattered." During the conference a somewhat cynical man came to me after one of my later lectures and said, "I wouldn't believe a word you say—except that you are sitting in that chair!"

I'd had too small a dream. I just wanted my life to be easier by being out of that wheelchair; I hadn't asked God to fulfill His larger purposes of deepening someone's faith precisely because I was in it.

Imagine how a sense of the larger story you are in can give you hope and wellness—knowing that even your infirmities will be used by the Trinity to God's glory.

The Creator of the swirling galaxies has created a place for us in the triune purposes. Can we learn to dwell in God's larger story and thereby imagine bigger dreams for our lives?

> Lord, you have been our dwelling place
> in all generations.
> Before the mountains were brought forth,
> or ever you had formed the earth and the world,
> from everlasting to everlasting you are God....
> Let your work be manifest to your servants,
> and your glorious power to their children.
> Let the favor of the Lord our God be upon us,
> and prosper for us the work of our hands—
> O prosper the work of our hands!
>
> Psalm 90:1-2, 16-17

The eternal God in whom we abide looks on us with favor and graciously prospers all our work. May all that the Trinity has done on our behalf fill us all with Joy and free us from the disappointment of our small dreams in the hope of God's everlasting future!

Methodist minister and author Ernest Fremont Tittle (1885–1949) penned this pastoral prayer that reminds us we are participants in a great meta-narrative.

The LORD be with you. [And also with you.] Let us pray:

Almighty God, who has brought again from the dead our Lord Jesus Christ and given him the name which is above every name, we rejoice this holy day with unutterable joy in thy great power and glory. By the might of thy Spirit quicken us also, we beseech thee, that we may rise to newness of life, and have a part in the working out of thy purpose of good for the world. Pardon and deliver us from all our sins. Bestow upon us thy healing and thy peace. And we beseech thee, grant us light upon our way and needed strength for our pilgrimage, until at length by thy great mercy we come to everlasting life.

We pray to thee for those dear to us who have gone before, whom we now name in our hearts before thee. . . . Grant them thy peace, and in thy perfect wisdom and love fulfill thy good purpose for them.

We beseech thee for our brethren in all parts of the world, and most especially for those who are now in sorrow and affliction. O thou who art Father of mercies and God of all comfort, draw near to those in every place who cry for succor, that they may have hope both for this life and for the life to come.

Pour out thy Spirit upon thy Church, that it may do all which may serve and set forward thy blessed kingdom. And we beseech thee, hasten the day when thy holy will shall be done on earth as it is in heaven; through him who for our sake died and was raised, even Jesus Christ our Lord, to whom be glory for ever and ever. Amen.[2]

3. A Vacuum without God— Spiritual Practices

As a deer longs for flowing streams,
*   so my soul longs for you, O God.*
My soul thirsts for God,
*   for the living God.*
When shall I come and behold
*   the face of God?*
My tears have been my food
*   day and night,*
while people say to me continually,
*   "Where is your God?"*

Psalm 42:1-3

In the last chapter we pondered the overwhelming flood of too many losses—losses of physical capabilities and of our dreams. Now we contemplate perhaps the biggest loss of all—the drought when we can't find God.

The poet of Psalm 42 captures well the yearning and yawning vacuum we experience when we don't feel God's presence. Not only do others say to us continually, "Where is your God?" but we wonder the same ourselves. Even if people say, "God is here with you," we don't *feel* any presence of Christ, any comfort of the Holy Spirit, any love of the Father. All we feel is emptiness, a silent void.

The more our losses pile up, the more God seems absent. The more we struggle to find Him, the farther away He seems. We get caught in a downward spiral of longing that receives no satisfaction, so the hunger becomes intensified, then the lack of an answer becomes all the more apparent, the yearning multiplies, and the vacuum expands immeasurably.

Perhaps you yourself are experiencing such a deep hole of dead feelings, an emotional drought. Where is the delight that you once found in God? Is God even there if we can't feel His presence?

Reasons That Our Emotions Seem So Important

I have felt the emotional drought of not experiencing God's presence since my kidney transplant. It has been a spiritual struggle for me for two years now, but it hit me especially hard this Easter season. I was singing for three different Easter worship services in both a choir and a special ensemble, but the singing didn't lift me to the heights of ecstasy as it had always done in the past before my transplant. Singing for Maundy Thursday and Good Friday services seemed to match my emotional state much more, for if there were any feelings at all they were ones of mourning.

I name this struggle here because some of you reading this book might be experiencing emotional drought for the same reason as I—certain medications level our emotions or amplify our low moods. Also, depression, which we will discuss more thoroughly in chapter 18, robs us of our positive emotions.

At first, many of us blame ourselves. We wonder what is wrong with us that we don't get exhilarated in God's presence (as perhaps we once did). In addition, the more we berate ourselves the more important having positive emotions becomes to us, and we plummet into another downward loop, this one spiraling between self-accusation and a magnified sense that we are missing something critical to our well-being. We equate the actual presence of God with our ability to feel it.

Furthermore, other factors contribute to this over-emphasis on *feeling* God's presence. One element that afflicts many in today's technological society is that children are not hugged enough and affirmed by their parents and grandparents or another individual totally devoted to them, with the result that they do not feel loved and in moments of crisis—such as the onset of debilitations or severe illness—feel abandoned by God.

As an example of technology replacing needed intimacy,+ consider this: a friend who taught in a Christian elementary school once asked her fourth-grade students how their parents tucked them in at night. One boy replied, "Oh, my parents don't tuck me in; they just say 'Goodnight' over the intercom." I worry whether that child or so many other children like him will ever feel embraced by God.

A very significant compendium of educational research reports that children who have not been consistently cuddled, responded to, and affirmed in their first 18 months will have difficulty trusting the rest of their lives. They might be able to learn intellectually to trust, but in stressful situations they will customarily revert to their emotional experience of abandonment.[1]

This research has rung true for several people who have talked with me about their emotional problems as they struggle physically with various limitations and illnesses. They have been hit with a double whammy: first, the sense of abandonment from their childhoods has been a contributing psychological factor in the development of their chronic illnesses, and then that same perception of abandonment prevents them from experiencing in their affliction any feelings of God's love and presence.

Their enormous sense of loss because they do not feel God's love is aggravated by the abnormal priority placed on feelings in U.S. culture. Most advertisements are geared toward emotions, not reason. Decisions to change jobs are often based on sentiments—for example, that the job is not "exciting" enough or not enough fun or not emotionally fulfilling. A high proportion of divorces in our society are rooted in one party feeling that he or she no longer loves the other. Love is treated as a gushy sensation, rather than an act of will.

This cultural fetish with feelings is profoundly disturbing to me. In working with young people I have noticed over the past 30 years that the question concerning moral issues has changed from "What do you think about it?" to "How do you feel about it?" Even more unbiblical is the fact that many people in our society judge a worship service by whether or not it made them feel "uplifted" or "excited." They place more emphasis on what they get out of worship (usually assessed in terms of emotional bolstering), rather than on what they put into it in terms of adoring God, who is, after all, both the Object and the Subject of our worship.+

We bring the same attitude into our personal devotional times and thereby expect that they should result in feelings of closeness to God, rather than in the formation of our selves to become more like God.

"Advice on Disregarding Spiritual Sweetness"

In contrast to our society's mistaken emphasis on positive emotions in our relationship with God, the great Spanish mystic and poet John of the Cross (1542–1591), who is most famous for his reflections on the "dark night of the soul," also wrote a piece called "Advice on Disregarding Spiritual Sweetness." In this work St. John compliments the person who loves God without feeling any emotional sweetness, for that individual is focusing on truly loving God and not the feelings.

To set our will on gratifying and soothing sensations, to concentrate on capturing them and basking in them, is simply to set our will on what God has created, instead of God Himself. Thereby, we turn those created feelings into the end instead of a means—and a non-necessary means at that.

According to St. John, we are ignorant if we suppose that because we fail to have any sweetness or bliss God is failing us. Similarly, we are uninstructed if we presume that in having such delectable emotions we have God. But the height of ignorance, he claims, is if we would follow God only to seek the sweetness and consequently stopped our yearning for God to wallow in delightful feelings when we acquired them.

As St. John concludes, in all these cases we do not purely fix our love on God above all things. If we cling to and long for only what is God's creation, then we actually miss God's true presence, and our will can no longer soar to God.[2]

Even if medicines or depression rob us of feeling God's compassion and presence, even if we suffered abandonment in our childhood and therefore can't feel God's love, and even if our society constantly highlights feelings as the most important part of our existence, we can overcome all these things by realizing that to *feel* God's enfolding is not necessary. The truth is that the Trinity embraces us nonetheless.

The Difference between Reality and Truth

I want to emphasize that word *truth* because it is a concept generally doubted in our present postmodern society. Two of the principal tenets of postmodern philosophy are that there is no such thing as a universal truth and that claims to truth are instead covert power plays. Indeed, the latter has been the case for most ideological truths espoused by governments and for many of the assertions of advertising.

But some truths can't be disputed and are not named to gain power over another. For example, the truth of gravity can't be doubted (apples always fall *down* from a tree), and usually it is mentioned in service to someone else (to warn someone standing under the tree that she might get hit on the head during this season when apples are ripe).

The truths of Christianity have indeed in the past been used to subject peoples of other faiths, and in those cases the violence certainly wasn't in keeping with the way of Jesus! But in general we believe certain truths about the Triune God and the Trinity's compassionate way of dealing with humankind, as briefly outlined in chapter 2 in the sketch of the biblical meta-narrative. We state these truths not to exert power over other people, but to invite them into the glad good news of God's desire to deliver us from our sinful attempts to rescue ourselves.

Furthermore, our belief moves toward knowing because of the testimony of all the eye-witnesses who recorded truths about God in the Scriptures and the millions of saints who have trusted the biblical record throughout history. Consequently, in our faith we count on the truth of God and God's grace and love toward us, even when we can't feel anything.

I write all this about truth because of a very important insight I learned from French sociologist and lay theologian Jacques Ellul. In a very important book for understanding the evisceration of language in our times, Ellul distinguishes between reality and truth.[3] This is an extraordinarily fruitful insight for dealing with the vacuum that we experience when we can't feel God's love or presence.

Reality is what we notice on the surface—what we feel or see, what superficial perspectives we might gain, for example, from television's evening news. Truth is much larger. It encompasses everything that genuinely *is* going on.+

The reality might be that our world looks totally messed up, that war and economic chaos seem to control the globe. But the truth is much deeper—that Jesus Christ is still (since His ascension) Lord of the cosmos, and the Holy Spirit is empowering many people to work for peacemaking and justice building as part of the Trinity's purpose to bring the universe to its ultimate wholeness.

The reality might be that you do not feel God, but the truth is that God is always present with you, perpetually forgiving you, and unceasingly caring for you with extravagant grace and abundant mercy. Not only that, but the very process of dealing with our lack of feelings and our resultant doubts about God is one of the ways by which our trust in the Trinity is deepened. As news reports and a recent book have shown, even Mother Teresa wrestled with her feelings that God was absent.[4]

Thus, we have discovered two very important spiritual practices—I call them practices rather than disciplines because the latter word sounds too much as if we have to force ourselves to engage in them, whereas we engage in practices, such as eating, quite happily. The practice of distinguishing reality from truth helps us not to overestimate the importance of feelings, and then we can find more contentment when we don't have them. The practice of focusing on trust enables us to find value even in the lack of feelings, for the struggle eventually deepens our trust.

Author Flannery O'Connor (1925–1964) is known for her novels and short stories dealing with people's vain attempts to escape God's grace. Before she died of the lupus that crippled her for the last 10 years of her life, she recorded some of her struggles in letters to friends. In one letter to Louise Abbot she wrote,

> I think there is no suffering greater than what is caused by the doubts of those who want to believe. I know what torment this is, but I can only see it, in myself anyway, as the process by which faith is deepened. A faith that just accepts is a child's faith and all right for children, but

eventually you have to grow religiously as every other way, though some never do.

What people don't realize is how much religion costs. They think faith is a big electric blanket, when of course it is the cross. It is much harder to believe than not to believe....

Whatever you do anyway, remember that these things are mysteries and that if they were such that we could understand them, they wouldn't be worth understanding. A God you understood would be less than yourself.

... I don't set myself up to give spiritual advice but all I would like you to know is that I sympathize and I suffer this way myself. When we get our spiritual house in order, we'll be dead.... You arrive at enough certainty to be able to make your way, but it is making it in darkness. Don't expect faith to clear things up for you. It is trust, not certainty.[5]

The spiritual practice of recognizing that Jesus called us to take up our cross (and not our teddy bear!) enables us to live with the uncertainty of abiding in faith. Even though we cannot know or feel with certainty, we can know the Trinity with trust because throughout history God has proved Himself trustworthy and trustable. We find, then, that sharing in the cross is possible because we participate in it with Jesus, whose cross conquered sin and death forever. That we know!

Spiritual Practices in the Word

Have you ever noticed how often the Bible stresses *knowing* God, rather than *feeling* His presence and love? Ponder such texts as "Be still, and know that I am God!" (Ps. 46:10), which is actually referring to resting from warfare and learning to trust that the LORD will provide for our future. In the same way, we can cease from struggling to acquire feelings and let God provide them if they will be spiritually profitable for us.

Or consider this prayer from Ephesians:

I pray that, according to the riches of his glory, he may grant that you may be strengthened in your inner being with power through his Spirit, and that Christ may dwell in your hearts through faith, as you are being rooted and grounded in love. I pray that you may have the power to comprehend, with all the saints, what is the breadth and length and height and depth, and to know the love of Christ that surpasses knowledge, so that you may be filled with all the fullness of God.

Ephesians 3:16-19

We can know that love with all its "breadth and length and height and depth" because God's love has been demonstrated universally and endlessly (notice that the phrase is four-dimensional because of this display throughout space and time).

By what spiritual practices can we know the Trinity's grace and love more deeply? Of course, the foremost practice is reading and meditating upon the Scriptures. Contemplate, for example, this passage from Psalm 146:

The LORD sets the prisoners free;
    the LORD opens the eyes of the blind.
The LORD lifts up those who are bowed down;
    the LORD loves the righteous.

Psalm 146:7c-8

Let us ponder this text especially in terms of our failure to feel God's love. The verses suggest that God will be the one, rather than we ourselves, who will free us from the bondage of needing to feel. Also, the LORD will open our eyes to see ways in which His love has been and is being demonstrated to us. Thereby, the Trinity will lift us up from the discouragement about feelings that has weighed us down. Finally, lest we be dismayed that God loves only the righteous—and we feel anything but!—let us remember that it is the LORD Himself who makes us righteous.

That last sentence offers us another find, the spiritual practice of remembering. Not only do we read and mull over the Scriptures, but we also remember what we have learned thereby so that the truths can continue to help us overcome realities that dishearten us. As Kathryn Greene-McCreight accentuates in her powerful book on spirituality and mental illness, "What will allow for our survival is not how we feel but what we remember."[6]

Let us, then, reflect on and remember three more texts that assure us of the Trinity's love for us. The first comes from the First Testament prophet Isaiah and refers specifically to God's chosen people.

> *But now thus says the LORD,*
> *he who created you, O Jacob,*
> *he who formed you, O Israel:*
> *Do not fear, for I have redeemed you;*
> *I have called you by name, you are mine.*
> *When you pass through the waters, I will be with you;*
> *and through the rivers, they shall not overwhelm you;*
> *when you walk through fire you shall not be burned,*
> *and the flame shall not consume you.*
> *For I am the LORD your God,*
> *the Holy One of Israel, your Savior.*
> *I give Egypt as your ransom,*
> *Ethiopia and Seba in exchange for you.*
> *Because you are precious in my sight,*
> *and honored, and I love you,*
> *I give people in return for you,*
> *nations in exchange for your life.*

Isaiah 43:1-4

We might wonder if such assurance that the people of Israel are precious and honored and loved applies also to us, but remember that the New Testament establishes that believers in Jesus have been grafted onto the root of God's covenant people and that thereby we share in the LORD's promises to them. When I temporarily lost my vision several years ago, a student of mine in a seminary class gave me a Braille pendant that says, "you are precious in my sight." I love touching those words and thereby trusting them more tangibly. Oftentimes in the midst of physical afflictions, I should return to that memorial and thankfully remember how eye surgery effectively restored my vision in one eye.

The spiritual practice of making memorials enables us more deeply to remember what we have learned about God's love. Some people who have spoken to me of their memorials have used their artistic gifts to create paintings, sculptures, calligraphied Bible passages, or other tangible reminders of times and ways in which God has demonstrated His love for them. Others find keepsakes or tokens that signify such events. At the Easter vigil this year, the preacher showed us some shells found on her beach vacations that she puts in her pocket to stir her to remember God's grace. She gave one shell to each family whose baby or toddler was baptized so that together parents and children can remember the baptismal covenant that God makes with us.

As far as I know, Isaiah 43:4 is the only text in the whole Bible in which God specifically tells us that He loves us, but there are plenty of other texts that *show* God's love for us. For example, let us study these words from 1 John:

> *God's love was revealed among us in this way: God sent his only Son into the world so that we might live through him. In this is love, not that we loved God but that he loved us and sent his Son to be the atoning sacrifice for our sins.*

1 John 4:9-10

These words from John's letter have been especially comforting to me ever since a discouraging day many years ago when

I telephoned my college organ teacher and, in despair, asked him, "How can I *know* God loves me?" His response came promptly, "Look at the cross." That very evening the book-marked prayer in the volume I was using at the time began,

> O Thou whose eternal love for our weak and struggling race was most perfectly shown forth in the blessed life and death of Jesus Christ our Lord, enable me now to meditate upon my Lord's passion that, having fellowship with Him in His sorrow, I may also learn the secret of His strength and peace.[7]

God's love is made clear to us at the cross and everything else that surrounded it in Jesus' life. John the Gospel writer highlights this by beginning his account of the night of Christ's betrayal and the rest of His passion with these words: "Now before the festival of the Passover, Jesus knew that his hour had come to depart from this world and go to the Father. Having loved his own who were in the world, he loved them to the end" (John 13:1). He loved us to the end—to the end of His life, to the extreme end of what love could endure, to the end of our ability to imagine such amazing love.

As a third text, let us delve into one of my favorite biblical accounts, that of the raising of Lazarus in John 11:1-44. I memorized that text once in order to preach on it, and the long procedure of committing it to heart gave me plenty of time to ponder it deeply. That leads me to recommend highly to you the spiritual practice of memorization, not just of truths that we know, but also of specific texts.

By the way that Mary and Martha call for Jesus with the words, "Lord, he whom you love is ill" (John 11:3), we can see their confidence in His affection for their brother Lazarus. Can we apply such texts to ourselves? I believe so, for Jesus came to earth precisely to show us the nature of God's love for us. No doubt Mary and Martha had the courage to send for Jesus because they knew that He loved them, too.

John, the Gospel narrator, assures us that the sisters were right by reporting that "Jesus loved Martha and her sister and Lazarus" (11:5), even though His fondness and compassion for them led Him to the strange action of waiting two days longer before He began walking to Bethany. Even so, sometimes God's mercy and love for us take strange forms. That is why we find it helpful to engage in the spiritual practice of resting in the mystery of God's grace.

The Practice of Gratitude

In John 12:1-8, Mary responds to Christ's tremendous love for her family by anointing His feet with costly perfume. By what practices can we demonstrate our thankfulness to the Trinity?

Of course, there are all sorts of ways to express our gratitude, but the most basic one, which we don't do nearly often enough, is simply to say, "Thank you." Or perhaps I should only confess, I do not thank God in any minuscule proportion to the amount of gifts that God showers upon me.

Expressing gratitude is one of the best ways to get past the lack of feelings that I experienced on Easter, as recounted near the beginning of this chapter. We can thank God for the Joy of the Resurrection even if we don't feel it, and, indeed, it is a very tangible offering of gratitude to worship especially when we don't feel like it. Sometimes the very practice of offering appreciation causes us to experience feelings, but that isn't necessary if it doesn't.

Numerous verses in the psalms invite us to bring our thanksgiving and thank offerings to God—to express our recognition of His grace and gifts in words and tangible contributions. Thus, we can pass on our gratitude monetarily or with concrete acts of service to others.

The great wonder of the spiritual practice of gratitude is that usually it enables us more often and more deeply to notice the specific ways that God has manifested His love for us (see chapter 21). I remember once long ago leading a "stacky-uppy" prayer with elementary school children at a camp and urging them to thank God for the gifts from Him that they had seen that day. One of the first participants said, "Thank you, God, for toilet paper." To my shame I realized that I had never before so appreciated that gift. Several years later, when I spent three weeks teaching in Madagascar, I remembered that child's prayer as I first responded to the harsh tissue with complaint, instead of thankfulness that here in the United States we are so spoiled with soft paper.

Other Spiritual Practices

We have found many spiritual practices in this chapter to help us surmount our loss of feelings. We will grow in trust that God is there for us, even when we can't sense it, by distinguishing between reality and truth; recognizing that Jesus called us to take up our cross to follow Him; knowing God better by reading, meditating upon, and memorizing the Scriptures, as well as by remembering truths that we have gained from the Bible; building memorials; resting in the mystery of God's grace; anointing Jesus' feet with our expressions of gratitude.

Besides these practices, we can grow in our assurance of God's love through the testimony of saints throughout time and space. That is why the chapters in this book include prayers and hymns from some of those saints. Other spiritual practices, then, such as singing hymns, utilizing prayer books, reading Christian biographies, pondering Christian art works, and corresponding with missionaries or believers in other countries, give us a much broader, wider, higher, and deeper sense of the love of God the Father, through Christ, by the power of the Holy Spirit.

By means of these and all the other practices sketched in this book—for, indeed, all the "finds" in these pages are spiritual practices of some sort—we can be well, even though our illnesses and disabilities cause us not to feel well or even to feel that the God of wellness is with us. We will be well with the wholesomeness of trusting that God is there, of knowing that the Trinity's grace enfolds us, of remembering all the ways that the LORD's love has been demonstrated to us. As we offer our gratitude to God—whether or not it is with feeling—God will be glorified and the world around us will be blessed, and in that we will be well.

 The LORD be with you. [And also with you.] Let us pray:

I believe, O Lord, but help my unbelief! Do not break the bruised reed, nor quench the smoking flax. O Jesus Christ, Thou who sittest at the right hand of God[,] make intercession for me that my faith fail not. Be the author and finisher of my faith, that I may be able to quench all the fiery darts of the wicked one. Though I see not, let me yet believe and thus be saved. Amen.[8]

4. Meaninglessness—
Looking for Grace

Vanity of vanities, says the Teacher,
vanity of vanities! All is vanity. . . .

Ecclesiastes 1:2

Again I saw that under the sun the race is not to
the swift, nor the battle to the strong, nor bread to
the wise, nor riches to the intelligent, nor favor to
the skillful; but time and chance happen to them all.
For no one can anticipate the time of disaster. Like
fish taken in a cruel net, and like birds caught in a
snare, so mortals are snared at a time of calamity,
when it suddenly falls upon them.

Ecclesiastes 9:11-12

The Teacher Koheleth[1] certainly has it right, doesn't he? The worst problem with chronic illnesses and impairments is that they are often so meaningless. Furthermore, they dominate our lives so much that they render all of life senseless. Truly, all is vanity. Calamity falls upon us, and we feel snared in an endless cycle of nonsense.

Cancer is probably the most meaningless of chronic illnesses. It strikes willy-nilly. We all know too many people who followed all the rules for avoiding cancer and were hit by it nonetheless. One very dear friend of mine lived a calm but active life out in the farmland, didn't smoke, and ate only wholesome food—and not too much of it—yet she died at a young age from metastasized breast cancer. Vanity of vanities!

Sometimes the meaninglessness pertains to non-life-threatening conditions. My left leg is crippled because a doctor misdiagnosed when my foot started to break down with what is called a Charcot joint. It was not his fault—the break was right along the joint lines and could not be seen on X-rays. Consequently, he thought that the swollenness my foot and leg manifested was due to retained fluids, and he recommended walking. Being duly obedient to doctors, I walked hundreds of miles over the course of four months and thereby shattered my foot.

A year after the original break, a renowned orthopedic specialist experimented—removing the middle-foot bones, screwing my metatarsals to my heel, and using pulverized bone to stimulate new bone growth. The result was "perfect," a nice new (and much shorter) foot. I kidded that I looked like two different people in the swimming pool—with one long, skinny foot and one short, thicker foot.

But that surgery changed my standing angle, my leg broke to compensate, and it healed crooked. The surgeon gave me three choices—to rebuild the leg (but then it would break higher up, and eventually we'd have to amputate), to wear a leg brace (which causes ulcerating wounds, which might lead to amputation), or to amputate right away to save the trouble.

I chose the leg brace and have lived in it now for 18 years, with lots of wounds and plenty of time on crutches and in wheelchairs. On all my speaking trips I carry crutches to get into showers or to move at night when my leg brace is off. It is all so meaningless, especially because perhaps 18 years of toils and troubles could have been prevented with the right diagnosis at the beginning.

As you will see below, this is not the whole story, but at times (especially when a brace-caused wound puts me on crutches again) I loathe the vanity of this adversity. The meaninglessness seems harder to deal with than the actual crippling.

The same might be true for you. You have perhaps learned to deal with the pain and the endless routines necessary to maintain your limited physical capacities, but the absurdity of the procedures' necessity is the most demanding burden. The senselessness of chronic illness and disability threatens us with the loss of intellectual, emotional, and spiritual well-being.

Our Attempts to Make Meaning Where There Is None

Our tendency in the face of incomprehensible suffering is to seek some sort of meaning, rather than to find spiritual wellness notwithstanding. I don't know about you, but I always think that if I could just grasp some sort of reason for adversity, then I could accept it. If we could discover some sense in things, we speculate, we could be more patient.

Most likely, we would find intellectual satisfaction if we took that progression in the other direction—that is, if we would simply accept the affliction, then perhaps we could find an answer for the "Whys." (We'll get to some "Why me's" in chapters 6 and 8.) Or at least, in acquiescence, we could stop asking the questions and tormenting ourselves.

We rebel against acquiescence to the state of things because that puts us out of control of our lives, and we have been thoroughly and ceaselessly trained by our society to be in command of our selves. Acquiescence seems like giving up or else like a submission that is slavery. The last thing we want is to be a vassal of our illness.

Emotionally we dig ourselves into holes because of meaninglessness. The harder we try intellectually to create some meaning, the more emotionally exhausted we become because our desire is set on making sense. That also escalates the spiritual danger because the more we long to make sense of things the more our desire is for meaning rather than for God in all God's mystery.

Then we get angry with God because He has made every-thing so obscure. This puts us back to the "Why?" questions. Why couldn't God reveal what value our suffering has?

All this is amplified devastatingly if our affliction leaves us helpless and we are compelled to endure endless days with no point to them. This agony is escalated still more when that persevering comes at cost to those who care for us.

I'm not talking here about the suffering related to an unnecessary prolongation of life. We will look at issues of dying in chapter 19. We are concentrating here on the sense-lessness of illness and disability when life is still strong, but rendered useless, or when less dire hardship prevents us from engaging in what once endowed our life with meaning.

Changing the Question

A first step toward finding intellectual, emotional, and spiri-tual well-being in spite of the absurdity of our physical circum-stances is to change the questions from "Why?" to "What?" and "Where?" and to ask these with an open-minded commit-ment to look for answers. More completely, the new questions are "What is God doing in the midst of this?" and "Where do I catch glimpses of the Trinity's grace?"

The first question is crucial because it changes the axis of our lives. We move from making ourselves the center with a focus on our own intellectual discovery of meaning or emo-tional relief to restoring the prominence of God in our think-ing. We also shift from demanding that God provide answers to our "Why?" queries to listening for what God might want to tell us about Himself and His provisions for us.

As a result we partake in several great finds—the gifts of letting God be God in our lives, of resting in God's mysteri-ous purposes, of humility.

Jesuit priest Marko Ivan Rupnik, who also draws inspi-ration from Orthodox spirituality, invites us into the spiritual attitude of listening. Thereby we are shaped into a constructive (rather than merely passive) "docility." Rupnik writes about humility

> in a spiritual-theological sense in which humble people are the ones who do not find anything certain in themselves to lean on because their only certainty is the Love that the Other has poured out into them. It is the Word that the Other has written within them and that mysteriously raises them up.[2]

Rather than leaning upon our own abilities to figure out a meaning for ourselves, could we humbly learn to rest in the Love that the Trinity pours into us? Can we learn a docility that receives the assurances of the Word Jesus Christ, who mysteriously raises us from our confusion and anguish over the senselessness of suffering?

In one of his reflections, Martin Luther said that it is indispensable that we be "destroyed and rendered formless" (he uses really strong language) so that "Christ may be formed within us, and Christ alone be in us." He even coins a word in Latin, *crucianus*, to say that true Christians necessarily bear a cross to be like Jesus.[3]

But if Christ is so formed in us, then we will trust Him even in the moments when we can't comprehend our suffering, even in the times when we bear what seem like useless crosses. I stress this because I know that my problem with the absurdity of afflictions is that there is still much too much of myself getting in the way of dependence on God and the mystery of Triune wisdom and sovereignty.

When I get so "inward turned," as Martin Luther called the sin of self-centeredness, I miss what God might be doing to bring me to that salutary humility that lets God be God in my life instead of me. When I forget to ask, "What is God doing in the midst of this?" with docility, then I get aggravated that the answers are not the kind I expected.

God has all sorts of responses other than explanations, most of which I neglect if I am so set in my own opinions of what kind of meaning matters. Perhaps the Trinity wants me to learn to rest so that I can receive more deeply the fullness of Three-Personed love. Maybe the LORD wants to show me a new avenue of service or wake me up to the needs of the people around me. No doubt God has all sorts of surprises in store for me if I would just cease my frantic struggling to find the kind of meaning I want.

What about you? Because I need them, too, let's ask the following questions of ourselves together so that they don't overwhelm us: Why do we trust our own intelligence to figure things out? Why do we want so zealously to be in control of our lives? Are we filled with anger against God for not making things understandable? How willing and ready are we to be rendered formless so that Christ alone can be formed in us?

How can we get to that point? We can't just tell ourselves to trust when we don't. And we can't very easily dig ourselves out of the emotional and spiritual holes we have fallen into because of our anger at the absurdity of illnesses and limitations.

What we need is a larger view, a perspective bigger than our own struggles, a vision of grace at work.

Becoming Grace Watchers

A very fruitful spiritual practice in which we can engage to help move us away from our wrestling with meaninglessness is offered by the second question raised at the beginning of the previous section. Instead of the "Whys" that we usually ask as we search for intelligibility, we could inquire, "Where do I catch glimpses of the Trinity's grace?"

This practice was an overwhelming blessing for me during the months when we first dealt with the shattered foot mess sketched at the beginning of this chapter. Myron and I were newly married, and he was busily engaged in teaching fifth grade, so I took the train to Seattle to wrestle with the orthopedic specialist about what we should do now that my leg had broken. I arranged for that appointment to be earlier on the Friday of a Bible study I was to lead for a church in the city.

The assembled group that evening took my prognosis in hand (all three options sounded like amputation to me so I was quite devastated) and decided that I shouldn't be alone for the weekend (I was scheduled to preach on Sunday for the congregation). Someone volunteered to drive three hours south on Saturday to get Myron and bring him to Seattle.

When Myron arrived, a couple from the group handed him the keys to their car and gave him instructions to get to an elegant restaurant. "Have whatever you like," they said. "Dinner is already paid for. You two go and talk this through."

I'm crying with gratefulness as I tell you this story, for the weekend was such a stunning surprise and magnificent gift of grace—and still today the grace of those people makes me wonder why so often I forget the momentous things that God has done in the midst of meaninglessness to help me be well.

Furthermore, at that beautiful dinner my husband of less than a year reaffirmed his commitment to me and promised that he would stand by me no matter what kinds of illness and disability afflicted me. And throughout the years of this particular handicap there have been zillions of glimpses of God's grace in the midst of the strains—train conductors who helped me board and disembark on crutches; an artistic brace maker (he's also a sculptor) who makes orthotics that fit well; multitudes of people at speaking engagements who've helped me get around on crutches; a great podiatrist whose surgical and caretaking skills keep wounds from immobilizing me. The list could go on and on.

What about you? From what surprising directions has generosity come to you? What people have been special bearers of God's grace for you? How have you caught glimpses of the Trinity's mercy even in the most arduous trials? Most important for the topic of this chapter, how have those glimpses enabled you to find wholeness and hope in spite of the loss of meaning in the situation?

Participating in Christ's Passion

One of the most important aspects of grace that we discover as we watch God is that the Trinity has specifically undertaken, through the Incarnation of Jesus in history, what was necessary to share our sufferings thoroughly. Consequently, another spiritual practice that enables us to find wellness—and meaning—is to recognize the mystery that even the most incomprehensible adversities knit us to Christ and the grace of His passion. Jesus bears our sufferings not only for us, but also with us.

The totality of our union with Christ in suffering is an awe-full mystery. It is astounding to think that the apostle Paul[4] could write to the Colossians, "I am now rejoicing in my sufferings for your sake, and in my flesh I am completing what is lacking in Christ's afflictions for the sake of his body, that is, the church" (Col. 1:24).

We don't participate in Christ's ordeals for the sake of the redemption of the world, of course, but for the sake of building up the Body of Christ, the universal Church. It is indeed a mystery, though. We never know how what we are going through can be beneficial for others or an offering to God, but it is. Even more, God takes everything—all that we are and experience—and knits it to Christ's cross.

Let us listen again to Marko Ivan Rupnik, who writes,

In pastoral work I have noticed that failures and sufferings of whatever type are great obstacles along the journey of the spiritual life. Every personal story leaves its marks on the psyche. . . . All these realities are in and of themselves very close to Christ, intimately tied to his paschal drama.

[The culture around us, however, in various ways] warps and blinds us, impeding us from seeing the relationship between our wounds and traumas and the drama of our Lord's Passion. . . .

I mean to say that even psychological suffering, even a disorder in our personal make-up, even a failure can communicate God, can become a remembrance of God and our participation in his Passion.[5]

What tremendous meaning it gives to our tribulations if they are enfolded in the Trinity's purposes and the global significance of Christ's trials!

Such good news might be hard for us to believe. Especially if we have contended with meaninglessness for quite a while, to catch sight of such a find full of meaning might be inconceivable or, perhaps, even too difficult to accept. How can our miseries accomplish anything? How can we in our weakness offer some good gift?

Seminary professor Chris Erdman recognizes our difficulty and writes, "Humanness, especially suffering, inducts us into the life of Christ, who suffers and is 'effective' *because* of suffering. That we don't understand this, or welcome it, doesn't make it untrue."[6]

If we have come to believe that the Trinity's love and grace compelled Christ to become incarnate to bear our humanness, then we realize that He probably was tempted to despair because of meaninglessness when He was on the cross. He who "in every respect has been tested as we are, yet without sin" (Heb. 4:15) indeed participated in the same

torments as we do, yet overcame them all by committing
Himself into His Father's hands (Luke 23:46).

As we learn ever more deeply that our miseries are "intimately tied to the paschal drama" (using Rupkin's words), the
more we can practice—with Christ—commending our spirits to the Father by the Spirit's power. In such a trinitarian
entrusting, we can rest from our attempts to find any other
meaning.

Learning from Hannah

John White, a psychiatry professor and author of a classic
book on prayer, draws from the biblical story of Hannah (in
1 Samuel 1–2) a lesson in finding meaning in the midst of
senselessness. Remember that Hannah was childless and bore
the taunts of her husband's other, fertile wife. But, according
to White, though Hannah suffered emotional agony, she was
never just "a pawn in God's historical chess game." Indeed,
the LORD had a much greater gift for Israel in the prophet
Samuel, and that larger design was lovingly connected with
His gracious intent for Hannah. "He led her gently through
suffering that he might enlarge her capacity for joy."

White deduces, "Personal suffering is never meaningless for the child of God. You may not know why you suffer,
and your suffering may seem to you too painful to bear." But
guided by Hannah, we can be bold to bring our concern for
meaning to God and implore the LORD to free us from it.
We can even praise God in the midst of our travails because
we have learned from the Scriptures that He is faithful and
committed to us. The Trinity might have much wider plans to
accomplish all sorts of things through our anguish that will
unfold considerably beyond our own existence and era. We
also may be increasingly equipped by our own suffering to
bring gifts of our finds to others in affliction.

As White concludes, "[God] may change the course of history through your pain, but you may never discover its wider meaning."[7] Even though we may never observe the significance, it is exceedingly comforting and meaningful to think that our little pebble of suffering offered in sacrifice to God and thrown into the pool of history might create endless ripples of blessings for others. Even now there are many who need to know what we have learned about meaning through Christ.

Passing on the Finds

One other find that helps me in the travail of looking for meaning is the realization that a good proportion of people in our culture are searching for it, too, even though their quest does not originate in the absurdity of physical suffering. I don't mean that I wish meaninglessness on anyone, but that it comforts us to know that the pursuit is not unique to those dealing with physical infirmities.

In fact, some of the people, especially youth, who have talked with me about the search for meaning have had too many good things. Folks discover, for example, that the acquisition of an elevated position, possessions, popularity, or power has not satisfied them, that such accumulations all turn up empty in the end. Those who locate meaning in their beauty or fame discover that it fades. People who place their lives' significance in what they accomplish encounter the truth that one will always long for ever greater achievements.

It is a biblical truth, noted especially by the Teacher Koheleth. "What do mortals get from all the toil and strain with which they toil under the sun? For all their days are full of pain, and their work is a vexation; even at night their minds do not rest. This also is vanity" (Eccles. 2:22-23).

There are innumerable reasons why people strive unsuccessfully for meaning. My point here is simply to suggest that as we find solace that frees us from the endless quest and as we discover our meaning in the Triune God we have enormous gifts to offer those around us.

Moreover, the very offering of these finds fills our lives with new meaning. We want others to know the Joy of entrusting ourselves to God, the relief that comes from letting God be our meaning, the rest that ensues when we give up the useless struggle to solve the intellectual problem of what seems to our human eyes to be absurdity.

A Concluding Word

Against the meaninglessness of our physical distresses, we have God's promises. One of my favorites is a promise given to the Israelites. It is a pledge made to that nation, so we can't too hastily apply it to ourselves as individuals, for it refers to the LORD's deliverance of His people from the Babylonian Captivity.

However, the more I have pondered the text, the more I observe that the Scriptures contain many such promises of God's covenant care for us and the more I comprehend the fullness of the Trinity's enfolding love. Therefore, I don't think we do a disservice to the original meaning of this text to let it speak to us afresh.

Perhaps you can find this text salutary for being well the next time you are tested by the apparent meaninglessness of your sufferings:

> *For surely I know the plans I have for you, says the LORD, plans for your welfare and not for harm, to give you a future with hope. Then when you call upon me and come and pray to me, I will hear you. When you search for me, you will find me; if you seek me with all your heart, I will let you find me, says the LORD . . .*

Jeremiah 29:11-14a

The LORD be with you. [And also with you.] Let us pray:

Merciful and healing Lord, for some reason which I do not understand the usual pattern of my daily life has been disrupted. . . .

Lord, sit beside me now and help me to learn the purpose which this illness is to accomplish. Help me to see how much and how often I have relied on my own strength, my own cleverness, my own ability.

Forgive my pride that will not let me depend on you.

In my illness help me to see that I am truly well when I remember that I belong to You. . . . Fill me with the life of the Spirit, that in Christ I may be blessed and be a blessing to others.

Hear my prayer in Jesus' name. Amen.[8]

5. Loss of "Innocence" — Lament

Help, O LORD, for there is no longer anyone who is godly;
> *the faithful have disappeared from humankind.*
They utter lies to each other;
> *with flattering lips and a double heart they speak.*

Psalm 12:1-2

O LORD, how long shall the wicked,
> *how long shall the wicked exult?*
They pour out their arrogant words;
> *all the evildoers boast.*
They crush your people, O LORD,
> *and afflict your heritage.*
They kill the widow and the stranger,
> *they murder the orphan,*
and they say, "The LORD does not see;
> *the God of Jacob does not perceive."*

Psalm 94:3-7

Our personal suffering from chronic illnesses and disabilities almost always brings to our attention the greater sphere of suffering in the cosmos. We "lose our innocence" about the goodness and safety of the world, and we feel more vulnerable to its malevolence and insecurities. Though events in history constantly alert us to tragedies on a societal scale, our own particular struggles against forces larger than ourselves more deeply link public and private disorders in our consciousness and amplify our introspective awareness of the reign of evil.

Initially that might happen, for example, because as we try to care for our maladies we catch ourselves battling against medical costs, government regulations, health maintenance organizations' (HMOs') restrictions, or other forms of injustice. We cry with the poet of Psalm 12 that people in the medical system seem only to "utter lies . . . with flattering lips and a double heart." No one appears any longer to be godly.

Then we begin to recognize that other people are also contending with the same systems that oppress us. With dismay we look around our nation and then, with more horror, the world, and we realize with the author of Psalm 94 that the wicked seem to be triumphing. People throughout the globe are being crushed and afflicted. Especially the poor—the psalm's "widows" and "orphans"—are being killed. As I write this, "universal" (that is, for U.S. citizens!) insurance coverage has become a primary campaign issue because such a large proportion of the nation's population exists without it. But what about all the people in other nations who have no access at all to even the most basic health care?

It might not have been your own battles against medical injustices that awakened you to the greater sufferings of people throughout the globe, but perhaps you agree that one of the "benefits" of living with infirmities is that they cause us to be much more sensitive to others' afflictions. I put the word *benefits* in quotation marks because some might wonder if it really is an advantage to be more aware of, and usually thereby more depressed about, all the evils we see. But the meta-narrative of how the Triune God cares for the cosmos frees us to bear the pain of awareness and to become more astute in finding ways to counteract the destructive forces that cause suffering. This chapter will explore how we can truly be well (rather than "innocent") in the midst of the world's evils.

Meta-Narrative

Chapter 2 introduced the find of the Christian meta-narrative to help us with our lost dreams by immersing us in a bigger story, the vision of our participation in God's grand work to recapitulate the cosmos. The meta-narrative is particularly important also for this chapter because it enables us to hope with a hope that will never disappoint us (Rom. 5:5) in the face of our growing recognition of all the evils and sufferings in the world. Then, because we are buoyed by that unshakeable hope, we are more able to become involved in the Trinity's purposes to bring healing and justice to those afflicted and oppressed.

The structure of the chapters in this book with their two major parts—grieving our various losses and focusing on particular finds that help us move beyond those losses—reflects the meta-narrative of the cosmos. The Bible is full of descriptions of evil, all the forces that cause it and all the forms it takes. This is the reality of the world, and Christians are not unrealistically optimistic.

On the other hand, the Scriptures constantly affirm the greater truths that God cares about all who suffer because of this evil, that the Trinity has done and is doing all that is necessary to conquer it, and that we have the privilege of participating in what God is doing to rescue the world. So Christians are not disbelieving pessimists. The truth sets us free to be realistically hopeful.+

So that we can be hopeful realists, we need to understand more thoroughly the larger forces that constitute some of the sources of pain and suffering. In this chapter we will not discuss Satan or the devil, evil angels or demons, or any other non-material beings. Nor will we reflect on human beings gone amuck. Our concern instead is for discernment of the workings of the principalities and powers, for this is a level of evil that is often misunderstood and not attended to frequently.

Principalities and Powers

The biblical vocabulary shows that the principalities and powers are neither unearthly entities (as some modern novels claim) nor simply human beings operating in devilish ways. Rather, the powers are on an intermediate level and combine elements of the other two—exhibiting supernatural power, but linked to human institutions or cultural fabrications.

These three levels of evil are emphasized in Martin Luther's explanation that our life in the Trinity is always being opposed by "the devil, the world, and our flesh"—that is, the supernatural forces of evil, those principalities that are superior powers in our world, and our own sinful inclinations. The baptismal services of many denominations include these three tiers of evil when the candidates and all those present who would like both to renew their baptismal covenant and thereby to reject evil respond, "I renounce them," to the following three questions:

> Do you renounce Satan and all the spiritual forces of wickedness that rebel against God?
>
> Do you renounce the evil powers of this world which corrupt and destroy the creatures of God?
>
> Do you renounce all sinful desires that draw you from the love of God?[1]

It is the middle level of evil that we are fighting when we have to deal with the various systems that make taking care of our chronic illnesses and disabilities difficult.

For example, think about the power of money. It becomes a god in our lives when we let it usurp the place of the only true God (see 1 Cor. 8:4-5). Then we call it Mammon, a term which enables us to distinguish between the goodness of money and the evil of letting it become lord of our lives.

Mammon is one of the principalities and, as such, it exerts undue power in such dimensions of life as medicine.

For example, sometimes pharmaceutical corporations make bad decisions because they are too influenced by the goal of making a huge profit. Some systems, such as Medicare or HMOs, are occasionally prevented from doing what is best for a patient because of financial restrictions.

That is why it is important to understand the principalities and powers. Ephesians 6:12 tells us that our battle "is not against enemies of blood and flesh," but against the powers as well as "spiritual forces of evil in the heavenly places." The latter we can't understand, but the powers we can recognize and do something about.

By acknowledging the power Mammon, for example, in many medical decisions, we will not blame flesh-and-blood doctors or pharmacists. By not seeing evil in them personally, we are more likely to be able to work in partnership with them to find the best way to offset the workings of Mammon.

Don't be bothered if you can't understand the principalities. The Bible never describes them or tells us their essence. We only know how they function, as described below. And we do know what to do about them. We can, for example, sometimes bring about changes in our medical systems so that they serve us better.

If we briefly sketch what we do know from the Scriptures about the powers, we will be more prepared to recognize their functioning in the distresses of the world around us. We will also be empowered by that understanding to engage in combat against them for our own sake and on behalf of others. By dealing with the powers of organizations, such as HMOs, we can often benefit other patients beside ourselves.

Colossians 1:16 makes it clear that all things, including the powers, were created in, through, and for Christ. Along with all the rest of creation, the powers were created for good. This is important to remember because it gives us courage to work to restore the powers to their proper vocation. For example, government (one of the powers) was created for the well-being of the citizens it rules. When government regulations harm those who are ill or disabled, then the way to proceed is to help the administration and legislature recover their warranted roles.

We are vigilant to hold the principalities to their divinely-given vocations because the powers do indeed share in the fallenness of the cosmos. As Romans 8:19-22 accentuates, the creation "was subjected to futility" and is in "bondage to decay." Paul adds that "the whole creation has been groaning in labor pains until now."

Because the powers are fallen, we need to watch them closely. We constantly have to guard lest money become a god in our lives, through coveting or hoarding or because we're not generous or gracious with it. In the same way, but on a much larger scale, the financial dealings of medical corporations will tend to act fallen, so we all need to be watchful lest patients suffer because of corruption, dishonesty, fraud, and deceit.

We are encouraged by knowing that none of the powers can ultimately keep us from God's care for us. Romans 8:38-39 underscores that nothing in all creation, particularly the powers, "will be able to separate us from the love of God in Christ Jesus our Lord." Since we know that God is on our side, we have more courage whenever we have to engage in combat against the powers, and we know that God is with us even if we can't do much about them.

Though we keep remembering that the powers were created for good and keep offering excellent gifts for human life, we also realize that various powers continually interact with one another and amplify each other's ill effects. This explains, for example, why people in the Two-Thirds world are so poor.

Wealthy nations and their consumerism, multinational corporations and their global dominations, the World Bank and its interest, the effects of technology and the media, and

so forth all work together to prevent poor nations from getting out of debt. Furthermore, poverty prevents the people
from getting proper nutrition and medical care, and that in
turn makes them even less able to work to get themselves
ahead. Texts like Ephesians 6:12 and Colossians 1:16 list "the
powers" along with other forces to indicate this kind of inter-
action between various agents of evil.

Furthermore, aspects in one power are linked to elements
in others, and these, too, multiply the ill effects. For example,
so much money is needed to win elections in the United States
(19 months before the 2008 election newsjournal columnists
claim it will be a $5 billion election!) that many superb aspi-
rants cannot compete for any government office. The result in
the past has been that some of those who care most for the
poor and ill are not those elected to do the congressional vot-
ing that affects government budget allotments for economic
aid to developing nations and those in poverty or ill health in
my own nation.

The great good news that commissions Christians to contend against all the powers is that Christ has conquered them
at the cross and empty tomb. They are ultimately defeated!
Meanwhile, we engage in skirmishes with them to prevent
their fallenness from dominating the world. But texts such
as 1 Peter 3:22 and 1 Corinthians 15:25-26 reassure us that
Christ will finally put all enemies into subjection to Him.

How We Battle the Powers

Two texts are especially important for our knowing how to deal
with the principalities. Colossians 2:15 gives us the model of
Jesus, who made a "public example" of the powers (by reveal-
ing the workings of Mammon in Judas, unjust government in
Pilate, and adulterated religious institutions in Caiaphas and

others), thereby "disarmed" them, and triumphed over them. In the same way, we often can take away the power of principalities by making public their misdealings.

For example, when the amount of interest that world financial institutions were charging poor nations became more widely known, many citizens became involved in the Jubilee 2000 campaign to forgive poor nations their debts so that they could use their limited funds for more constructive projects than interest repayment. Similarly, as more people become aware of the huge number of people, especially children, who have no medical coverage in the United States, government leaders are recognizing that this must change.

The other crucial text is Ephesians 6:10-20, which underlines that we deal with the powers by becoming "empowered in the Lord and in the strength of His might" (my translation of the Greek text of v. 10). That triple enablement gives us hope for the struggle! The text also emphasizes that we "stand against" the powers with weapons of truth (see chapter 15), righteousness, a readiness to bring peace, faith, salvation, the Scriptures, and prayer.

We don't have space here to delineate all the kinds of principalities that we deal with among various human institutions, nor to sketch ways that righteousness, faith, and salvation become important weapons for our combat against them.+ But we should certainly stress how important it is that we conduct our methods peacefully. Our goal is to win people over to biblical ways of thinking about human suffering, and that, of course, cannot be accomplished violently. The better we know the Scriptures, furthermore, the more thoroughly we will know that our calls are in keeping with God's will.

Verse 18 accentuates prayer as an especially crucial weapon for contending against the powers. That is why the main find of this chapter is the gift and tool of lamenting.

Lament

For this chapter principally, but also in other instances in this book, it is vital that we know not only that laments are expressions of deep sorrow or grief and that to lament is to weep, rage, or mourn, but also that the biblical laments are held collectively by all of God's people. Even though individual laments constitute the largest category of prayers in the Psalter, yet those personal cries have been made communal by including them in the Scriptures.

In other places in this book that mention our lamenting cries to God, we might emphasize more our private groaning, but, when we are concerned for larger societal or global ills, the more public the lament the better.

In keeping with the Colossians text above that showed Christ making a public example of the powers, ethics professor Stanley Hauerwas defines a lament as "the cry of protest schooled by our faith in a God who would have us serve the world by exposing its false comforts and deceptions."[2] That is, the people of God (Jews and Christians) have given us (through teaching us the Psalms) a pattern by which we can reveal to others the workings of the powers.

The Church not only teaches us how to lament; it also joins in with our laments as a social body. Even more than that, through the Church's instruction in the Scriptures, we have learned that we lament along with God, who surely grieves all the world's evils. In fact, no one can be truly well (or in tune with God) who does not, with the wholeness of God Himself, lament all the suffering throughout the globe.

We see that wholeness in all the psalm laments, for every one of them (with the notable exception of Psalm 88) makes a dramatic turn from pouring out grief, rage, or bewilderment to a promising trust and hope in God. And even Psalm 88, though ending in solitary darkness, contains many cries to the

LORD, which indicates that the sufferer still hangs on to hope in God's covenant faithfulness.

The psalm laments are very realistic—they wail out the poets' anguish because of illness, death, allegations, imprisonment, or adversaries. But laments include not only complaints; they also contain specific cries to God for deliverance from those woes and then usually end with an affirmation that the LORD is trustworthy and attentive to our sorrows. Different psalms give various proportions to these aspects.

The same is possible for us. Sometimes when we lament, we might spend days (or months or years) in the complaining stage. Usually, though, we come to the end of confidence in ourselves quite soon and move to the stage of crying out to the LORD for rescue. But even if we can't make that shift for a while, the lament is good for us because God hears our complaint no matter if we don't direct it to Him.

As we grieve (or whine, which God also receives) and scream for release from our woes, the Holy Spirit starts speaking to our hearts and minds and gives us not only assurance that God indeed listens to our cries and answers them with love, but also ideas for what we can do about our situations. Then we progress to the stage of putting legs on our laments.

Of course, the most important arms and legs of action to put on our laments are those (metaphorically) of God. We don't know how it is that our petitions for ourselves and intercessions for others cause the Trinity's engagement, but the Scriptures constantly assure us that they do. It is important for us to note this specifically that God Himself answers our prayers because of two extremes that sometimes characterize Christians' doubts—one, that God expects us to do all the acting on our prayers or that prayer simply changes us and not God and, two, that it demonstrates a lack of trust in God if we ourselves take action to have them answered.

The latter causes a passivity that denies God's call for us to be engaged in the Trinity's purposes to bring about the well-being of the world. The very facts that the LORD chose a people to be His own and that Jesus began the Church by selecting disciples to become occupied in fulfilling His mission show us our own vocation in the meta-narrative of the Kingdom.

The first extreme that causes people to bear all the burden of answering prayers doesn't recognize all the ways that God acts, including stirring up other people to join in our lamentings and undertakings. This extreme perspective imagines that God is passive.

Let us, then, for the rest of this chapter envision just a few ways that God and we can be engaged together in answering our laments to expose, disarm, and triumph over the principalities and powers.

Putting Legs on Our Laments

I hesitated to put this chapter in this book because some might wonder why they should bother with the principalities and the powers when they have enough on their plate just to deal with their own afflictions. And it is true that many who suffer from chronic illness and impairments are not able to be very energetic or to do much to combat the powers' workings—EXCEPT that they can be vitally engaged in laments and intercessions for those oppressed by the powers. Such prayers are actually the most important thing we could do, though in our activist culture many people think of prayer last. The Scriptures promise us that "the prayer of the righteous is powerful and effective" (James 5:16b). Prayer is the culminating weapon in the Ephesians 6 list of the armor we put on to deal with the principalities, so it is a crucially significant ministry that the suffering world needs many of us to undertake.

Sometimes our laments take practical shape, and we can be God's servants in effective change. As a very minor example, many years ago I whined frequently because the blood glucose meter supported by the HMO to which we belong was not very easy to use if a person has visual limitations. Then I started complaining to my doctor, who shared my concerns. That led to writing out a lengthy list of disadvantages to the machine and a suggestion for an alternative that worked much better.

I'm sure mine was not the only complaint that precipitated an adjustment, but the HMO did switch to the alternative meter. Perhaps in a small way my lament contributed to making things easier for other diabetics.

On a much larger scale, our laments can instigate changes that help multitudes of people. A prominent example is the ONE campaign, designed to persuade the U.S. government to devote an additional 1 percent of the whole national budget to poverty-focused development in the world's poorest countries.[3] The cries of many people on behalf of the poor could lead to a major change in budgetary allotments and development policies and then in the state of poverty worldwide.

Many people are concerned for medical care in the United States. The more of us who convey those laments not only to God, but also to our representatives, senators, and president, the more we put legs and arms on our prayers.[4] There is great power in communal lament! If our elected leaders hear from enough of us, they comprehend the "will of the people" and are more likely to act on our wishes.

Of course, we can't limit our dedication to decent medical care to just U.S. residents when so many in the world suffer from chronic illness. Laments are especially urgently needed for the widespread sufferers from the AIDS epidemic and from the ravages of malaria, which is being extended by global climate change. Our prayers are given hands when we contribute financially to networks that provide medical expertise, medicines, education, and care for the orphans left behind—such as the Evangelical Lutheran Church in America's "Stand with Africa" program.*

We can also pass our desires for change on to agencies that advocate on our behalf. I'm thinking of such conduits as the American Association for Retired People (AARP) or the Gray Panthers, who have done much to secure justice for older people. We can lament to a host of organizations committed to specific medical needs.

It is also especially valuable if we lament in ways that raise awareness. Probably the most famous person doing that is the rock star Bono of the band U2, who has done more than perhaps anyone else to awaken people to issues of global poverty.

Of course, we don't have the stage that Bono has, but we can lament in public by writing letters to editors or articles for newspapers and other journals. More simply, writing a bulletin announcement or a piece for our church newsletter can enlist our local congregation in lamenting and standing against the workings of the powers.

These are just a few examples to set your ingenuity going. When we bring our laments to God frequently, the Holy Spirit moves in us to help us discern ways that we can live our laments for the sake of being well in the face of the powers. May the Trinity enlarge our imaginations!

And may the LORD bolster our hope as we reflect on the final lines from some laments that were assigned for my

---

* Because this book is devoted to alleviating the sufferings of those with chronic illness and impairments, all its royalties are being directed to "Stand with Africa," specifically to fight AIDS and malaria. For more information, please contact 1-800-638-3522, ext. 2757, or to contribute financially, send your gifts to "Stand with Africa," ELCA World Hunger Appeal, P.O. Box 71764, Chicago, IL 60694-1764.

prayers today. I'm frequently astonished at how the readings for the day match my needs. (Talk about the mystery of God—I think the Holy Spirit moves the bookmarks!) Contemplate these concluding verses in terms of our combat against our non-flesh-and-blood enemies, the principalities and powers:

Declare them guilty, O God;
    let them fall, because of their schemes.
Because of their many transgressions cast them out,
    for they have rebelled against you.
But all who take refuge in you will be glad;
    they will sing out their joy for ever.
You will shelter them,
    so that those who love your Name may exult in you.
For you, O Lord, will bless the righteous;
    you will defend them with your favor as with a shield.

Psalm 5:10-12

The Lord has heard my supplication;
    the Lord accepts my prayer.
All my enemies shall be confounded and quake with fear;
    they shall turn back and suddenly be put to shame.

Psalm 6:9-10[5]

O Lord, you will hear the desire of the meek;
    you will strengthen their heart, you will incline your ear
to do justice for the orphan and the oppressed,
    so that those from earth may strike terror no more.

Psalm 10:17-18

The LORD be with you. [And also with you.] Let us pray:

We pray especially for the government [and health organizations] under whose care and protection you have called us. Bless [them] with success and prosperity. May the word of God, decency, and all honesty be advanced; may all of the offense of which there is so much be prevented; and may the common welfare be properly and peaceably provided. Make us obedient and devout. Amen.[6]

6. Retribution and Other Bad Ideas— Biblical Theology

As [Jesus] walked along, he saw a man blind from birth. His disciples asked him, "Rabbi, who sinned, this man or his parents, that he was born blind?"

John 9:1-2

If you have chronic illness or a disability of any sort, you have probably had people ask you questions like this one that the disciples asked Jesus. For some perverse reason, outsiders want to blame us for our maladies. It is horrible theology—that our diseases and handicaps are direct punishment for our sin or someone else's.

I am forever grateful that Jesus firmly rejected this erroneous theory when he answered, "Neither this man nor his parents sinned; he was born blind so that God's works might be revealed in him" (John 9:3). The proper question is not "Who is to blame?" but "What good might God reveal through this affliction?"—and the answer to that question might not even be known in this life. It is a mystery that we will only fully understand at the end of time.

But in the meanwhile, we can be well intellectually, emotionally, and spiritually because we trust the words of Jesus that through whatever illnesses or impairments we might suffer "God's works" will be revealed in us. God's work might be to take us home to be with Himself, but what better work could we imagine? Or the LORD's work might be to reveal His sustaining grace throughout our afflictions. No doubt God has some surprises in store for us as to how the Trinity might act in partnership with us to accomplish divine purposes. The endless possibilities enable us to be well in trust and hope.

"We Have to Blame Somebody!"

But some people seem to have an inordinate need to blame somebody. Perhaps it is because then they don't have to face the fact that the same infirmities could strike them. Maybe it is because they feel more in control of the enigma of evil if they can accuse someone.

This was brought home by the headline news today. A gunman killed 32 people yesterday at Virginia Technical University, and immediately people began blaming the administration for not letting students know sooner after the first two people were killed in a dormitory. Leaders, voices complained, should have canceled classes so that the students would not have been endangered.

One sane voice on the radio said that the university's administrators could not have known that the student was going to strike again in a classroom. From all appearances, the killings were random violence by a strange student who was not originally suspected of anything but a personal grudge that might have been satisfied with the dormitory slayings. But the brutality of the destruction terrifies us; we feel a need to blame someone.

Sometimes people think that they soften the blame for our chronic problems by berating us for a specific action or lack of action on our part. One of my friends who is in a wheelchair for quadriplegia—I refuse to call him "a quadriplegic," since he is so much more than that—doesn't like to go to Christian bookstores any more because someone will invariably tell him that if he just prayed right he would be able to get out of that chair!

Similarly, I was told by one well-meaning student that there must be some unconfessed sin in my life that causes me to be blind in one eye. (When my right eye hemorrhaged, two surgeries to clear the blood failed, and now the retina is irreparably damaged.) The collegian thought he was helping me, but, intentions aside, his comment was bad theology, as were the other remarks mentioned above. In my case, I memorized as a child the verse "Cleanse thou me from secret faults" (Ps. 19:12 KJV) and have continued my whole life to pray in the words of the liturgy for forgiveness for sins "known and unknown." It is not God's character to punish me with blindness if I forget one!

The bad theology that people express to us is extremely harmful. It not only cuts us to the quick and damages our sense of ourselves and our ability to be well, but it also sabotages our understanding of the nature of the Trinity. Often it arises from the speaker's own faulty conception of God—in many cases the idea that God the Father is a wrathful and stern Judge whom Jesus had to placate by His sacrifice of Himself on the cross.

This is one reason that I so often emphasize that God is Trinity. All three Persons share the same gracious essence. All three Persons were willing to go to the extreme lengths that it took to reconcile us to God's Self, and all three participated in the act of redemption. All three Persons love us unconditionally and perfectly. The Triune God desires our salvation and does not operate on the basis of retribution.

Retribution and the Book of Job

Retribution is such bad theology that an entire book of the Bible is devoted to denouncing it. It is the notion that makes us ask, "Why is this happening to me? What have I done that I should be assailed in this way?" It is the doctrine that God gives "tit for tat"—a specific punishment or reward when we do evil or good. It is the tenet posited by the disciples when they asked who sinned that the man had been born blind. In other words, was it his fault or his parents' that he was suffering this affliction? Even though the apostles should have known better—after all, the book of Job was in their Scriptures—it requires a firm rejection by Jesus for them to give up the idea.

A wonderful Jewish scholar named Matitiahu Tsevat helped me to see that retribution is the main issue in the book of Job and demonstrates its structure.[1] Various Hebrew words for the idea of retribution occur more than 40 times throughout the first 37 chapters of the book—until the LORD answers Job out of the whirlwind. Once the LORD appears, no such words occur. In contrast, now the text includes terms like *foundation*, *bases*, and *cornerstone*, and then the LORD sketches in words all the drama of the Creator's accomplishments in constructing the cosmos and all that it contains. The contrast between the book's first part emphasizing retribution and its ending suggests that we ask what the foundation of the world is.

Both Job and his friends, throughout their three rounds of argument, are not able to dispense with the doctrine of retribution. The friends assert that Job must be guilty or else why would God have punished him with so many troubles. Job, however, insists that he is not guilty—at least not to the extent of his massive suffering, for he readily admits in various verses that he is a sinner. Yet retribution, his prevailing philosophy, turns up especially when he claims that he should have been rewarded, but received evil instead. For example, he maintains,

> *Did I not weep for those whose day was hard?*
>   *Was not my soul grieved for the poor?*
> *But when I looked for good, evil came;*
>   *and when I waited for light, darkness came.*
> *My inward parts are in turmoil, and are never still;*
>   *days of affliction come to meet me.*

                                                    Job 30:25-27

Yet Job also, to his credit, does not give up on his relationship with the LORD, even though he frequently blames

Him for his sufferings. Instead, he keeps asking that somehow he be given the opportunity to discuss the matter with God. In three noteworthy places he requests an umpire, a witness, and a redeemer (see 9:33, 16:19, and 19:25-27) to intervene on his behalf. We who know Christ as a Redeemer can cherish that gracious gift of the Trinity.

God answers Job by giving him precisely what he most profoundly desired: Himself. When Job has the opportunity to converse with God Himself, the LORD unfolds a dramatic tour of the creation to reveal that He did not construct the earth with retribution or retaliation as the basis, but with a wisdom beyond human understanding.

When God revealed Himself in all the fullness of His glory and generosity, Job responded with repentance. He didn't "despise [himself], and repent in dust and ashes" (42:6) because God had lambasted him into submission, but because Job had discovered that the LORD "can do all things," that he had uttered what he "did not understand, things too wonderful for [him] which [he] did not know" (42:2-3). Our human ideas of God's character and goals are simply too small; our perceptions of our participation in the Trinity's meta-narrative too trivial. How inadequate are our comprehensions of the mysteries of the universe!

Through Job's afflictions God reclaimed him from his pride and fears and doubts. Instead the LORD enfolded him more deeply in His own presence. That gift was infinitely superior to even the doubling of Job's possessions and family (which was also doubled because his original children had also been and eternally remained members of the community of faith).

Job is thus not a model so much of patience (he does not seem overly patient in all the chapters of argument with his friends), but of learning good theology. His book, then, is a great find for us when we need to counteract those who advocate a doctrine of retribution and suggest that we have done something to deserve our sufferings.

The cosmos is not founded on retribution. Its cornerstone is the character of God, who is boundlessly wise, everlastingly gracious, and unceasingly mysterious. God does not blame us for our sufferings (see chapter 16 on forgiveness); instead He wants to dwell with us in them and show us Himself. The theology in the book of Job enables us to learn this more deeply and thereby to be well in the midst of our tribulations.

"It Was God's Will"

Because of a further misunderstanding of the book of Job, many people subscribe to another bad idea, the theology that everything that happens is God's will. (We could wrongly get this idea from Job if we don't read carefully because God seems to relish the duel with the satan [see below] at great cost to Job—but we're not done yet with what we can find for our well-being in Job.)

A young woman once came to me in tears because her baby had died from SIDS and her friends were saying it was God's will. One even declared decisively to her that "God needed your baby more than you did," to which she replied, "Then why did God give her to me in the first place?" If the cruel loss of her infant was God's perfect will, then she wanted nothing to do with such a God.

Her friends were no better than Job's friends in offering her bad theology instead of simply weeping with her over her tragic loss. Why do we and other people so often feel that we have to give explanations? Could we not rather learn in the face of calamity to grieve over it first and leave the mysteries in God's gracious care?

I'm always leery of anyone who confidently claims to know God's will. There are so many other factors involved in our tragedies. It would require an entire book to explicate the problem of evil—and then we still wouldn't completely comprehend it, for evil is an enigma beyond our human understanding. Philosophers and theologians have tried for centuries to explain the cause of evil with countless debates and books, and their efforts have always come up wanting.

However, the book of Job gives us a clue (but only a clue) in that the satan—the Hebrew word means "the accuser" and is not a proper name in Job—causes all the trouble, but disappears after the first two chapters of the book. God also puts a limit on him, beyond which he cannot go in afflicting Job. Through these pointers we can find better theology than the bad idea that our sufferings are God's will.

Let me simply list some of the things that we can know, though how they all fit together is beyond human comprehension:

- We know that God does not send evil. (Passages in the Scriptures that seem to indicate that God creates it were written before the Babylonian Captivity, through which the Jewish monotheists learned that they could recognize a power of evil without diminishing the utter sovereignty of the LORD.)

- We know that many forces of evil—Satan and his minions, the principalities and powers, and wicked human beings (including ourselves at times)—cause the pain and sorrow in the world.

- We know that God in His cosmic Lordship puts a limit on what the forces of evil can accomplish. That limit is sealed by the death and resurrection of Jesus Christ, whose triumph announces that all evil

is conquered and will be done away with forever at
the close of time.

Some of the finds in this book's other chapters teach us more
things that we can know about God and evil.

Sometimes people say that even though illness and
impairments are not caused by God, still God must will them
since He allows them. I think we can best ponder that issue
by distinguishing between God's perfect will and what has to
take place secondarily to bring about that perfect will. I use
this vocabulary carefully to prevent the bad theological idea
that everything that happens is God's best will.

God's perfect will is our well-being. But the Trinity is
working with us in a broken world that contains evils caused
by many other forces. It is not that God doesn't have the
power to supersede the will of these forces, but that out of
His perfect love He will not mess with our free will and the
natural laws of the creation.[2] So tragedies happen because this
is an evil world, presently under the reign of its ruler, as Jesus
acknowledges Satan to be and yet asserts that he has been
judged and driven out (John 12:31; 14:30; and 16:11).

Sometimes also, for our well-being, God does allow tribulations to enter our lives. Here we truly must apportion wide
space for mystery, because we do not and cannot know what
purposes God might accomplish through our sufferings, nor
should we try to distinguish decisively (as some actually try!)
between what troubles are sheer tragedies of evil and what
are permitted in order that we might be changed. We simply
know that evil is evil and that we will no doubt be transformed
if we rest in God in the face of it.

To think that everything that happens is precisely God's
will is to malign God's character and to ignore human free
will and all the forces of evil at work in the world. We can,
however, certainly believe that even in bad situations, evil
times, and dangerous places God will be at work. God never

abandons us, but He will always be there with us to give us help and abiding hope.

When we give up the idea that chronic illnesses and disabilities are God's will, we are more able to find peace and spiritual well-being. Then our eyes and ears and hearts are also more open to find God at work in the midst of and through our travails.

"Just Thank God for Your Handicap"

Another example of bad theology that we will glance at in this chapter (other chapters indirectly deal with other false, faithless, or insidious ideas) is the notion that we should plead with God for release from our tribulations just once and then start thanking Him for it.

Some of my disabled friends and I met one year on a December day for a "Handicapped Persons Christmas Singalong." We sang carols with all kinds of instruments (one man on kidney dialysis played guitar; two people with quadriplegia whacked rhythm instruments; others dabbled with recorders or guitars) till we felt quite glad. Then we told each other horror stories of all the nasty things that people had said about our impairments, so that we could share our hurts and laugh together over the silly theologies those annoying comments exhibited. This gathering was a great way for me to find support for coping with chronic limitations. From it came the story above from the man who won't go to Christian bookstores any more.

Another narrative concerned the person who was told that she still suffered because she kept praying for God's healing. Her erroneous adviser told her that she would be made well if she started only thanking God *for* the handicap.

This recommendation is faulty in two ways. First, the Scriptures encourage us to lament as long as we need to. For example, consider this psalm portion:

As for me, I call to God,
*   and the LORD saves me.*
Evening, morning and noon
*   I cry out in distress,*
*   and he hears my voice. . . .*
Cast your cares on the LORD
*   and he will sustain you;*
he will never let
*   the righteous be shaken.*

Psalm 55:16-17, 22 TNIV

"Evening, morning, and noon" denotes set times for prayer, but it also is a Hebrew idiom that corresponds perhaps to our phrase "all day and all night." Notice that the LORD does not turn away from us if we repeat our cries for help, no matter how often we plead with Him. The psalm verses promise that we will not be totally shaken by our struggles; whenever we feel that we are being overwhelmed we are invited instead to "cast [our] cares on the LORD and he will sustain" us (TNIV). That first part of verse 22 is such an important truth that Peter paraphrases it as "Cast all your anxiety on him, because he cares for you" (1 Pet. 5:7).

What a wonderful find good biblical theology is! We can weep and cry out to God all the time. There is no stage at which we *should* switch to thanksgiving instead. In fact, if we are still burdened, it would be a lie to stop lamenting.

The second reason that the supposed adviser's counsel is flawed is that the one suffering was told to thank God *for* her disability. I do not thank God for my pile of limitations. I thank God that He is there in the midst of them. I thank God for people who are helpful, for medicines which combat them, for scientists who invented those treatments, for the intellectual lessons I've learned because of them, for the emotional changes that have developed over time through them, for the spiritual transformations that have been great finds. But I do not thank God for the evils themselves because I don't believe that God's creation intention was for us to be ill and handicapped.

The Bible does not command us to thank God *for* evil. Instead, 1 Thessalonians 5:17-18 invites us to "pray without ceasing" and to "give thanks *in* all circumstances; for this is the will of God in Christ Jesus for you." We are encouraged to lament and ask the Trinity for help at all times and to give thanks in the midst of every situation. God's will is not for us to be afflicted, but for us to turn to Him within those afflictions.

Similarly, Ephesians 5:20 doesn't exactly say that we should give thanks for our troubles. Instead, building on verse 17, which urges us to "not be foolish, but understand what the will of the Lord is," verse 20 calls us to be "giving thanks to God the Father at all times and for everything in the name of our Lord Jesus Christ." To do something in Christ's name is to do it according to His character.

It was never His character to approve of evil or to thank His Father for it. Rather, he combated evil when He could and submitted to it when it was necessary. Above all, He entrusted Himself to His Father in the midst of it. It seems that to follow His model would not cause us to thank God for evil, but to thank God "about" or "because of," which seem to be more accurate translations of the Greek word *huper*, which is rendered "for" in the NRSV. Thus, the text seems to imply the same thing as the 1 Thessalonians passage, for we are urged by it to thank the Father about everything that surrounds our difficulties with the character of our Lord Jesus. We thank God because He enables us to be well in spite of them.

"We Claim Your Healing, O God!"

One final example of bad theology that should be discounted here is the attitude of those who pray brazenly, "We claim your healing, O God." Again, there are two false assumptions in this statement. The first is that we have the right to claim anything from the Trinity. God is the generous Giver. What can we do but respond with humble gratitude for whatever He wants to give us?

We can't twist His arm or impose our will on Him. We are mere human beings, and not very wise at that. How could we possibly know enough to stipulate what we desire from God? We can't be well if we are arrogant or demanding.

The second problem is that those who pray in this way usually order some sort of physical healing. The truth is that God has many other ways to heal, and we might need social or emotional, intellectual or spiritual healing far more than physical in order to be well.

It is good to be confident when we pray, but our boldness should be based in good theology and follow the model of Jesus. It is a gift to have the privilege of praying for healing, but we will find that to do so humbly and with total openness to the transformations that God wants to accomplish will truly enable us to be well.

The LORD be with you. [And also with you.] Let us pray:

I love you, God, who heard my cry and pitied every groan.
Long as I live and troubles rise, I'll hasten to your throne.

I love you, God, who heard my cry and chased my grief away.
O let my heart no more despair while I have breath to pray.[3]

Amen.

7. Making God Too Small—The Mysterious Love of the Trinity

Turn, O LORD! How long?
Have compassion on your servants!
Satisfy us in the morning with your steadfast love,
so that we may rejoice and be glad all our
days.
Make us glad as many days as you have afflicted us,
and as many years as we have seen evil.

Psalm 90:13-15

This psalm section, attributed canonically to Moses, is nestled in a poem that also affirms a strong faith in God's creation power and eternal existence, confesses the sinfulness of the people of Israel, and asks the LORD to teach them wisdom. Otherwise we might suspect that the lines above hint at the doctrine of retribution (see chapter 6)—that God should give "tit for tat," a large enough reward to cover all the days we've been afflicted and the years that we've suffered from evil.

My culpability is that I tend to think that way and demand that God should heal me because I've suffered enough. Then I twist such prayers into only a plea for healing without either an attendant sense of who God is or a love for the Trinity alone. In the process I lose the true God Himself.

Do you do that too? Why do our petitions occasionally turn God into merely a cure dispenser? Sometimes our desires focus not on the Giver, but rather on His gifts, specifically of healing.

We make God extremely small because we want Him only to fix us. We become so overwhelmed by our maladies that we slide toward what Martin Luther calls being "inward turned" instead of well. All our attention is on ourselves, so we want only what others, especially God, can do to help us feel better.

Not Being Able to See Past Ourselves

I caught myself doing that far too often in the last two years since my kidney transplant. Before the procedure I had had great expectations that the treatment would enable me to feel better and function more effectively for my work as a writer and speaker. The transplant was indeed a phenomenal success: I no longer feel poisoned, as I did when my failing kidneys could not clean out the toxins. The new kidney is performing superbly, and I am enormously grateful to the donor, Connie Johnson.

But I had not counted on how much the various medications that prevent rejection and balance my body's nutritional needs would sap my energy and take away the strong will I once had to work in spite of how I felt. Because of extremely low blood pressure, it is harder to function now than before the transplant.

The result has been a frequent flow of complaint and a self-centeredness that keeps asking how this state of affairs can be remedied. It has narrowed my relationship with God and thwarted my prayers by reducing them to a constant whine to make things better. What has happened to my personality is totally disgusting to me.

I hate to have you see me at my worst, but perhaps writing it here might be helpful to you if you have sometimes exhibited the same sort of self-centeredness. It is true that we can hardly help it (from a human perspective). This chapter is not included in this book so that we blame ourselves when our infirmities drive us to want only improvement (see chapter 17 on guilt), but it is inserted here so that we can find spiritual practices that enable us to stop shrinking God in our lives, so that we can again become truly well.

Side Effect—Diminishing Ourselves

When we constrict God's role to being only that of a healer, we typically diminish ourselves too, for we start to gauge ourselves solely by the state of our health. If it doesn't improve, we not only think less of God, but we can't help but begin to think merely of getting better. When I was combating the exhaustion after my transplant and did not know it was due to medications and blood pressure, what was going wrong consumed our conversations as my husband and I walked every day over to the place where we exercise. The subject of my fatigue and lack of willpower demanded almost every spare thought when I wasn't studying or teaching.

I no longer took delight in the beauties of God's creation. I didn't enjoy concerts as much because whenever my mind wandered from the music it nosedived into the ever-deeper hole I was digging for myself. Even in the midst of worship services, my mind would bolt to the subject. In these and many other ways, my self was lessened because I had reduced God.

How does your being become diminished when you become absorbed in getting healed, when you make God too small because you turn to Him only for healing? Does your mind wander—or rush!—to the subject inordinately? What are some of the aspects of you that get sidestepped as a result? Once we realize what is happening, how might focusing on those elements restore our balance as we find more of ourselves and thereby expand our vision of God?

What might we discover if we intentionally follow the final chapters in Job and spend special time noticing the panorama of God's magnificent creations? How might that enable us to find more of the Trinity's majesty and splendor?

Side Effect—Reducing Others

Another side effect of our reducing God is that we become so turned in on ourselves that even other people become mere objects of our jealousy. We make God a petty tyrant because we presume that it is not fair that others seem so healthy and fit when we have to struggle so much to survive.

That reminds me of Psalm 73:4-5 wherein the poet Asaph describes his envy of those who are prospering when he himself has difficulties. He protests,

> *For they have no pain;*
> *   their bodies are sound and sleek.*
> *They are not in trouble as others are;*
> *   they are not plagued like other people.*

Notice that once we want God mostly as a Healer, we slip into a downward and tightening loop that makes us ever more self-centered and thus even less of ourselves. Furthermore, we become jealous of others instead of rejoicing in God's creation of them. Thereby we accuse God of being unjust.

We won't spend much space here on our envy (see also chapter 9), but it is necessary to mention it because it both comes out of our diminished self and dwindles us further. It is part of the decline that catches us in a whirlpool.

The spiral reaches bottom no doubt when we go so far as to name God as our enemy. As Job blurts,

> *If I speak, my pain is not assuaged,*
> *   and if I forbear, how much of it leaves me?*
> *Surely now God has worn me out;*
> *   he has made desolate all my company.*
> *And he has shriveled me up,*
> *   which is a witness against me;*
> *my leanness has risen up against me,*
> *   and it testifies to my face.*
> *He has torn me in his wrath, and hated me;*

he has gnashed his teeth at me;
my adversary sharpens his eyes against me.

Job 16:6-9

Those are strong words—that God has worn us out (or has it been our pity party?), that He made desolate our company (or did we do that to ourselves by our self-absorption?), that He has shriveled us up (or did our own anger and miserable questioning?), that He has torn us, hated us, gnashed His teeth against us. The more we ponder such texts, the more we realize that the LORD is not the one who hates us, but that we have deduced that from the fact that He hasn't healed us in the way we have wanted.

Look at the extent to which we have reduced God!

Why We Reduce God

We usually lose the true God Himself because we want to stick with our own ideas about who the Trinity is and what the Three Persons want to do for us and for the universe. The God we have manufactured in our minds is small enough for us to contain Him, to be comfortable with Him. But then we have not understood God's character. If we really let God be GOD, the Sovereign Lord of the cosmos, He will be too vast and mysterious for us ever to be comfortable!

Using the narrative of Abraham pleading for Sodom as a model, psychiatry professor John White reminds us that God never defends Himself when we come to Him in our "perplexity." We keep wanting God to go on being the one we have always known.

When God reveals different dimensions of Himself, we find ourselves asking, "'Lord, how could you *be* like that?'" White then exclaims, "And his answer has always been to show me more of himself than I had seen before, so that my tears and perplexity gave place to awe and to worship."[1]

God's revelation of Himself won't lead us to awe and love if we remain obstinately stuck in our own conceptions of who God is and how He works. With those reduced ideas we tend to blame God and drift or run away from Him.

But God Loves Us Anyway!

The astonishing thing is that our gracious God still loves us even at the time that we accuse Him and turn against Him— and that is the major find that can start to deliver us out of the deep hole into which we've fallen. When the poet of Psalm 73 ponders what his self-pity has done to him, he confesses,

> *When my mind became embittered,*
> *I was sorely wounded in my heart.*
> *I was stupid and had no understanding;*
> *I was like a brute beast in your presence.*
> *Yet I am always with you;*
> *you hold me by my right hand.*
> *You will guide me by your counsel;*
> *and afterwards receive me with glory.*
> *Whom have I in heaven but you?*
> *And having you I desire nothing upon earth.*
> *Though my flesh and my heart should waste away,*
> *God is the strength of my heart and my portion forever.*
>
> Psalm 73:21-26[2]

I have included such a large portion of this psalm here because it embodies such an enormous transformation. The poet moves from self-pitying and jealousy to a grand tribute to the amazing character of God. He stops reducing God to his enemy and recognizes that even while he was being foolish and obtuse, very much like a hippopotamus toward the LORD, still his God held him in fellowship (the meaning of the "right hand" for Semitic peoples).

Repeatedly I find this text to be a treasure to restore me to my right senses. Once we acknowledge how embittered we've become and how faithful God has been to us in spite of it, then our soul springs free into a larger vision of God. We discover that we don't want to desire healing more than God. We don't desire anything but Him. We want the LORD to be the strength of our hearts and our portion forever.

This is what God longs for! As psychiatry professor and author John White asserts, the Trinity listens when we pour out our agonies, "but he longs to be something more than a celestial pacifier. He wants people in their suffering to come to him. For he is himself the gift we really need."[3]

When we have been sucked into the downward spiral for quite some time, we will not be able to come back to the surface and move in another direction very quickly. We need to be patient with ourselves—and probably because we are having a hard time of it all, we will need others to urge us to be more merciful to ourselves. I am so grateful that my husband put up with me day after day as I bemoaned my losses and always assured me of his love.

A strong Christian community is essential if we don't have family members to encourage us to look beyond ourselves (see chapter 9), but lacking any people we still have the most important tool of all—the Trinity's own Word to speak to us over and over about the breathtaking greatness of God and His love.

Getting into the Light

I realize that it is hard to turn to the Scriptures when one of our very problems might be the lack of willpower to get moving. Sometimes we find that it takes just plain grit to force ourselves to do it, to shake off our self-absorption, but the self-discipline gets easier when we discover that such sternness with ourselves pays back great rewards when our reading lifts us to God. We are also helped if we establish good habits of daily devotions in our better times, so that those practices carry us through the seasons when we are less inclined to let the Bible be the means for restoring a greater vision of God.

This might even be one way that God could use us—that as we recognize the importance of personal spiritual traditions to prepare us for the times when God doesn't do what we want (in the case of this chapter, to heal us as we'd like), we will more strongly urge others to develop those habits before they hit such periods.

If we would simply look at the plants, we would discern the importance of reading the Scriptures and other practices that open us to Christ, the Light of the world, and through Him to a wider and grander perception of the Triune God. Helen Barrett Montgomery (1861–1934), the first woman president of the Northern Baptist Convention and first female leader of any mainline denomination by a quarter of a century, translated the Greek New Testament into a published version, then called *The New Testament in Modern English*. In a sermon printed as a devotional pamphlet, she cites trees as a model for us of living in the Light of Christ, for both trees and human beings "are born of the light and live and thrive only in the light."

Mrs. Montgomery notes that the way the limbs are characteristically spread and even every branch or twig is patterned demonstrates the tree's tenacious search for light. She continues,

> Yet humans often forget this primary lesson of spiritual and physical health, and struggle into shadows as if they belonged there, cherishing their griefs, wrapping themselves in their sorrows, refusing the comforts of God's warm sunshine. They lead defeated and thwarted, and selfish lives.

How much more whole we are when we follow any plant's example and extend ourselves to be in Christ's Light. When we do, we can "rejoice in God even from prisons of disease, poverty and death." When we abide in the Light and the wholeness God gives us, we will join the trees in clapping their hands, can "rejoice in God forever more," and will continue to bring forth fruit for God and humankind.[4]

Realizing the Fullness of the Trinity's Love

The question remains: Why should we love God when we aren't healed? Or, put another way, why is loving the Giver more valuable than loving the gift of physical cure?

When the question is put the second way, we realize our folly in making God so small that we think He has turned against us when He doesn't heal us. Throughout the Scriptures we behold momentous revelations of the immensity of the Trinity's love for us.

For example, when we envision the brilliance of our creation, we are overwhelmed with gratitude that through and in Christ by the power of the Holy Spirit the Father has made us to be so much more than physical beings. God has also breathed into us the breath of social, intellectual, emotional, and spiritual life so that we can be well, even when we are chronically ill or physically impaired.

I listed the names of all three Persons in the Trinity in the paragraph above because, of course, all of God was involved in our creation. Similarly, the whole Trinity participated in our redemption and continues to act in and through and on us for our sanctification. When we observe the prodigious love behind all that God has done and does on our behalf, how can we not but respond with love? Truly, the LORD's love, His covenant passion for us and devotion to us, is unfathomable. The more we discern of it, the more we react with adoration and wonder and love, however feeble our response might be.

The very names of the Three Persons connote their love. What is central to God's character is relationship. This is suggested by the intimacy of Father and Son through the fellowship of the Holy Spirit.+ And to our utter amazement, Jesus assures us that we are enfolded in this union, that there is a place for us within that triune intra-mutuality (see especially John 13–17).

The Son reveals the Father's love for us throughout His teachings. Whereas in the First Testament the name *Father* had been used for God only 11 times, Jesus speaks of or to God with the term *Father* more than 170 times,[5] most prominently in Matthew and John, and in many of those instances He extends His own intimacy with His Father to make Him our Father, too. "See what love the Father has given us, that we should be called children of God; and that is what we are" (1 John 3:1)!

Christ also demonstrated His own profound love for people wherever He went and whatever He did. John the Gospel writer announces that "Having loved his own who were in the world, [Jesus] loved them to the end" (John 13:1b)—the end of His life, the extreme end of all that love can be, the end of our ability to imagine it. In light of this eternal love we find hope.

Even in Christ's treatment of the Pharisees—those who had made themselves His enemies—we see love. When He says to them, "Woe to you," the Greek word *ouai* expresses His agony over them. He longs for them to come to their senses to comprehend who He is and the grace He would like to offer them.

In the same way, His love is always with us—even if we turn against Him in our self-absorption and confusion. He longs to make us well, even if that might not include physical healing.

And He has sent His Holy Spirit—who is not called the Comforter for nothing!—to create in us that wellness. The

Inspirer inflames our reading of the Scriptures so that we encounter in them the Trinity's love for us. The Intercessor pleads for us when we are discouraged and tempted to make God too small. The Counselor guides us so that our vision of God's will expands beyond our tendency to concentrate on physical healing. The Empowerer gifts us with abilities to find wholeness and hope in spite of our impairments.

See with what love God has loved us, that we should be enfolded in the Trinity's embrace and welcomed as God's children—for that is what we are! As we relish our place in God's family and abide in the Trinity's love, our conception of God keeps expanding. The more we know of and know God, the more well we will be, no matter what our physical status. God is love, and we are the glad recipients!

 The LORD be with you. [And also with you.] Let us pray:

Divine and gracious Savior, I beseech Thee to take full possession of my heart and life. Let me know that each moment of this day Thou art with me, protecting me with Thy grace and preserving me through Thy love. Help me to overcome the discouragements which are coming into my day, and ease my pain. Remove from my heart all self-pity, take all resentment from my mind, and let me live trustingly one day at a time as I lean on Thee. Give me a hopeful outlook for this day, and remove all irritation from the coming night. Let my patience increase as I ponder upon Thy mercies, previous Savior. Amen.[6]

8. Loss of Trust, Bitterness— God's Discipline

I will speak in the bitterness of my soul.
I will say to God, Do not condemn me;
*   let me know why you contend against me.*
Does it seem good to you to oppress,
*   to despise the work of your hands*
*   and favor the schemes of the wicked?*

Job 10:1c-3

When Job speaks in the "bitterness" of his soul and asks God not to condemn or oppress him, he is thinking in terms of retribution (see chapter 6), the idea that God punishes us "tit for tat"—an equal amount of oppression in relation to what one has done. Job thinks, however, that God has tipped the scales with a different sort of weighting of good and evil, for the LORD seems to be favoring the wicked and that makes no sense to him.

We get bitter, too, when God appears to be unfair—especially in the times when we feel like we have "out-Jobed Job" with the pile of sufferings we have had to bear. We lose our trust in God's purposes, that the Trinity really has our well-being in mind.

It has been noted by theologians and psychologists alike that such bitterness as a response to suffering seems to be primarily the reaction of more affluent peoples. Those whose lives are more desperate instead turn to God as their only source of hope and help. Here let us add to the previous chapter that it is crucial for us to let not only God be bigger in our lives, but also to widen our world so that we put our adversities in a global perspective.

In this chapter we bring to the culmination a series of theological considerations that must be handled before we can begin to think about God's discipline in a positive way. It was important for us to recognize earlier that some of our sufferings are caused by the principalities and powers (chapter 5), that God does not deal with us in terms of retribution (chapter 6), and that we often make God much too small and don't acknowledge both the immensity of the Trinity's grace and the unfathomableness of divine mystery (chapter 7). Bringing all these insights together, we find that God's discipline is not a direct cause of our adversities, but what the sovereign and covenantly committed Lord brings out of our infirmities.

God's Discipline

The idea of God's discipline has gotten a bad name because most people associate it with wrath and punishment. After studying both the original Hebrew text of Proverbs 3:11 and the Greek of Hebrews 12:5 where that verse is quoted, I am convinced that the NRSV translation of the latter misconstrues the meaning of God's discipline.

The NRSV quotes Proverbs 3:11-12 in Hebrews 12:5b-6 as

> *My child, do not regard lightly the discipline of the Lord,*
> *or lose heart when you are punished by him;*
> *for the Lord disciplines those whom he loves,*
> *and chastises every child whom he accepts.*

However, the NRSV renders the original Proverbs text in this way without using the idea of punishment:

> *My child, do not despise the Lord's discipline*
> *or be weary of his reproof,*

for the LORD *reproves the one he loves,*
*   as a father the son in whom he delights.*

The original Hebrew text of Proverbs 3:11 does not carry the harshness of the idea of punishment, but contains a Hebrew word that is better translated "reproof" or even "correction." Reproof is not punishment, but warning, urging one to change rather than retaliating against one for something already done wrong.

It is crucial that we see the difference, because God's discipline never lambastes us for our failures, but always works instead toward transformation. Eugene H. Peterson's *The Message* captures the sense of the original Greek text of the Hebrews 12:5-6 quotation of Proverbs 3:11-12 with this version:

My dear child, don't shrug off God's discipline,
*   but don't be crushed by it either.*
It's the child he loves that he disciplines;
*   the child he embraces, he also corrects.*

This version comprehends much more deeply the profound love that undergirds God's discipline and invites us neither to treat it lightly, nor to think that it is punishment. God desires that by it we shall be cultivated. Peterson conveys this superbly in his rendering of Hebrews 12:7-10:

God is educating you; that's why you must never drop out. He's treating you as dear children. This trouble you're in isn't punishment; it's training, *the normal experience of children. Only irresponsible parents leave children to fend for themselves. Would you prefer an irresponsible God? We respect our own parents for training and not spoiling us, so why not embrace God's training so we can truly live? While we were children, our parents did what* seemed *best to them. But God is doing what* is *best for us, training us to live God's holy best.*

Remembering this conception of discipline, we can return to the NRSV translation of the paragraph's end in Hebrews 12:11. The writer of the letter concludes, "Now, discipline always seems painful rather than pleasant at the time, but later it yields the peaceful fruit of righteousness to those who have been trained by it."

With this understanding of God's discipline as training rather than retaliation, we find ourselves thankful for it rather than bitter; we change our attitudes about it. Our chronic illnesses and disabilities are not God's punishment, but the Trinity uses them to train us for living in greater holiness and wellness. Of course, Christ's work of redemption makes us all holy, but the Holy Spirit always dwells within us to empower us to act more like the saints that we are, to the glory of the Father who embraces us as beloved children and thereby enables us to be well.

I'm convinced that thinking of our infirmities in terms of God's discipline is a positive way to find deeper wholeness. One Lent when I had to be on crutches because of a bad burn on my crippled foot, my attitudes about the difficulties involved at a speaking engagement on a college campus were dreadfully negative. But at dinner one day, the students were comparing what they had given up for Lent, such as desserts or chocolate. I joked (I confess, somewhat angrily), "I gave up walking for Lent."

That remark spun around to become a turning point. If the challenges were seen as a choice, as a deliberate acquiescence to God's discipline, then they would train me in positive ways for the sake of righteousness. God's reproof came through that joke, and I heard how much I was missing the good education of the adversity.

The Cost of Following Jesus

We can also rethink what we mean by God's discipline if we pay attention to persecutions that come to us because we are committed to following Jesus. Truly to be like Jesus will cost us. People won't understand our passion for justice and peace and spreading the good news of the Trinity's love and grace. We will have to take up the crosses that are imposed upon us. As 1 Peter 4:12-13 encourages us,

> *Beloved, do not be surprised at the fiery ordeal that is taking place among you to test you, as though something strange were happening to you. But rejoice insofar as you are sharing Christ's sufferings, so that you may also be glad and shout for joy when his glory is revealed.*

We are not surprised at such troubles because the Bible testifies frequently that we will be mistreated for righteousness' sake, and we willingly choose to bear it because Jesus has called us "blessed" when we are reviled and persecuted and falsely accused. Indeed, then we can even "rejoice and be glad" (Matt. 5:11-12).

Johann Sebastian Bach's *St. Matthew Passion* captures our willingness explicitly in this bass aria, sung just before the narrative of the crucifixion itself:

Come, sweet cross, I will say;
My Jesus, give it to me always.
If my afflictions one day become too heavy for me,
then You Yourself will help me bear them.[1]

The crosses that we bear become sweet to us when we know specifically that we bear them because we are following Jesus. Furthermore, we know that in their heaviness Christ Himself is enabling us to endure them.

It is harder, however, to bear our chronic illnesses and disabilities, because they don't seem to have any relation to

Jesus' suffering, other than that they mysteriously enfold us in His passion, as we learned in chapter 4. We don't have infirmities specifically because we are following Jesus in His ways. But the Bach aria encourages us, in this case too, to turn to Christ for assistance to accept and abide in our trials.

God Wants Us to Turn to Him As an Act of Will

Rather than slip into bitterness when our afflictions cause us to lose trust in God's purposes, faith summons us to turn to Him, no matter what our doubts are. In addition to what we discussed in chapter 3 about not feeling God's presence or love, here we add the emotions we experience when we have lost our confidence in the Trinity. At such times we begin to move away from bitterness by remembering that faith is not a feeling but an act of will, for indeed it is "the assurance of things hoped for, the conviction of things not seen" (Heb. 11:1).

That disposition of will can say with John White, "'Whether I feel that God is there or not, whether I feel he will heed me or not, his Word tells me he hears and answers and I am going to count on that.'"[2]

Such a stance of will is another find in this chapter, for the way God's discipline works is that our very infirmities train us in acting out of what we know instead of what we feel. Then that discipline carries into other areas of our lives.

C. S. Lewis (1898–1963) recognized further that the discipline of acting from our will is a great weapon for all our battles against temptation. In his classic book, *The Screwtape Letters*, in which the "senior devil" Screwtape writes to his nephew Wormwood, a "devil in training," about various issues, the eighth letter concerns times when God does not comfort us in our loss of trust with tangible evidences of His good purposes for our sakes. In this long excerpt, necessary to get the whole logic of Screwtape's argument, remember that the Enemy of these two devils is God:

> You must have often wondered why the Enemy does not make more use of His power to be sensibly present to human souls in any degree He chooses and at any moment. But you now see that the Irresistible and the Indisputable are the two weapons which the very nature of His scheme forbids Him to use. Merely to override a human will (as His felt presence in any but the faintest and most mitigated degree would certainly do) would be for Him useless. He cannot ravish. He can only woo. For His ignoble idea is to eat the cake and have it; the creatures are to be one with Him, but yet themselves; merely to cancel them, or assimilate them, will not serve. He is prepared to do a little overriding at the beginning. He will set them off with communications of His presence which, though faint, seem great to them, with emotional sweetness, and easy conquest over temptation. But He never allows this state of affairs to last long. Sooner or later He withdraws, if not in fact, at least from their conscious experience, all those supports and incentives. He leaves the creature to stand up on its own legs—to carry out from the will alone duties which have lost all relish. It is during such trough periods, much more than during the peak periods, that it is growing into the sort of creature He wants it to be. Hence the prayers offered in the state of dryness are those which please Him best. We can drag our patients along by continual tempting, because we design them only for the table, and the more their will is interfered with, the better. He cannot "tempt" to virtue as we do to vice. He wants them to learn to walk and must therefore take away His hand; and if only the will to walk is really there He is pleased even with their stumbles. Do not be deceived, Wormwood. Our cause is never more in danger than when a human, no longer desiring, but still intending, to do our

Enemy's will, looks round upon a universe from which every trace of Him seems to have vanished, and asks why he has been forsaken, and still obeys.[3]

We can find in Lewis's brilliant insights many treasures that enable us to be grateful for the Trinity's discipline in our lives. God does not show to us evidences of Himself that are Irresistible and Indisputable because then we would be merely robots responding as programmed. Though God is almighty, He can't force us to believe in Him or to trust His purposes. He wants us to turn to Him with trust, but He can't coerce us.

Earlier in our life, or before the onset of our chronic illnesses or disabilities, we might have had much more "emotional sweetness" in relationship with God. In those times it was probably easier to deal with our doubts.

But now we are in what Lewis calls "trough periods," times when it is tough to hang on to God. Infirmities leave us without supports and incentives to love and trust God. As we try to live for God, much of the delight is lost, so we must live by will alone. The great blessing of such times, which is why I stress that God's discipline is a positive thing, is that our learning to act more and more by virtue of our will alone is causing us to grow exactly into the kind of people the Trinity has designed us to be. God is indeed most pleased when we pray in spite of our feelings of dryness, when we keep trying to "walk" spiritually despite our stumbles.

Screwtape's warnings to Wormwood are hilarious—how much danger the devils are in when we start learning to live virtuously solely by acts of will, for then we are immune to their temptations, especially to bitterness. May our laughter at their plight equip us with new strength to do precisely what puts their work in danger: to keep intending to do God's will even when we no longer desire it, to obey God even when His purposes are obscure.

God Works through Weakness

The more we act out of sheer will, the more we find another treasure, the truth that God works best in weakness.+ When we don't think our will is very strong and yet we are able to cling to God, we know more surely that God is working through our weakness, holding on to us, and not willing ever to let us go.

But God working through weakness involves much more than our discovering at times that our very feeble mustard seed of faith can "move mountains." We learn a theology of weakness best by looking at Jesus.

According to our human logic, if God were going to destroy the principalities and powers, we would think that the best method would be to destroy them utterly by outright demolition. But violence cannot be abolished by more violence. So Jesus took the path of submitting to the powers of Mammon, unjust government, and adulterated religious institutions in order that they might be exposed, disarmed, and thereby triumphed over (as we saw in chapter 5). Christ defeated death by going through it.

That was a major reason why the disciples were so confused by Jesus. They couldn't understand why He didn't fight His enemies. They had expected an aggressive Messiah who would defeat the powers of Rome and set the people of Israel free from their oppressions. Instead, He willingly suffered those oppressions and thereby exposed them for all the world to see. As the apostle Paul testifies, "he was crucified in weakness, but lives by the power of God" (2 Cor. 13:4).

Following the model of Jesus, Paul could exclaim,

I will boast all the more gladly of my weaknesses, so that the power of Christ may dwell [the Greek word is "tabernacle"] in me. Therefore I am content with weaknesses, insults,

*hardships, persecutions, and calamities for the sake of Christ;
for whenever I am weak, then I am strong.*

2 Corinthians 12:9b-10

This is the main result of God's discipline: we find that we can be content in our infirmities because we discover more richly God's power working through our weaknesses and the tabernacling of Christ, who pitches His tent in us and abides there. The hope that enables us to trust this truth is the promise that God gave to Paul after he appealed to the Lord three times concerning his thorn in the flesh. That assurance is usually rendered, "My grace is sufficient for you, for power is made perfect in weakness" (v. 9a).

My study for my M.Div. thesis made it apparent to me that this verse could be translated more accurately+ and strongly, "My grace is sufficient for you, for your power is brought to its end in weakness." Then the text emphasizes that the sufficiency of grace frees us to rest in the weakness that we experience when our power is brought to its end. No wonder we can boast about our afflictions, for in them Christ dwells more fully and works more powerfully. As long as we are trusting our own strength, we hinder the Trinity's work through us.

For example, if we trust our own strength to get us out of the struggles of chronic illness or disability, we can easily get bitter when we make little or no progress. Being content in our weakness instead is what will keep us from bitterness, not strength or arrogance. When we remember the immense physical, social, emotional, and spiritual agonies that Jesus endured throughout His life and death and what the Trinity accomplished by means of His weakness, we are enheartened to trust that God will work powerfully through ours.

From our infirmities the Lord brings the discipline of learning to be content in our weakness and believing that the Trinity will make us strong in divine ways.

God's Discipline Makes Us Well

When the chemotherapy for my cancer was too tough for me 15 years ago, it pushed my kidneys into serious decline, which eventually led to my transplant two years ago. But the transplant wasn't necessary for so many years because of the strict low-potassium, low-phosphorus, low-protein diet the doctors put me on. The regimen of sticking to that diet was great for me not only because it held my kidney functioning quite steady for more than a decade. Indeed, the persistence helped me in many more ways than simply tightening my ability to be disciplined about bodily care. It strengthened my willpower in many other aspects of life, and, I pray, caused me to be more sensitive to other people's stringencies. The situation enabled me to receive God's discipline in order to be well, in spite of low functioning kidneys.

Against the bitterness that sometimes stirs in my mind and heart when I doubt the LORD's purposes in the face of escalating infirmities, God's discipline calls me instead to a deeper relationship with Him, to a more profound awareness that God's will is best. During my annual Good Friday afternoon listening, I was thrilled to find this exceptionally comforting chorale in Johann Sebastian Bach's *St. Matthew Passion* concerning the Trinity's discipline:

> What my God wills, may that always be done.
> His will—it is the best;
> He is ready to help those
> who believe firmly in Him.
> Such an upright God, He helps us out of affliction
> and disciplines us in due measure.
> The one who trusts God and builds firmly on Him
> He will never abandon.[4]

The LORD be with you. [And also with you.] Let us pray:

O God, whose love is unlimited and whose ways are marvelous, we pray Thee to give Thy comfort to all who are ill. Enable all patients to know Thy love even in moments of pain. Reassure them of Thy forgiveness, and renew them in the faith that through Christ Jesus all sins have been removed. Displace the despair of doubting hearts with the certainty of Thy love even in tribulation. Send Thy Spirit that all who are ill may know that all things work together for good to those who love Thee. Thou great Physician, we commend to Thee all in hospitals and homes. Grant them recovery from illness, according to Thy gracious will. To those whose burden is heavy and whose illness is prolonged, give the ability to suffer all things and to know Thy joy in Christ, who strengthens with His presence. Amen.[5]

9. Loneliness — Community

Be gracious to me, O LORD, for I am in distress;
my eye wastes away from grief,
my soul and body also.
For my life is spent with sorrow,
and my years with sighing;
my strength fails because of my misery,
and my bones waste away.
I am the scorn of all my adversaries,
a horror to my neighbors,
an object of dread to my acquaintances;
those who see me in the street flee from me.
I have passed out of mind like one who is dead;
I have become like a broken vessel.

Psalm 31:9-12

Though the poet David's situation was vastly different from ours in terms of enemies, this psalm excerpt captures acutely the profound loss that accompanies our adversarial physical maladies and impairments—that we are usually rendered terribly lonely as a result. Then, in a vicious cycle, that loneliness can make us more ill. If our life is spent in sorrow and sighing, that causes our strength to fail and our body's frame to waste away.

The psalm comes from a time when physical afflictions were often thought to be God's punishment (see chapter 6), so the poet David underscores how alienated his friends and neighbors had become; they didn't want to associate with him if he was cursed. His enemies took advantage of his situation and made him an object of their scorn. But mostly people forgot about him as if he were dead.

Though retribution is not so common a doctrine these days—various disability movements have caused people to rethink their attitudes toward those who suffer physically—still, as we saw in chapter 6, some people espouse the bad idea that we experience chronic illness or handicaps because we have done something wrong. Then such people try to help us fix it, which leads to a different kind of isolation.

But even without that complication of bad theology, many people who suffer feel as if they've been dropped out of the world when they become isolated in their homes by their infirmities. One of our friends, who is afflicted with multiple sclerosis, felt outrageously sequestered when his wife broke her ankle and they could no longer go for drives. For many long months they saw very few people beyond those of us who brought them groceries, took the wife to the doctor, or cleaned their house.

Another couple kidded to us that their marriage was severely tested because they saw only each other when the wife was immobilized by hip replacement recovery and her spouse was receiving chemotherapy for cancer. When people are confined to their homes, the sense of detachment can become crushing, almost a greater trial than the chronic illness or disability itself.

Equally grievous, or even more so, are all the other kinds of isolation that make us feel lonely. Journalist Norman Cousins presents a long list of the ways that being in a hospital magnifies the detachment, such as the use of machines instead of personal touch, the constant shifting of personnel, or the withholding of information we both fear and want.[1] We experience enormous losses when we are severed from ordinary life.

Intellectual Isolation

Chronic illness and disabilities exclude us from all kinds of cerebral activities simply because our afflictions might prevent us from attending plays or concerts or worship, might make it necessary for us to stay away from possible infections, might limit the number of conversation partners we encounter, might inhibit our use of libraries or other educational resources. I write this not so much for those of you who suffer those limitations, but so that those who care for us might recognize the other kinds of losses that we experience besides those of physical health.

A few people with partial hearing impairments have told me that the onset of their difficulties almost immediately made them feel intellectually isolated because they could no longer engage in stimulating conversations held in groups. As their disability worsened, they were less able to hear news and music and face-to-face interchanges. Of course, eventually these people could find plenty of mental inspiration in the deaf community, but in the meanwhile they suffered because they were not yet fluent in lip reading, their friends did not yet know sign language, and they wanted to maintain their relationships in the hearing world.

Similarly, those with visual impairments who do not know Braille miss the literary input from books and other reading. I know from my own experience of being totally blind for seven months when my seeing eye hemorrhaged that I felt isolated simply because I couldn't see the flowers or architecture or whatever else was being conversed about by others. For many of us these lonely losses lead to deeper emotional scars and, frequently, envy.

Emotional Isolations and Envy

Those of us with physical impairments feel inordinately left out when other people see things or hear things that we miss or when we can't join in their games or hikes or dances. Last night my husband was exuberantly enthusiastic over an unusually close conjunction of Venus and the crescent moon, so he took me outside to see it. However, my visual limitations made them both look fuzzy to me, so I felt emotionally empty and hugely disappointed. We tried looking through the binoculars, but then I couldn't see both at once.

I should add that there was an emotional gift in that with the binoculars I could see both the moon's crescent and, nestled within it, its full earth shine. Also, Myron's patience with my inabilities saved me from a further isolating jealousy. But still there is always a bit of emotional aggravation when I'm left out of the complete experience.

Perhaps you endure the same sorts of psychic loneliness when you can't participate in things as fully as you would like because of your afflictions. There is no way to fix it so that we don't miss out. Our only immediate help is compassionate people who work to make sure we can participate in the experience as fully as possible. I also find myself longing more for heaven when I won't be left out of anything. Through these two gifts and others, we can discover ways to cope with the scars of these emotional upheavals so that we don't become bitter or envious.

Emotional traumas from moments that segregate us are bad enough, but we separate ourselves further when we allow them to cause us to envy other people. As we noted in chapter 7, craving others' health pushes us away from God, for those whom we resent are God's beloved too and their gifts which we begrudge are the Trinity's brilliant creation.

We make God too small by thinking that we are less loved if we are not as physically healthy. We also reduce God if we do not believe that He can enable us to flourish in other ways besides those in which our afflictions hamper us. Most important, we diminish God by not trusting that He can enable us to be well in spite of our emotional scars.

Of course, envy pushes us away from those whom we turn into adversaries. We start judging them, demeaning them in our minds, disliking them, changing them into rivals for others' attention or affection. All too easily those attitudes break into our behaviors, and we treat them with anger or disdain, distance or animosity.

Jealousy also pushes us away from our true self, for our human nature longs for human companionship and it is difficult to be friends with those whose capabilities we covet. Have you experienced a lessening of yourself and a loss of relationships with others because of the emotional wounds caused by your impairments? When that happens, we intensify our social isolation.

Social Isolation

We've seen examples of social isolation throughout the above comments, but what people outside of those of us with infirmities don't understand is how much we are separated from the human community simply because we can't participate in ordinary things that healthy people take for granted.

For example, ever since a college concert tour around the world awakened me to the needs of the poor I have been deeply concerned to take every action possible for me to alleviate their destitution. It is therefore another type of social isolation that the combination of my crippled leg (so my footing is not sure), blind eye (so that I have little depth perception), and lack of an immune system prevent me from helping with a soup kitchen or homeless shelter.

Probably you have experienced the same—some sort of limitation caused by your handicaps or illnesses that keeps you oddly separated from social relationships and usefulness. That detachment heightens the loneliness we already feel simply because we have to bear our ailments alone. No one can help us live through the sick feelings, the pain, the physical inconveniences, and the stresses of being chronically ill or disabled. Infirmities in and of themselves are excessively isolating.

Solitude can be a great gift for those who need to pull away from their overly busy schedules in order to spend time with God, to ponder their involvements, and to take sabbath rest. But for those of us whose solitude is forced upon us, too much time with just ourselves quickly becomes onerous. We can hardly help but become inward turned and thereby augment our own loneliness.

Misunderstanding

Furthermore, our loneliness is magnified when others don't understand the disparate kinds of losses that we have considered in this chapter and others. Various kinds of isolations are sketched here so that you won't feel so misunderstood in experiencing some manifestations of these different types. But our need to be accepted by those in our immediate surroundings is acute. As seminary professor Arthur Paul Boers notes,

> I learned long ago in giving pastoral care that in stressful situations people feel not just severely alone but profoundly misunderstood. The sense that "I'm the only one who knows, understands, or feels this" may be ever more difficult than whatever appears to be giving the pain. . . . It is important to name and share the details and to have someone else listen to them.[2]

Professor Boers makes specific what has been only suggested in the paragraphs above that usually a first move toward dealing with our loneliness comes from us. It profits us if we find some person—a family member, neighbor, member of our Christian community—to whom we can "name and share the details" of our isolation, of all the kinds of loneliness and separation we are feeling, of all the dimensions that other people don't seem to understand. We will look more closely at finding such a person after we look at one more kind of detachment.

Spiritual Isolation

As discussed in previous chapters and emphasized through the Scriptures, the Trinity is never apart from us, even when we feel that we are enduring a dark night of the soul. But our various kinds of isolation and the deep loneliness that results usually make us feel that God is absent too.

That is why it is so important that we establish habits of reading the Scriptures, so that we can trust what we know over what we feel. When we feel most estranged from God, we find great treasure in texts that assure us of the LORD's presence.+

For example, we felt a kinship with David at the beginning of this chapter because he expressed so well the alienation that we experience because of our infirmities, that we are incredibly lonely because we seem to be passed out of the mind of those who once paid attention to us. But in that same psalm two verses later David undauntedly affirms his confidence in God's care.

> *But I trust in you, O LORD;*
> *I say, "You are my God."*
> *My times are in your hand;*
> *deliver me from the hand of my enemies and persecutors.*
> *Let your face shine upon your servant;*
> *save me in your steadfast love.*

Psalm 31:14-16

When we read words like *enemies* and *persecutors*, we can imagine our adversaries like *chronic illness* and *loneliness*, for indeed those are our antagonists at this point in our lives. And let me encourage you to ask specifically for the Lord to shine His face upon you and to save you from your loneliness by His unceasingly enduring love. Who knows how God will answer? What surprises in a sense of His comforting presence and affection might we find?

For me the music of the Church throughout the ages is a great treasure in times of loneliness. Listening to tapes or CDs of hymns or singing them myself enables me to find the solace that poets and composers have conveyed to God's people over the centuries.[3] Singing especially pulls me out of myself, but that is because I have always loved to sing.

Perhaps the practice of doing so will also benefit those who have not been particularly fond of singing before. In fact, singing is the one human activity that involves every part of our body if we breathe deeply and enter into it with as much gusto as is available to us. By engaging all of ourselves wholistically, singing gets our endorphins moving and is often a mood lifter, not only through the content of what we sing, but also by our actual involvement in it.

Of course, this practice is all the better if we can invite some friends for a songfest. Then we find the spiritual benefits greatly increased and the sense of God's presence more sure because the saints are gathered.

The Sacramental Work of the Church

We cherish the sacrament of the Eucharist, for it gives us bread and wine so that we can *know* Christ's presence in a tangible form. In the same way, the sacramental work of the Church is to be a physical sign of the Trinity's presence for the sake of everyone, especially the lonely. We find both when someone from our local community comes to give us the Lord's Supper. Then we experience Holy Communion not only in Christ's body and blood, but also with those present with us for the feast.

This double find is especially critical to us when our infirmities and loneliness have made us incapable of turning to God or even of establishing relationships with others. Theologian Marko Ivan Rupnik writes of the importance of receiving sacramental care and attention from a Christian community.

He stresses that when a person who is enduring afflictions is lovingly recognized by a brother or sister in the faith, even though the agony continues, still "that suffering will slowly be mitigated through the one reaching out to the other." One's pain, then, is "lived within a relationship of charity," which in turn helps the one with infirmities to remember the larger bonds of love with God and His people, for "Where there is charity, there is God."

The brother or sister who attends to us in our trials enables us to be aware of our various kinds of isolation and the depth of our loneliness without overstating them. As Rupnik emphasizes, "What is truly important is to lovingly acknowledge our psychological world, [even what is] unknown or unrecognized, so that we might welcome, accept, and wholeheartedly entrust it to God."

One of the most important things that Rupnik says is that we don't have to reach complete "psychological tranquility" to be well, for to attain it can easily become an idol in itself. Instead, "What counts and what is really healthy is discovering that our lives are gathered and hidden with Christ in God. . . . It is necessary that I find a way to see these events transfigured in Christ for eternity."[4]

What a find! How good it is to remember that all our lonelinesses, all our isolations and deprivations will someday be transformed. Realizing that, we can offer them up as sacrifices to God to be changed into the Joy of heavenly fellowship to be experienced thoroughly someday, but meanwhile to be briefly tasted whenever we have the opportunity to receive Holy Communion in its multiple meanings.

The Worship of the Christian Community

Every book I've ever read on suffering has accentuated the importance of community for dealing with our afflictions. However, perhaps you are too shy or too encumbered by your infirmities or too depressed by your loneliness to ask for help from others. Then our best help, if possible, is to attend worship services.

Kathryn Greene-McCreight, superb theologian and author on mental illness, quotes Psalm 42:5-6a to emphasize the importance of holding on to the expectation that we will praise the Trinity: "Hope in God; for I shall again praise him, my help and my God." She encourages us to gather with the community for worship, to ask fellow members to pray for us, to participate in common prayer, to "borrow from the faith of those around you."[5]

The great gift of public, corporate worship is that for those who are too timid, burdened, or discouraged to ask for help, faith can be borrowed from our worship partners without our needing to ask. Even if we are silent, we draw inspiration and hope from listening to the hymns and Scriptures, from hearing our neighbors' voices and inflections and testimonies of faith in the Creed, prayers, or personal prayers of thanksgiving (if those are offered in the worship setting you attend).

Sometimes it is difficult to make ourselves get up and go to a church building to participate in the services offered. But professor Norman Wirzba encourages us. He write that even with "Stress, guilt, fatigue, self-pity, embarrassment, frustration, obsession," which are "the daily accompaniments of chronic, debilitating disease," these "griefs can be borne within a worshiping community that welcomes and cares without fear or judgment for others no matter who, or how healthy or 'normal,' they are."

Wirzba says these things in the context of telling about a woman whose son was severely impaired. She found that "worshiping and joining with a Christian community in an area of social deprivation helped her understand our collective vulnerability and our need for relationship and mutual help."[6] I have found this to be true for both individuals and churches: the Christian people and communities who are strongest in nurturing those of us with afflictions are those who have suffered themselves in some way.

Perhaps if your own church has not been very helpful to you in your adversities and sorrows, it might be necessary to make your needs known or to find another Christian community. The first alternative is preferable, of course, for indeed you can be a great help to your congregation if you teach them how to minister to those who suffer.+ Many people have told me that their own churches were appalled at their failures when afflicted or lonely persons got up the courage to explain their struggles.

After all, the entire Christian community is sanctified together. Too often we think only about God working faith in us as individuals, but almost all the descriptions in the Scriptures are plural because the Israelites and the early Christians understood themselves primarily in communal terms.

For example, as you read the following text remember that every instance of the words *you* and *your* is plural in the original Greek. Notice how God's work of polishing His people is corporate and how every dimension of ourselves is part of His perfecting work.

> *May the God of peace himself sanctify you entirely; and may your spirit and soul and body be kept sound and blameless at the coming of our Lord Jesus Christ. The one who calls you is faithful, and he will do this.*

1 Thessalonians 5:23-24

When we are lonely in spirit or soul or body, we find that the Church is lonely without us, too. Therefore, we think about this community in our prayer.

 The LORD be with you. [And also with you.] Let us pray:

Almighty God, by your Holy Spirit you have made us one with your saints in heaven and on earth: Grant that in our earthly pilgrimage we may always be supported by this fellowship of love and prayer, and know ourselves to be surrounded by their witness to your power and mercy. We ask this for the sake of Jesus Christ, in whom all our intercessions are acceptable through the Spirit, and who lives and reigns for ever and ever. Amen.[7]

10. Physical Pain— Ministry to Others

Why is my pain unceasing,
my wound incurable,
refusing to be healed?
Truly, you are to me like a deceitful brook,
like waters that fail.

Jeremiah 15:18

Jeremiah's situation is much different from ours—his pain comes because he is caught between a rock and hard place, having been called by the LORD to prophesy to Israel concerning their future captivity and being persecuted by those he is trying to rescue. However, he voices the feelings that many of us have when we experience excruciating pain in connection with our chronic illnesses and disabilities.

We wonder why God lets us suffer such relentless pain, why it remains irresolvable. The LORD seems to have failed in His covenant love—we are so thirsty for relief and yet the waters perpetually fail. We start to wonder if the LORD really cares for us, whether the promise can be trusted that "God is faithful, and he will not let you be tested beyond your strength, but with the testing he will also provide the way out so that you may be able to endure it" (1 Cor. 10:13).

The task of this chapter, then, is to find some possibilities for the "way out" so that we may be able to endure our pain. Other chapters deal with our emotional anguish, our intellectual turmoil, our spiritual distress; here we will focus specifically on physical pain.

Pain in the Bible

It is interesting to me that the Bible speaks very little about pain. Job cries out about his pain as we saw in 16:6 (chapter 7), but usually he is more concerned about his mental torment and spiritual travail than his physical pains. Other uses of Hebrew words for "pain" are usually interpreted in English Bibles as "sufferings" or "distress" or "sorrow."

Even the Suffering Servant songs, which refer to a person or Israel in the time of Isaiah and are used by New Testament authors as prophecies of Jesus the Messiah, tell only of the "diseases" or "sorrows" that the Servant bore for others (see, for example, Isa. 53:3-4).

Otherwise, Hebrew words for "pain" are used in connection with sin (see Ps. 38:17) or the pains of Sheol (Ps. 116:3, for which the NRSV uses "pangs"). Again, these are primarily spiritual pains, though they might have physical manifestations.

To our surprise (and contrary to the focus in Mel Gibson's movie about the Passion of Jesus), the New Testament says nothing about the physical pains that Jesus experienced; the texts only record, quite briefly, the tortures that were administered to Him. The focus in each Gospel lies elsewhere.

In fact, the Greek word *ponos*, the primary word for "pain," is used only four times in the New Testament—once to describe Epaphras's efforts on behalf of the Colossians (4:13), over whom he took "great pains"; twice to describe the pains of those in eternal torment (Rev. 16:10-11); and once in a way that is useful to us here, God's promise that there will be no more pain when we live with the Trinity in the new Jerusalem (Rev. 21:4). That last text echoes several promises from Isaiah (25:8; 35:10; 51:11; and 65:19), but none of those four contains any word for actual pain.

The more my quest for Hebrew and Greek texts dealing with physical pain turned up almost empty, the more I questioned why the Scriptures, especially the Psalms, which seem to contain every human feeling and need, do not seem to care about it except in relation to sin. Two possibilities particularly suggested themselves.

The first might be that the people of Israel and the early Christians suffered such physical pain regularly in their difficult lives that they simply took it as a matter of course. The same is true still today in countries characterized by poverty, where people are accustomed (but still suffer, of course) to the pains caused by hunger, the elements of nature, disease, and arduous labor. We who are among the more wealthy citizens of the globe are mostly comfortable in our daily existence and therefore notice our physical pains much more sharply.

I do not write this to discount anyone's pain, especially those of you who suffer from severe or untreatable pains. We simply should acknowledge that our lives are much easier in so many other ways than that of people who existed in earlier times or those who inhabit poorer places of the world now.

Modern Medicine and the Advance of Pain

Another reason that we are more troubled by pain today is that the advances of medical science have been so extensive that we live much longer and survive many of the diseases and disablements that would have killed people in an earlier time. This is important to say so that we do not blame ourselves if we are bothered by physical pain more deeply than the Bible seems to reflect.

For examples, soldiers are usually rescued (by high-tech vehicles) when they are wounded in battle and often come through serious injuries, such as those which require amputation, which would have been fatal to warriors living in times without anesthesia, antibiotics, and advanced surgical techniques. But they might be left with fierce phantom pain or misery related to the troubles of fitting and using prostheses.

Realizing that pain has taken new forms and extremes in our times because of modern medical advances can also help us find one way to cope with the agony, and that is to be grateful that we have survived the originating causes. This is apparent to me because of the three primary sources of pain in my own life—my crippled leg, nerve damage from a mastectomy, and scar tissue from an intussusception.

Only in a wealthy modern age would the three originating difficulties have been discovered and surgeries made possible. I am especially grateful for pain in connection with the intussusception (when my intestine caught on a polyp and folded over on itself). The pangs caused now by scar tissue obstructions remind me of the miracle 25 years ago that a Christian doctor couldn't sleep after wondering all day why I was in such pain to necessitate an emergency rush to the hospital from a retreat center two hours away. At 10 P.M. he opened me up to find out what was going on and found 15 inches of my intestine tucked into itself and gangrenous. He operated just in time to remove it and resection the rest. Praise God for his sensitivity to the Spirit's nudgings, so that the unusual occurrence (intussusceptions usually happen in babies) didn't become fatal.

Indeed, in that case and many others pain is a gift because it enables us to find its cause and to deal with it. Lepers lose their limbs because their degenerated nerves do not record pain when they are injuring themselves. Dr. Paul Brand tried for years to equip lepers with pain-sensing devices, but people would usually shut them off. We don't want to experience pain, and yet, how good it is that it alerts us to dangers.

Sometimes thanking God for the good things that lie behind our pain can enable us to be well in spite of it. But we receive enormous spiritual benefits also when we seek medical help to alleviate or eradicate our pain.

Modern Medicine and Pain Management

The same medical advancement that has kept us alive to face the physical pain of chronic illnesses and disabilities has also produced numerous medications and treatments to eliminate it. Yet many do not take advantage of the resources available in the very practical coping strategy of seeking professional help with our sufferings.

Between 15 and 20 percent of U.S. residents live with chronic pain, and less than half of those get adequate care. The American Pain Foundation estimates that one in four U.S. residents has one day of pain a month and 10 percent of these say they have had pain for more than a year. It is crucial to explore the sources of that pain and possibilities for its alleviation.

Pain management consultants insist that there is no reason for anyone to live in unreasonable pain. What is needed is an appropriate diagnosis of the sources of pain and an applicable prescription for the best medications. Almost always good treatments and therapies can be found. A pain clinic supervisor pointed out to me that the prevailing axiom is "something works for anybody, and nothing works for everybody."

We shouldn't just "grin and bear it" when we are in pain, because that actually impedes healing by increasing our stress. Some of us grew up in households, however, where the "bear it" notion was encouraged as our first and only recourse, so we must reject that advice adamantly and seek professional medical help to get the kind of pain relief that we need. Furthermore, if past attempts to get medical help have proved fruitless, the lightning advances of medical knowledge and treatments should encourage us to try again with a pain specialist.

The most important gift that these professionals offer us is an assessment of our entire life to find out what aggravates our pain and what reduces it. There are no doubt many things we could change to mitigate our pain—ranging from improving our eating habits, to choosing different chairs or rearranging pillows for the sake of better positioning, to learning relaxation techniques for better sleeping (since increases in pain and lack of sleep form a vicious downward cycle). Beyond these very practical helps, pain specialists teach us skills for governing our minds so that we can channel them away from our torturous hurts.

Other remedies are also available, such as self-hypnosis, bio-feedback practices, or, at the extreme, spinal cord stimulation, which blocks the transmission of pain signals to the brain (though it carries the risk of infection). Detailing specifics of all these treatments is beyond the scope of this book, but I briefly mention them to invite those with lingering pain to investigate the multiple possibilities.[1]

Spiritual Resources

Besides the very practical medical treatments that God bestows upon us through the gifts of trained professionals and medical science, our best resources, of course, are spiritual. Six out of ten people who live in the United States say that prayer has been helpful to ease their pain. This is a quite surprising figure when we consider how irreligious the media often claims this nation is.

One of my dearest friends, who still battles exceptionally severe pain in spite of multiple kinds of treatments including nerve blocking, insists that being pain-free is not the goal. The goal is to make the pain manageable so that it doesn't possess us—that is the truth of the "grin and bear it" axiom. We use the best resources we can find for managing pain, and these enable us to bear it with a greater possibility for smiles. My friend finds that her best treasure for handling pain is to meditate with Christian music.

All kinds of emotional, intellectual, social, and spiritual methods enable us to be well. Most of these work by taking our mind away from focusing on the pain. For example, another friend with painful cancer said that she is helped by becoming involved in working on a very complicated quilt pattern. But when we can't get away from dwelling on the pain because it is so incapacitating, our best resource is one that serves us well at all times in connection with our infirmities and that is to cry out in our bewilderment to God.

Even though the Bible doesn't seem to deal much with physical pain, still its psalms and other prayers are very helpful to us for lamenting to God. Many of the passages in this book that help us with our emotional and spiritual pain are excellent texts for our meditation when we suffer physical torments.

We might be wailing or barely whimpering, but we know that Jesus understands. We have already glanced briefly at Hebrews 4:15 in chapter 4, but here let us look more deeply at its context since we can draw such profound comfort from it:

Since, then, we have a great high priest who has passed through the heavens, Jesus, the Son of God, let us hold fast to our confession. For we do not have a high priest who is unable to sympathize with our weaknesses, but we have one who in every respect has been tested as we are, yet without sin. Let us therefore approach the throne of grace with boldness, so that we may receive mercy and find grace to help in time of need.

Hebrews 4:14-16

Most of Hebrews 4 is concerned with entering into God's rest, which we are able to do both now and eternally because Jesus has made it possible for us to be reconciled to God. Because He is both God and our Mediator with God as the entire book of Hebrews emphasizes, we can hold fast to our confession of faith in Him.

That is why it is so helpful to realize what an extraordinary High Priest He is, for He understands us completely, having suffered every kind of affliction imaginable. We can cry out to Him and know that He compassionately shares our agonies, for in human form He went through not only the brutal agony of social, emotional, and spiritual dislocation, but also the most severe physical pains.

We are not alone! Christ is totally with us in comprehending our woes, in bearing them with us, in bringing us to healing—both now and eternally.

Not too long after my kidney transplant and before the doctors had figured out all the medicines I would need to keep all my bodily systems in balance with the depleting effects of the immuno-suppressants, I spent an agonizing night in horrendous pain from which at the time I knew no relief. I sat in my rocker in my "quiet time" (devotional) corner crying out, reading the Scriptures, praying the psalms about various categories of distresses and sorrows, looking at icons, and crying out some more. There was no relief from the pain that night, but there was rest in God's embracing grace. Our High Priest heard me, accompanied me (I know, though I didn't feel it at the time), and furthermore escorted me to a miracle.

The next day when I went to the hospital to deal with the pain, blood tests revealed an unrelated dangerously low amount of sodium in my system. Thank God for the pain, which led to urgently-needed attention to a perilous deficit that could have caused convulsions, coma, or even death because of swelling of the brain cells.

Not all pain leads to such a miracle, but I believe our cries to Jesus do result in His abiding with us in our crises. That is a great gift we can trust, even when we don't necessarily feel it (see chapter 3).

Alternatives to Complaining

Probably all of us with chronic infirmities have learned that complaining does no good. (Then why do I so often fall into it? What about you?) To whine about our woes merely focuses our attention on them and, it seems, actually increases our pain because we become so conscious of it. We have so many better choices for greater wholeness.

One choice is to concentrate on our language, so that we discipline ourselves simply to report our pain, rather than gripe about it. Informing other persons about our pangs is usually necessary so that they don't touch us where we hurt, hug us too tightly, or make noise that will increase our headache. But we can do that in a way that only asks them to take proper precautions to prevent further injury and does not request prolonged conversation that will intensify our attention to the pain.

Once people have become acquainted with our needs, then we do well to urge them to avoid the subject, unless we need the emotional therapy of disclosing more about our affliction to a lovingly listening ear. In an excellent book that I just found, former pastor and present psychiatrist Jeffrey Boyd interviewed many people with chronic illnesses to make a list of coping strategies. One of the most delightful came from a woman named Mary.

Mary, in her 70s, suffers from severe rheumatoid arthritis, but does not want to talk about her pain or infirmity. Her sister Rose reported,

> At one family gathering she got a brown paper bag and said that anyone who mentioned anything about disease would have to put five dollars in the bag. With the threat of losing five bucks, everyone avoided talking about her illness. The conversation was about the exciting things

that we were doing, about . . . Mary's grandchildren, and about the exhilarating side of life. Mary loves that kind of talk. She thrives on it.[2]

If I had done such a thing in past times of struggle, I would have gotten rich paying my own self! My own chronic complaining taught me a strong lesson about losing the opportunity to be well. Perhaps I should keep a brown paper bag on my desk to remind me not to be so stupid again. Thank God for His forgiveness for my foolish ways.

The bag would also help me laugh at myself—and humor is one of our best gifts for dealing with pain. Many years ago Norman Cousins helped himself out of a serious illness by emphasizing the body's own natural recuperative mechanisms, including laughter. Walter B. Cannon calls these mechanisms "homeostatic responses—namely, the natural processes that enable the organism to return to the 'normal' state in which it was before being disturbed by a noxious influence."[3]

Cousins tells stories about Dr. Albert Schweitzer and the way he used humor to encourage the exhausted staff at the medical center he had established in 1913 in Lambaréné, in what is now Gabon. He also reports that numerous philosophers and scientists have pointed out the physical benefits of mirth. For example, Sir William Osler, who developed the methods of modern hospital-based medical education through his work at Johns Hopkins University, to which he was appointed in 1889,

> regarded laughter as the "music of life." His biographer, Harvey Cushing, quoted Osler as having advised doctors who are spiritually and physically depleted at the end of a long day to find their own medicine in mirth. "There is the happy possibility," Osler wrote, "that like Lionel in, I think, one of Shelley's poems, he may keep himself young with laughter."[4]

It may seem a bit too pedestrian to mention it here, but since the finds delineated in each chapter of this book pertain to other chapters as well, let me suggest the importance of keeping humorous materials available to us for our arduous times. I especially love children's stories or funny movies, while others might like CDs of humorists or joke books.[5]

One main reason that I especially love films and fiction for children or from older eras is that they usually don't contain risqué materials that offend. Healing purposes get lost if we are disgusted. I probably err on the prudish side, but I don't find it funny when people are demeaned or when comedians stretch the boundaries of morality. The goal is well-being in spite of pain, so we want to find resources that give us an alternative focus not only to change our mindset, but also to lift our emotions and spirits into greater wholeness.

Exercise and Other Natural Pain Relievers

This writing got interrupted for an hour while I went for my physical therapy appointment. (Long ago I started naming my workout that because people didn't think that it was a sufficient excuse for not being able to meet with them at a certain time.) Exercise is on my daily schedule because of all its health benefits, such as alleviating depression, controlling blood glucose levels and weight, maintaining sound bones, improving cardiovascular systems, and so forth.

With the advice of a physician I recently learned that I could also deal with my arthritis pain by switching from swimming to bicycling on a stationary machine that also lets me exercise my arms. The pedaling strengthens the muscles around my arthritic knee even as it circulates my blood faster to bolster the pain-decreasing work of endorphins.

Walking outside is an especially good exercise against pain if people are capable of doing it. Not only do we get the benefits of the workout itself, but we also have our attention diverted from our pain by meeting and conversing with neighbors, smelling the flowers along the way, and noticing the progression of the seasons—which gives us a different sense of time from that which endless pain conveys.[6]

All kinds of other natural, home remedies help us handle pain. I mention them here simply in case readers haven't thought about them or to spark your memory or imagination. Such things as warm baths and ice packs (according to the source of pain), chicken soup (which decreases my headaches), humidifiers, naps, breathing exercises, back rubs, foot massages, and so forth help us to find more wholeness.

Someday I would like to learn the pressure points on human feet because of an amazing experience over 20 years ago when I was at a remote retreat center and in severe pain that kept me from sleeping at night because of a weirdly broken finger (which became permanently bent). A woman who was trained in foot massage offered to give me one, and I thought it was funny to rub feet for the sake of fingers. How little I knew—and how blessed the sleep that her soothing work put me into!

Ministry to Others Who Suffer

One exceptionally important gift we gain from pain is an increased sensitivity to those who suffer in any sort of way. This is significant for every chapter in this book, but it is especially of benefit for this chapter because to reach out in aid to others is one of the best ways to disregard our own pain.

My close friend, mentioned above because her pain is so severe, recognizes that her pain is secondary to the ache of how pain reduces her ability to function as before (see the following chapter). Though we live far apart, we have discovered that we are helped by the extent of each other's struggles to continue facing our own. When I mentioned in a phone conversation recently that simply knowing she exists helps me, she responded, "We feel each other's pain more deeply than words can convey." Friendship is surely one of God's greatest gifts for our pain. It helps to relieve our own agonies to share with others whatever we find to sustain us.

Paul lets this attitude dominate his reaction to all his adversities, as this excerpt from his letters displays:

Blessed be the God and Father of our Lord Jesus Christ, the Father of mercies and the God of all consolation, who consoles us in all our affliction, so that we may be able to console those who are in any affliction with the consolation with which we ourselves are consoled by God. For just as the sufferings of Christ are abundant for us, so also our consolation is abundant through Christ. If we are being afflicted, it is for your consolation and salvation; if we are being consoled, it is for your consolation, which you experience when you patiently endure the same sufferings that we are also suffering. Our hope for you is unshaken; for we know that as you share in our sufferings, so also you share in our consolation.

2 Corinthians 1:3-7

Out of our own experiences and knowledge of the Trinity's consolations, we realize how much we have to give to others who are enduring adversities. We discern what soothes us and might be of solace to them. We are also more alert to those who are suffering but trying to hide it, and thereby we can both assist them and encourage them to let their needs be known to a community of support.

Pain makes us more attentive to the ways in which every person is hurting. Arthur Paul Boers passes on these words from Philo of Alexandria, an ancient Jewish philosopher: "Be compassionate for everyone you meet is fighting a great battle."[7] Out of our battle with pain comes not only the recognition of others' struggles, but a deepened passion to do something about it.

An outstanding young-adult book about a teenager named Hope, whose mother had abandoned her when she was a baby, intertwines her story with that of a man with leukemia, who becomes mayor (amidst all kinds of political trouble) in order to stop the corruption in the town. After he is elected, he calls on the teenagers in town by asking them, "What's the best we can be?" Hope narrates these results of his inspiration:

> And together we came up with a plan to do volunteer work for people who were short on cash.
> We helped at the expanded day care facility....
> We manned the Gospel of Grace's new twenty-four hour family shelter....
> We fixed fences, mowed grass, and painted houses. We were only okay house painters....
> But we kept trying.
> And we learned that you don't have to be famous or rich or physically healthy to be a leader. You just have to try to be a true person. We learned that helping other people brings out the good in everybody.[8]

What a great double find! We read about a man who inspired an entire town even as he struggled with infirmity. We also discern that we can become more whole when we thwart our pain by serving others and that they, too, are made more well.

The LORD be with you. [And also with you.] Let us pray:

Lord Jesus Christ, by your patience in suffering you hallowed earthly pain and gave us the example of obedience to your Father's will: Be near me in my time of weakness and pain; sustain me by your grace, that my strength and courage may not fail; heal me according to your will; and help me always to believe that what happens to me here is of little account if you hold me in eternal life, my Lord and my God. Amen.[9]

11. Unproductivity—
The Mysterious Workings of God

Turn, O LORD, save my life;
deliver me for the sake of your steadfast love.
For in death there is no remembrance of you;
in Sheol who can give you praise?

Psalm 6:4-5

The Bible seems not to mention our contemporary anguish over not being able to be productive. As I thought about and searched through the Scriptures, I could find no texts that say anything about an incapacity to serve God when our infirmities encumber us. In several passages such as the portion above (see also Ps. 30:9; 88:10-12; 115:17; Eccles. 9:10; Isa. 38:18) the poet asks to be delivered from death and the grave because no one can praise the LORD there.

Some days in our infirmities we feel that way. When we are immobilized by our chronic illnesses or disabilities, we experience a kind of death because we can no longer do the things we were once able to do. Our lives appear useless.

People in biblical times seem not to have been so bothered if they were still alive, but not productive. The culture then was obviously more accepting that "For everything there is a season, and a time for every matter under heaven" (Eccles. 3:1). Did those times and seasons include a time to give up being productive—or, better put, a time to refrain from needing to be productive?

Why do we feel such a need in present society to be useful?

A Culture of Productivity

We live in a culture that primarily assesses someone's worth by what he or she accomplishes. We send out résumés that list our achievements. Even at parties we judge one another's productivity because the usual question upon meeting a stranger is "What do you do?"—as if by gathering such information we will really know who that individual is.

That societal attitude has probably invaded our own. One of the worst problems with which we struggle (or at least I do) in our infirmities is that we are slowed down or even incapacitated by them. We develop an inferiority complex because we haven't fulfilled all of our goals or been as productive as someone else. When we get into such comparisons, we are really in trouble because we can always find someone who performs better than we.

That has been my biggest problem after my kidney transplant. I have to spend so much time dealing with medications (taking them at 11 times a day) and am so exhausted from unreasonably low blood pressure that I cannot do as much work. I know that my exhaustion is nothing like that of people with such illnesses as chronic fatigue syndrome, but it causes me to spend a lot of time napping and lying down. And I feel guilty for doing so.

The need to produce has caused our society to have a terribly frantic notion of time. I once had a tee-shirt that read "So many books . . . So little time." After pondering that slogan for a while, I had to give the shirt away because it was increasing my "need" to work harder "to get everything done before I die." One of the greatest finds in my life was learning to keep the Sabbath so that one day a week was set apart to cease this need to be productive. If we can learn that attitude on the Sabbath day, then perhaps it can also temper the compulsion on other days.+

However, so many things in our society keep contributing to this pressure to accomplish plenty. Cell phones make us more accessible so we can take on more conversations; e-mail demands that we respond faster to urgent messages; computers enable us to do so much more work.

Even our language betrays this need to get a lot done. We "do" lunch as another thing on our list of accomplishments, or, even worse, we "do" an art museum in a short period of time. (Why bother to visit it at all if there is no time to immerse oneself and revel in the paintings?)

Let us acknowledge that this compulsion to pile up achievements is a mistaken response to the deepest hunger of our lives—a longing for God. No matter how much we produce, there will always be more things we could have done. We will never be satisfied, no matter how much we do. For as the early Church bishop and theologian Saint Augustine (354–430) confessed, "Oh, Lord, thou hast made us, and our spirits are restless until we rest in thee."

We will never quell our yearning for God by means of all the output of our frenzied efforts, so why do we keep longing to do more? Why do we judge ourselves when we can't do much, since to pile up accomplishments never gives us ultimate satisfaction anyway? And why do we let others judge us if we are not very productive? Does it matter to God?

Incapacitation

Those of us who are limited in what we can do by our chronic illnesses and disabilities often think that others are judging us when they're not. And if they are, usually it is simply because they don't know enough about us. I just came home from today's workout and felt judged by someone who said that my heart rate should have gotten higher when I was walking on the treadmill. She doesn't know much about my crippled leg, lower metabolism rate, and so forth. I wish I could inoculate my mind against judgment so that in such cases other people's misguided comments would quickly pass out of my brain.

Usually, however, we feel judged or let others judge us because we have already judged ourselves—we who already know that we are doing the best we can at the moment! Why can't we learn to stop being so harsh with ourselves?

One insight came to me from reading an interview concerning a book by Mihaly Csikszentmihalyi called *Flow: The Psychology of Optimal Experience*, in which the author argued that "the most rewarding happiness lies in the skillful performance of meaningful work that fully occupies one's attention."[1] In addition, then, to society's push for us to be productive and our own haunting yearning for God, which we try to fill with accomplishments, there is a very real elation that we are missing when we can no longer invest ourselves as fully as we would like to in weighty work that we could execute well.

It seems therefore that the tendency aroused in us by our society to demand productivity from ourselves is coupled with our own deep desire to do what we have loved in the past. Thus, we feel both guilt and an absence of pleasure and think (mistakenly) that we should somehow make ourselves capable of accomplishing things again.

Standing and Waiting

The masterful poet and essayist John Milton (1608–1674) went blind in 1652. That same year his wife died and a short while later his son died also. Talk about debilitating trauma!

Three years later Milton wrote his famous poem, "When I Consider . . . ," which questions how God expects us to keep serving Him when we are incapacitated.

When I consider how my light is spent,
Ere half my days, in this dark world and wide,
And that one talent which is death to hide,
Lodged with me useless, though my soul more bent
To serve therewith my Maker, and present
My true account, lest He returning chide:
Doth God exact day-labour, light denied,
I fondly ask; but patience to prevent
That murmur, soon replies, God doth not need
Either man's works or His own gifts; who best
Bear His mild yoke, they serve Him best; His state
Is kingly; thousands at His bidding speed
And post o'er land and ocean without rest:
They also serve who only stand and wait.[2]

This poem has been powerful in my life to help me real-ize how much I need to learn to rest in God's will. God does not require our "works," nor the "gifts" He created in us in the first place. Besides, the Trinity has "thousands" more who can do the work we think we should have done.

God does not demand anything from us when we are incapacitated, and His judgment is the only one that counts! Can we learn the "patience" that prevents our murmuring? Can we learn to bear "His mild yoke" together with Jesus who obeyed God's will best when He was totally incapacitated on the cross?

Most of all, we are immensely encouraged by the final line: we serve the Trinity well when all we can do is "stand and wait"—or sit or lie down while we wait, if that is required by our infirmities. The key both to not judging ourselves and also to discovering new delight when we are denied the work we love is to find contentment in learning to wait for God, with God, and on God.

Knowing That We Are Accepted

We learn such waiting best when we remember what we *know* about the Trinity's love and don't count on what we feel. That is especially true because we so often feel guilty about not accomplishing anything or we feel self-disgust because we can't fix the problem.

Psychiatrist and Christian leader John White addresses that problem at length in this excerpt from his powerful book on prayer:

> It really does not matter how small we are, but how at peace we are with ourselves. And he is at peace who has seen himself appropriately placed in the total scheme of things. The problem is not that we are small but that we are competitive and therefore displaced persons in the mad scramble for a place in life. . . .
>
> To know that we are small yet accepted and loved, and that we fit into the exact niche in life a loving God has carved out for us is the most profoundly healthy thing I know. . . . Most of all we are left free to wonder at the glory and majesty of God, drinking in drafts of living water and knowing what we are created for.[3]

And what we are created for is simply to wonder at God's exalted and gracious magnificence, to drink in the glories of His life in us, to wait in His presence with praise!

White's comments help us realize that sometimes we don't feel accepted and loved by God because of our pride. We are not willing to take our small place in the midst of the billions of people God has created. Let us remember, then, that we don't have to prove ourselves to others or to ourselves. Even if we are totally immobilized by our illnesses or handicaps, still we are in God's hands and can respond with praise.

Small Fidelities

God doesn't ask anything of us, except to be faithful in whatever situation and with whomever we are at the moment. Notice I didn't say "to be faithful with whatever we can do." That is our society's chief problem—that we are a people of "doing" instead of "being." As a result, people are not free to *be* well when they can't *do* well.

That is not the biblical perspective. Rather, the Scriptures invite us to entrust our lives to God so that we can be well by grace, no matter what we can or cannot do.

This is crucial for everyone to learn—not only those of us who are limited in our productivity by our infirmities. Seminary professor Arthur Paul Boers, who was walking a 500-mile pilgrimage in Spain, recorded this insight:

> Later I became stymied with fear about my incapacity to achieve full Christian faithfulness. I gradually overcame my frustration when I remembered that Jesus counseled followers to "take up their cross *daily*" (Luke 9:23, emphasis added). I took this to mean that I did not have to do and achieve everything all at once. Rather, I just need to be faithful each day in whatever is put before me, the small achievable piece of fidelity God calls me to in that moment. That still requires hard work and daily commitment and recommitment, but it seems ever so much more doable.[4]

The key for us in that passage is the phrase, "the small achievable piece of fidelity that God calls me to in that moment." In our limitations, our achievable piece of fidelity might be simply to rest in grace, to refrain from fussing about not accomplishing anything, but to learn to wait.

Such non-activity equally "requires hard work and daily commitment and recommitment," but God is not asking us to accomplish that for the rest of our lives all at once. We are only asked for the small fidelity of waiting today.

In our case, we are called to be like Mary instead of Martha—attentive rather than active. Perhaps you might want to insert your own name in this text instead of Martha's so that you can hear Jesus speaking to you: "_____, _____, you are worried and distracted by many things; there is need of only one thing. Mary has chosen the better part, which will not be taken away from her" (Luke 10:41-42).

May we find peace in being devoted to listening to God! How much better to think of it not as the only thing left to us since we can't do anything else, but as our choice for faithfulness.

And how much more well we are when we so learn to rest in grace and faithfulness. I truly regret all the energy I have wasted fretting that I can't accomplish much being so exhausted after the transplant. I could instead have been resting more fully and waiting to see what God would do with the situation. (New balancing of my medications eventually has led to some improvement.)

It also helps us learn to rest in our non-productivity if we keep remembering, as Elizabeth O'Connor's *Cry Pain, Cry Hope* taught me 20 years ago, that in a time of infirmity, the illness IS one's work.[5] Taking care of all the disciplines that our health problems require IS the other part of the small daily fidelity to which we are called, beside the faithfulness of being attentive to God. We can be well simply by our diligence in being who we are at the moment.

Alternative Methods

Occasionally, over time, we learn alternative methods to do some of the things we could do in the past. I add this not because it is necessary—for the main find of this chapter is the assurance that we don't have to be productive, in spite of our society's implicit demands. But a word is called for because someone might protest that Milton might have written "they also serve who only stand and wait," and yet 15 and 19 years after he went blind he wrote his masterpieces *Paradise Lost* and *Paradise Regained*. It is even said that his daughters read to him in Latin, Greek, and Hebrew, even though they didn't understand those languages.

Milton didn't write his major works immediately, and it must have taken his daughters quite some time to learn to pronounce the Greek and Hebrew characters. Other resources for participating in modified ways in our past activities might become apparent to us, too, over time.

Perhaps in our time of waiting we might get insights into alternative means by which we might enjoy some of our past pleasures. Let me stress that if we look for those substitute measures not out of a compulsion to be productive, but out of the gladness of delighting in certain activities, that will free us to be imaginative.

I can't shoot hoops on a basketball court any more, but I relish daily games of tossing papers to the recycle bin and socks across the bedroom to the clothes hamper. Of course, that is a silly illustration, but I admit the sport helps to keep me from being envious of those who can still play ball.

There might come a day when I will no longer be able to play in these ways. Rather than worry about it (see the following chapter), it is important now to practice the small daily fidelities of rejecting any compulsion to be productive and of discovering instead to stand and wait with God.

Resting in Grace and Mystery

Have you known a person who by age or infirmity has been rendered generally helpless and yet is characterized by an incredible serenity and contentment? Such people grace our lives in powerful ways because they have learned to rest radiantly in the mystery of God's infinite love. It is a sheer gift that thereby the Trinity uses them in spite of their condition. When it seems that we can't do a thing for God, the small fidelity of resting in Him is always a glowing witness.

Let's expand the apostle Paul's testimony to state the goal for this chapter. He wrote, "I have learned to be content with whatever I have" (Phil. 4:11b). Can we learn, by waiting with God, to say, "I have learned to be content with whatever I can do"—even if that is nothing?

It is the mystery of God's tabernacling in our weakness (see chapter 8). It is the mystery that we are wrapped up in the Trinity's meta-narrative, and therefore the Lord uses even our waiting for His eternal purposes. We can rest content in the Father's grace, entrust our incapacities to Jesus who understands them, and rejoice in the Holy Spirit's companionship. Then we will learn the small fidelity of this praise:

> *Now glory be to God who by his mighty power at work within us is able to do far more than we would ever dare to ask or even dream of—infinitely beyond our highest prayers, desires, thoughts, or hopes.*
>
> Ephesians 3:20 *(The Living Bible)*

The LORD be with you. [And also with you.] Let us pray:

Heavenly Father, Thou art the Refuge and Strength of all who put their trust in Thee. Thou art a very present Help in trouble, and dost supply grace for every time of need.

Teach me by Thy Holy Spirit to glory in my infirmities and to discover the meaning of Thy gracious promise[s] . . . Help me to discover Thy strength when I am weak, that I may with fullness of heart praise Thee for Thy mighty care.

When I am tempted to moodiness and despair because of my affliction, . . . when others are thoughtless and unsympathetic, give me, dear Father in heaven, a clear vision of the Cross of Thy dear Son. . . .

Show me the advantages of my handicap and the blessings which are mine because of it. Especially do I praise Thee for the kindness of my loved ones, the thoughtfulness of my friends, and the opportunities I have to reflect the love which Thou hast shown me in Christ Jesus, my Lord. Amen.[6]

12. Worry—
Gratitude, the Peace of God

I cried out to God for help;
I cried out to God to hear me.
When I was in distress, I sought the Lord;
at night I stretched out untiring hands
and my soul refused to be comforted. . . .
"Will the Lord reject forever?
Will he never show his favor again?
Has his unfailing love vanished forever?
Has his promise failed for all time?
Has God forgotten to be merciful?
Has he in anger withheld his compassion?
Selah

Psalm 77:1-2, 7-9 NIV

I worry about a lot of things—like whether I might lose my remaining eye or when my good ear might go deaf suddenly like the other one partially did—but I never worried about a stroke because a doctor once told me that my low blood pressure and good cholesterol level freed me from that anxiety. But last week I had what seemed to be a TIA (transitory ischemic activity—when there is a lack of blood supply to an organ or tissue), and it seems that this small stroke was caused by my blood pressure being too low.

No one can say for sure, because a trip to the emergency room and a subsequent CAT scan of my brain and ultrasound of my carotid arteries didn't show anything conclusive. But my blood pressure was dangerously low (64/34), and the effects of the TIA are obvious: I'm having trouble writing with a pen, my typing is much slower than usual, and my right leg doesn't work very well in walking.

Now I've got a whole new set of worries. How long will these effects last? Will I be able to continue my traveling to teach? What does this mean for my future? A meeting with my doctor today (the earliest I could get in after my trip to the emergency room a week ago) didn't provide any answers to those questions, so I'm left with all my worries until I can finally get into a neurologist and an occupational therapist.

What about you? What worries keep you awake at night? What keeps your soul from being comforted? What anxieties do you have about your cancer? Or about the conflicts of various drugs you have to take? (I have to take Fosamax® for my osteoporosis, but research has shown that it can cause dental problems—and I have had those for years because my jaws are too small and because I have been a diabetic for almost 45 years. I feel caught between a rock and a hard place on this issue as on so many others.) In what ways do you worry because of the side effects of drugs that you have to take? What possible complications of your infirmities cause you the most anxiety? What dimensions of your future cause you worry because of your chronic illnesses or disabilities? How can we be well when we have so much hanging over our heads?

This new situation with the TIA changed the way I'm writing this chapter. The first psalm that I thought about because of these new worries was Psalm 77 because of the six questions that it asks about the seeming absence of God and His grace.

The poet's situation was the troubles of his country. He couldn't understand why God no longer seemed to be caring for the descendants of Jacob and Joseph (v. 15). But he speaks for the people and so his community lament takes a personal tone—he is the one who moans and his spirit faints (v. 3). He is the one who is so troubled that he cannot speak (v. 4). Things aren't the way they used to be, so he wonders if "the right hand of the Most High has changed" (v. 10). We wonder that, too, in our worries.

Worry, of course, is the most useless thing we do. We don't accomplish anything with it except put ourselves in a deeper stew. Scholars tell us that 95 percent of the things we worry about never take place—but that doesn't help us feel any better because our very chronic illnesses and disabilities convince us that we are the 5 percent exception, that most of the infirmities that we imagine *will* take place.

We *know* that worry doesn't do any good, yet we can't help it. Our lives are full of trouble, and we worry that we won't be able to handle it if we develop any more problems. Enough bad things have happened to us already, so we expect that they will keep on happening. Our fretting and fears have historical precedent. What can we do to keep ourselves from drowning in our trepidations?

Crying Everything Out to God

The first thing we can do is suggested by the psalm portion that heads this chapter. Rather than holding our fears into ourselves, it is far better to cry them out to God. We have considered this before in other chapters, but it is especially important in connection with our worries, for if we hold them to ourselves they always multiply in our imaginations. It is significantly more useful to our souls and spirits if we place our anxieties into God's hands.

I'm especially helped by Psalm 77 because it asks the fundamental question about God's presence in all our woes, and it asks it in six different ways (in the NIV translation). Each question is a rhetorical one, and the six are followed by the direction *Selah*, which most scholars agree means some sort of interlude, perhaps with music, during which time we can contemplate what we have just said. When we ponder these six questions, we will realize that they all must be answered with a resounding NO!

No, definitely not, will the Lord reject us forever. We know (remember the larger story that we investigated in chapter 2) that the LORD will ultimately bring His purposes to completion, so though we might suffer setbacks temporarily, we can know that ultimately our lives are safe in the Triune God's hands.

No, doubly no, will the Lord not show His favor again. In fact, if we think about it carefully, we can see signs of God's favor in our situation right now (see below).

We could easily answer the other four questions in a similar fashion. Of course, unfailing love couldn't vanish forever. Indeed, God's promises could not fail for all time; we have seen again and again in the Scriptures that the LORD always keeps His promises and is always faithful to His covenants with His people. And how could One whose very character is to be merciful ever fail to be benevolent? The same is true for the One whose character has been revealed throughout history to have compassion with a mother's "womb-love" (the actual Hebrew root of this noun).

The last question reminds us of the rhetorical question in Isaiah 49 that uses the same Hebrew noun *racham*, with its root meaning "womb-love." The prophet responds to Zion's complaint, "The LORD has forsaken me" (v. 14) with this question:

> *Can a woman forget her nursing child,*
> *And have no compassion on the son of her womb?*
> *Even these may forget, but I will not forget you.*
> *Behold, I have inscribed you on the palms of My hands;*
> *Your walls are continually before me.*

Isaiah 49:15-16 NASB

Just as the city of Jerusalem's walls are continually before the LORD, so are we as individuals inscribed with nail prints on the palm of the hands of the Savior who bought us with His blood. He will certainly never forget us after paying such an enormous price for us. Behold God's love! The Trinity will never cease to have compassion for us.

A Larger Historical Perspective

After wondering in his grief whether the fellowship (the "right hand") of the Most High had changed (v. 10), the poet of Psalm 77 decides that he "will call to mind the deeds of the LORD" and will remember God's "wonders of old" (v. 11). By means of meditating on all God's works (v. 12), he realizes that the LORD can absolutely be trusted. Indeed, in recognizing the larger purposes of God and all the marvels of past history, he completes the set of questions posed earlier by asking a seventh (the biblical number for perfection), "What god is so great as our God?" (v. 13b).

Thus this poem gives us a second find for dealing with our worries. Not only do we cry out to God, but we remember all the ways in which the LORD has worked on our behalf in the past. We, too, can join the poet in remembering God's mighty deeds through Moses and Aaron (v. 20), for this is part of our history also, and the Exodus is one of our foundations of faith.

We additionally have the entire history of Christianity to instruct us so that we remember God's mighty deeds, and events in our own pasts have further helped us to discover God's faithfulness.

When I look back at my own health history, I realize that there have been many times when I thought I couldn't go on—and yet each time God has made a way through the situation, though often He has not led me out of the physical difficulty.

The poet sets a model for each of us with his selection of verbs inviting us to think, meditate, consider, remember, search, call to mind, muse. The more we ponder the LORD's gracious wonders throughout history, the more they encourage us to trust God for the situation at hand and the less time we have to worry and fret.

Doing What We Can While We Can

A very practical find that always helps us avoid worrying by taking the time away for it and by taking our minds off of it is to stay busy with other things, to do what we can while we can. While I still have one eye, I want to concentrate on enjoying what I see, focusing on the goodness of seeing, rather than worrying about when I might lose the vision that remains. (We will look more at such strengthening what remains in chapter 14.)

In this most recent source of worry, my husband and I realized that the small vessel stroke had not affected my mind and my speaking, so it was possible five days later for me to go to Montana to help train the camp staff at Flathead Lutheran Bible Camp. To complete this speaking engagement last weekend my husband Myron had to travel with me to help me walk in the airport and to help with various elements of daily life that I couldn't accomplish because my right side is so uncontrollable. Even preaching on Sunday at a local church was possible as long as I didn't try to stand in the rest of the worship service and as long as there was a lectern to hold me up.

In the same way it enables us all to avoid worry if we do what we can do and find help with those things that we can't, so that we realize what capabilities remain and so that our active engagement in positive work or enjoyments carries our mind away from anxieties.

Gratitude

Certainly my going to Montana would not have been possible without the urging of the camp director, who invited me to come to staff training in spite of my limitations and who made it possible for Myron to get a plane ticket to accompany me. We have enormous gratitude for the generosity of the camp leadership, their encouragement and support.

Gratitude is the next find that can help us with our worries. We are instructed by Paul's letter to the Philippians to cry out our bewilderments instead of being anxious and to do so with gratitude. Paul writes this important sequence:

> *Rejoice in the Lord always; again I will say, Rejoice. Let your gentleness be known to everyone. The Lord is near. Do not worry about anything, but in everything by prayer and supplication with thanksgiving let your requests be made known to God. And the peace of God, which surpasses all understanding, will guard your hearts and your minds in Christ Jesus.*

Philippians 4:4-7

This guideline for handling worry is SO helpful to me whenever I remember it (but I confess that I oftentimes forget and dwell on my apprehensions instead). Even when we neglect Paul's instruction, it can be useful for us because it calls on the entire community, rather than on us as specific individuals.

The verbs throughout the passage noted above are plural and in the continuing present imperative. That is, we are commanded to rejoice at all times not by ourselves (which is impossible to do) but as a community. Furthermore, we can do so continually because we have each other to keep reminding each other that the Lord is the source of our Joy.

Thus, when we are tempted to worry, we can call on other members of the Body of Christ to help us rejoice, as the poet did above, in the greatness of God's deeds, especially with our

New Testament awareness of the multiple implications for us of the Resurrection. As we have recognized in previous chapters here, the Resurrection of Christ proves that God always keeps His promises, and it empowers us to go through tough times because we know that someday we, too, shall arise with glorified bodies freed from our limitations. The magnificence of our future in God's great design for the cosmos enables us to hope and to rejoice now in the company of our fellow believers.

The second sentence of Paul's instructions to the Philippians reminds us that we don't have to scramble for our future, but we can respond to whatever afflictions we might have with gentleness because we know that the Lord is near. That nearness might be taken in two senses—both that God is with us now and that the return of Christ might be soon. The latter might not seem true in the long waits that we often have because of our limitations, but, in terms of eternity, Christ's coming back is imminent. The former is especially helpful to keep us from worry because God's immediate presence in our struggles is constantly reassuring. We can cry to Him at any time, and we can know confidently that He will hear.

In fact, the crying to Him is given us next as the direct action that we should take against worry. Paul intensifies the invitation by saying that we should give all our requests to God "in everything" and by means of both "prayer and supplication." Our gracious God invites our pleas, our lamentations of fear, our expressions of bewilderment and anxiety, our shrieks for mercy. However we cry out, we are encouraged to do so with thanksgiving because the practice of gratitude helps us to realize that the Lord is near and already acting on our behalf.

I realize today as I write this how much gratitude relieves our worries because every time I start to think about the future and begin to wonder what my experience of the minor stroke means, I am prevented from getting too worried because of the immense debt of gratitude that I owe to all the people at camp who received me so graciously and supportively. In the midst of the community, my cries for God's compassion were turned to acclamations of thankfulness for the wondrous way in which the LORD was working through the camp leadership and counselors to encourage me and to reveal His covenant faithfulness.

Think in your own experience about how gratitude has relieved your worries. When we make it a practice to pay attention to all the positive gifts that we are receiving from God and through His people, we are turned from fearing what *might* happen to acknowledging the good things that *are* happening by God's grace. How blessed we are that the Lord is near and that we can rejoice in all circumstances together with the community of faith!

The Peace of God and the God of Peace

Let us turn now to the last find that Paul's instructions to the Philippians give us to free us from worry. We begin with the last sentence recorded above and expand it to develop a habit of mind, though we will set the stage for our consideration with a sidetrack into the words of Jesus first. Paul writes,

> *And the peace of God, which surpasses all understanding, will guard your hearts and your minds in Christ Jesus.*
>
> *Finally, beloved, whatever is true, whatever is honorable, whatever is just, whatever is pure, whatever is pleasing, whatever is commendable, if there is any excellence and if there is anything worthy of praise, think about these things. Keep on doing the things that you have learned and received and heard and seen in me, and the God of peace will be with you.*

Philippians 4:7-9

Our main problem with worry is that we try to figure out what is going to happen before it does and how we are going to handle it before we have to. In contrast to that, Jesus told us in Luke 12 that we don't have to worry for these seven reasons:

1. An argument from the greater to the lesser: If God can accomplish the greater deed of creating our bodies, can't He accomplish the lesser work of taking care of us? (vv. 22-23)

2. An argument from the lesser to the greater: If God can take care of birds (and unclean ones at that!), certainly He will take care of human beings who, Jesus asserts, are much more valuable. (v. 24)

3. An argument from negation: Could we add a single hour to our lives by worrying? (v. 25) (The verse could also be translated, could we add a single cubit to our stature by worrying—which is an even sillier picture to which we have to respond, Of course not!)

4. Another argument from the lesser to the greater: Why do we worry about such things as clothing when God clothes the lilies of the field with such beauty? (vv. 27-28)

5. We do not need to be in anxious suspense as are those who do not know God. We are rooted in the character of our God, so why do we hang in suspense as do the nations of the world? (vv. 29-30a)

6. Jesus reminds us that the Father knows what we need and is very caring to provide it. Why then do we doubt Him? (v. 30b)

7. If we strive for the Kingdom of God, we can trust
   that whatever we need will be given to us as well.
   Why don't we fix our attention on how we can
   participate in the Kingdom instead of worrying?
   (v. 31).

We looked at Christ's whole list of reasons not to worry
before studying Paul's words about peace because Jesus gives
us plenty of rational arguments against fretting. When we
begin to realize that our worry is irrational, we will be less
likely to let our minds (falsely used to plan the future or to
control things) get in the way of the peace that God wants to
give us.

Moreover, Paul reminds us that when we turn everything
over to God in our supplications with thanksgiving then we
will know the peace that surpasses understanding. I like to
translate that last phrase also as "the peace of God which
bypasses our understanding" because so often my mind wants
to understand and therefore can't accept simple trust in God.
I would be a much more peaceful person if I didn't always try
to figure everything out.

What about you? Does your mind get you in trouble
with worry, instead of resting in God's peace? Notice further that God's very peace will guard our hearts (the biblical
word emphasizes our will) and minds and keep them fixed on
Christ Jesus.

Besides, Paul gives us a long list of what can occupy our
minds instead of worry. Dearly beloved, he calls us (notice
again the emphasis on community), let us not think about
what we dread. Instead, let us contemplate those things that
are true, honorable, just, pure, pleasing, commendable, excellent, worthy of praise. That is an extensive enumeration—it
will keep our minds busy for a long time!

And then comes the surprise. Paul's catalog leads us to
new heights. When we are involved in the practices of faith,

such things as we have "learned and received and heard and seen" in Paul and other exemplars of godly lives, we will not only receive the peace of God, but the God of peace Himself will be with us!

That is the biggest problem with worry: it prevents us from knowing that God Himself is with us. It gets in the way of true perceptions. False anticipation inhibits us from discerning the very presence of God, with the fullness of His triune character of love and compassion.

The gifts of prayer and thanksgiving and of putting our faith into action keep us from worry. Because the LORD has lifted up the light of His countenance upon us (Ps. 4:6b), we can say with the psalmist,

You have put gladness in my heart
more than when their grain and wine abound.
I will both lie down and sleep in peace;
for you alone, O LORD, make me lie down in safety.

Psalm 4:7-8

Rather than worry, we can rest in peace, knowing that our deepest well-being lies in entrusting ourselves to the LORD.

Johann Sebastian Bach invites us to such peace in the presence of the all-sustaining God in the 44th Chorale of the *St. Matthew Passion*, which is sung after Jesus remains silent when accused by the religious leaders in front of Pilate. Surely, Christ's peace at such a time is a powerful pattern for us.

Entrust your ways
And all that grieves your heart
To the totally faithful care
Of Him who directs the heavens.
He who gives the clouds air and winds,
Their ways, course, and path,
Will also find roads
Where your foot can go.

The LORD be with you. [And also with you.] Let us pray:

I lift up mine eyes to Thee, O Lord, my Refuge and Strength. Trusting in Thy promises, I know that Thou wilt not fail me in this hour of trouble and that Thou wilt give me the strength I need and the help which is necessary. Today let Thy mercies again override all my worries. Keep me calm, untroubled, unalarmed. Ease my pain, and let Thy divine forgiveness speak peace to my soul through Jesus Christ, my Lord. Fill me with the grace of cheerfulness and patience, hope and confidence.

Bless our household with a greater faith and a larger hopefulness as we carry on from day to day in this trouble and in my illness. Remove from my heart all fears and misgivings. Give me a quiet and restful day and a peaceful night of sleep. I ask this in Jesus' name. Amen.[1]

13. Boredom—
Solitude and the Glory of God

My soul languishes for your salvation;
 I hope in your word.
My eyes fail with watching for your promise;
 I ask, "When will you comfort me?"

Psalm 119:81-82

This text does not exactly fit the topic of this chapter, but I can't think of a single text in the Scriptures that deals with being bored. That doesn't seem to be part of the cultural vocabulary until the 20th century and the onset of an entertainment society. Certainly, however, it is a serious problem for those whose infirmities keep them from engaging in the activities that they love.

Psalm 119, which is all about God's word, statutes, testimonies, ordinances, commands, and other words for the Torah (or God's "instruction"), includes this general cry for God's presence in our times of remedy-less sorrow. One of the most problematic times for those with infirmities is a season of boredom or the loss of interest in anything.

Surely boredom makes us languish. We spend endless hours watching the clock, or watching for God's promise (though we wonder whether the Lord's promises say anything about our situation), or watching for something to change. We can't find any comfort and wonder if there is not anything to hope for.

Boredom and Losses

I hesitated to write this chapter because boredom is not usually a problem for me. I am actually tormented by the opposite—

with too much to do and a reduced capacity to do it because of my physical limitations.

But I am convinced by many who have spoken to me out of their anguish that monotony is a chief enemy for those with infirmities. Actually, for the afflicted, boredom is often the consequence of other losses because the symptoms of chronic illness hinder them from doing what they usually did in the past or because a new disability prevents them from enjoying hobbies or work that once filled their time. This is especially a complication for the aged as their eyes dim and their hearing diminishes or their hands or legs become more arthritic.

For some, however, the dullness takes a unique form in that their state of infirmity leaves them so discouraged that they lose interest in anything unrelated to their afflictions. This can often be a symptom of depression and should be treated accordingly (see chapter 18).

One friend of mine broke her ankle and was confined not only to her home, but also to a wheelchair. Suddenly, she was deprived of all the homemaking, gardening, and car-trip-related endeavors that usually animated her life. She felt trapped.

Perhaps you are suffering from boredom now. What can you do with your life when the usual opportunities for spending your time are now closed to you?

Learning from the Orthodox

One of the great differences between the Eastern (Orthodox, Greek-based cultures) Church and the Western (Latin-based cultures) Church is that the former emphasizes the process of deification, how God is using the materials of our ordinary life to transform us into His likeness. Theologian Gerald Sittser encourages us to pay attention to this process and to ask such questions as these: "What is God trying to do in my life?" and "What choices can I make to give him freedom to work?"

Such questions are exceedingly helpful for our times of dullness (though also exceedingly difficult to ask) because we start to think in a very different direction. We begin wondering how God can use even periods of inactivity or limitations to form us for His glory. We inquire how we can learn to submit to that process, rather than to resist it. This investigation is useful at all times in our lives, including the busy periods.

I am aware that I have not been as open in the past as I wish I had been to the ways in which God wanted to change me through my experiences with chronic illness and disability. As a result, I have not reached the level of spiritual maturity that might have been possible were I more receptive to the mysterious ways in which God transforms even the evils in our lives into what is good for us.

Sittser gives us encouragement for undergoing this process in this hopeful summary:

> True maturity must be God's doing. Not that we are left with nothing at all to do. God calls us to trust him, pray to him, surrender ourselves to him, respond to his initiative and obey his commands. Above all, we should remind ourselves daily of the goal, which is complete transformation. What God has started, God will surely finish (Phil. 1:6).[1]

I bring up these practices of trust and prayer, surrender, response, and obedience here—though any infirmity can be a means for changing us more into God's likeness—because a period of boredom is an especially apt time for us to be more willing and eager to embrace God's actions in our lives.

I would guess that we would all admit there are many traits in our character that need changing, many attitudes that keep us from being the kind of people God has created us to be. When we acknowledge the flaws in our disposition, we can be enheartened by Sittser's observation that "God can purge us of the deepest sins of the heart. Sometimes he uses what we most dread—darkness and suffering—to accomplish this work."[2]

To know that God is using the very suffering or boredom that we dread to accomplish His purposes enables us to yield ourselves to His gracious work, and that very acquiescence frees us from our apprehension. We can be well even though we're in a time of monotony because we expect that God is doing something with us, even though we're not able to do much except to rest in that expectation.

Rituals

One gift that helps us with the burden of too much time on our hands is to develop rituals. I learned from a Jewish rabbi that our human psyche needs rituals or else all time seems the same. A ritual highlights a specific moment and makes it special.

That is why a family birthday ritual is so important to a child. For the birthday girl to do definite things in a distinct order—like making a wish, blowing out the candles, and then eating her piece of cake without talking or laughing (though others try hard to make her speak or giggle) in order for her wish to come true—makes the day meaningful and memorable, standing out from all the other days as truly unique.

Thus, if we have too much empty time, we can distinguish some of it by engaging in various rituals that set certain periods apart.

For example, we can develop rituals in connection with our meals so that they don't merge into the rest of the day. Something so simple as lighting a candle and asking God to be present reminds us that the Lord is always with us, but that this mealtime is a special moment to notice His companionship.

Various rituals in connection with our prayers can set them apart. Perhaps we move to a favorite rocker for our intercessions. Maybe we could begin a prayer time with meditating on an icon. Listening to music might set the stage for a distinct time of prayer. If we are physically able, we might incorporate different postures—such as standing with outstretched arms, kneeling in front of a window, or prostrating ourselves on a couch or the floor—into our rituals for prayer.

As we learned in chapter 1, the ritual that begins our closing prayers or hymn-prayers in each chapter reminds us that the covenant LORD is with us and that we are not praying alone, but in a community of believers who share this book. We have hope because we are part of God's larger story and participants (even when we don't know how) in the fulfilling of the Trinity's purposes.

When I was a child, I learned a daily ritual of crossing myself and remembering my baptism. This came from Martin Luther and reminds us to ask God to be the center of our thoughts (as we touch our forehead), of our will (as we tap our heart), and of all our actions (as we pat our shoulders). While we are making the cross on our body, we are saying, "In the name of the Father and of the Son and of the Holy Spirit. Amen," and thereby knitting ourselves to the entire Christian community that has been baptized in this Triune Name.

This ritual is wonderfully helpful, for it stirs us to recognize the Trinity's presence throughout our day, reminds us of the sure hope that in our baptism we were saved by grace and that we still remain in that grace, and suggests that even our times of monotony can be used for the sake of the community in which we are a part. Even if we are alone, as we shall see below, we can participate in the well-being of the community.

Solitude

One of the best gifts of a period of dullness is that it almost forces us to learn the value of solitude. In this positive aloneness we discover that we don't have to be busy all the time, that we can rest in the Trinity's presence, that God has things to teach us that we've been missing because our activity has prevented us from hearing.

Solitude provides us with both time and space to perfect many practices of the faith. We develop new ways to pray, including singing hymns to ourselves or crying out deeper laments concerning our sufferings. We expand our capacity to contemplate God's character and intensify our desire for union with the Trinity. We gain skills for listening to God and for discerning the Lord's will. Our awareness of the needs of the world stretches, and our prayer life grows to include more of the adversities of others.

In solitude we can meditate on Scripture passages that we know. This is possible for everyone, but especially useful to someone whose boredom comes from not being able to see or hear adequately. We can memorize long texts from the Bible as food for further reflection.

Solitude also prepares us for being in community, for, as we muse about the people with whom we will be, we gain insight into their needs and become more able to minister to them when we are in their company. God gives us all kinds of insights into others if we take the time to ponder their lives. I remember one time that a student of mine was shocked by a comment I made about his trouble and asked how I had become aware of his concern. The only answer was that the perception was sheer gift, an observation granted to me by a gracious and generous God.

Seizing the Moments

Once we are given new comprehensions of others, we can seize the moments and act on those insights. Perhaps we can call our friend or family member to help him talk through a situation, or maybe we can send a card to let her know that we are thinking about her and want her to know our prayers for her. In many ways we can open the door to further ministry by means of the sensitivities we have gained in our solitude.

What we acquire in our seclusion will affect the ways we act when we are with others. We will be more ready to listen to them, to check out whether our perceptions are accurate. We will be more gentle, knowing that they are fighting great battles themselves. We will be more ready to offer them whatever gifts we can to contribute to their well-being. All of this will come because we are more well ourselves, having learned in our solitude God's character for, in, and through us.

Once in a Christian school faculty restroom, I saw a poster that said, "Time is not measured by clocks, but by moments." That is an appropriate aphorism for those who suffer from boredom. Instead of watching the clock move slowly onward, we can look for moments that we can employ for the sake of others. The poster pictured a girl in a wheelchair pushing herself along as another girl walked beside her. If the latter was truly seizing the moment, she was probably learning much from the attitude of the former, who was smiling as she propelled herself forward.

What might we discover about others if we are open to the moment? What memories might we store for further reflection? What prayer requests surface? All three of these gifts enable us to fight boredom the next time it comes around—what we have learned, memories that cheer us, and how we can pray.

The Glory of God

The best biblical advice when we are immobilized or feeling weary with life comes in Paul's letter to the Corinthians, when he is giving them advice about whether or not they should eat meat offered to idols and then sold in the marketplace. His main concern is not to offend the conscience of others, so he writes, "So, whether you eat or drink, or whatever you do, do everything for the glory of God" (1 Cor. 10:31).

We no longer have the same quandaries, but the principle can help us know what to do with all of our time, whether it is monotonous or overly busy. Can we do what we are doing to God's glory—or, alternatively, can we rest in and to the glory of the Trinity?

This is an important instruction for me because I have trouble resting to God's glory. To rest simply in His love would honor Him. To believe that we are loved totally without efforts on our part would exalt His grace. Can we learn to channel our boredom instead into anticipatory waiting? To do so would turn our dullness into worship.

Once we start thinking about God's glory, we realize that there are many things that we can do to fill up our time. There are myriads of needs in the world that we can address if we spend the time to imagine ways in which we can be involved.

One friend of mine who had terminal cancer complained from her hospital bed that she was good for nothing, that time was heavy on her hands. At that time I was working for a church and involved in numerous ministries for which I needed her support in prayer. She began an intensive prayer routine for the various events for which I was concerned. I really could tell the difference her prayers made, and I missed the assurance of her support when she died. Her last days taught me many things about the power of prayer. Who knows what effects her intercessions had on all the people who participated in the events I was leading at that time?

We can never understand the mysteries of prayers and how they work, but we have God's promise in the Scriptures that "the prayer of the righteous is powerful and effective" (James 5:16b).

There are copious kinds of concerns about which we can pray. Rather than extensively listing them, let me focus on just one. Recent research showed that a huge majority of teenagers in our churches do not really know what it means to be a Christian. In general, they thought that Christianity helped them to be happy.

Remembering the meta-narrative, the larger story of who the Trinity is and what God is doing to restore the cosmos to His divine purposes in creation (discussed in chapter 2), we know that Christianity means much more than increasing our own happiness. Instead, it enables us to rejoice in what God has done to rescue us from our sin and rebellion and from our inability to fix ourselves (or to make ourselves happy). Furthermore, God welcomes us to participate in His intentions for the rest of the universe. We are invited to be part of an entire community, an alternative society, that resists the workings of the principalities and powers (see chapter 5) for the sake of the well-being of humankind and all the earth.

Young people who do not understand Christianity in this way can easily be caught up in the powers of our times— media (entertainments and information overload), money (Mammon), technology, violence, sexual immorality, and so forth. How much they need our prayers against these forces and for the sake of their faith!+ The Church needs our intercessions that her members can learn better to pass on their faith. Parents long for our supplications, for it is so difficult to raise a child in the faith when our society offers so many distractions and contradictions.

Out of our prayers and reflections, furthermore, can come new ideas for tangible ministry. For example, at one camp where I trained the summer staff for several years, their training period coincided with a retreat for senior citizens. That way, those experienced in the faith (though often suffering from chronic illnesses and the disabilities of age) were available to counsel the young people, to give them advice, and, above all, to invite them into deeper spirituality by means of the richness and radiance of their hope held for so many more years.

How might you minister to the young people in the congregation to which you belong? What might you teach your grandchildren or nieces and nephews? How might you be available for the needs of children in your neighborhood?

These are just a few ways that we might become more involved in serving the world around us. Our own solitude will give rise to more extensive prayer, and that, in turn, might lead to other avenues for ministry.

The Glory of God and the Well-Being of the World

When we are seeking God's glory, we will become much more alert to all the ways that we can contribute to the needs of the Church, the neighborhood, and our world. I focused on young people above because I am especially concerned for how hard it is to be Christian in our present society, which in so many ways is inimical to the Gospel, but your imagination can freely roam over all the needs that surround you and over ways in which you might become involved. As long as we live, God is not finished with us and the manner in which we can serve His Kingdom.

In one of the liturgies in a new Anabaptist prayer book, one section of the prayers incorporates the following series that gives us confidence for our periods of boredom. (This can be divided between one who recites the words in regular type and those who respond with the italicized sentences, or you can say it all to yourself and imagine the community with you.) Let this be our closing ritual for this chapter.

Ask, and it will be given to you;
   search, and you will find;
knock, and the door will be opened for you.
*The heavenly Father will give the Holy Spirit to those who
   ask him.*

God whose word is trustworthy, we bring our prayers to
   you with confidence, in the name of our Lord Jesus.
In your mercy, Lord, hear our prayer.

You entrust the seed of your word to the soil of our lives.
   We pray for ourselves and those dear to us.
(open prayers)
You can do more than we ask
or imagine, Lord;
hear our prayer.[3]

(That last set of phrases after the open prayers can be used
after every set of people or things for which we pray, even
as the refrain is used five times in the prayer book before this
concluding affirmation and the Lord's Prayer:)

Generous God,
you draw us into surprising stories.
Use them to disrupt our complacency
and remove our fear,
that we may follow you
into the joy of your kingdom.
In the name of the one
who taught us not to lose heart, we pray:
Our Father . . .[4]

14. Side Effects—Strengthening What Remains

I was pushed hard, so that I was falling, . . .
The LORD has punished me severely . . .

Psalm 118:13a and 18a

Sometimes we think that God is punishing us, though we know better (see chapters 6 and 8). Still we feel that we've been knocked over and cannot right ourselves.

Perhaps you feel this way especially when medicines that are supposed to help you also cause various kinds of side effects. Here we are, trying to be good and do what helps, we think, and yet we have to suffer more troubles.

Sometimes our side effects are minor (like headaches with certain pills). At other times they are actually embarrassing (my immuno-suppressants are causing my hair to fall out). Tragically, they can be really dangerous (the chemotherapy necessary for my cancer was too harsh for me and hastened my kidney failure; the kidney transplant works so well that my blood pressure is often perilously low). Once in a while we get caught between a rock and a hard place—not knowing which is worse, the side effects of the medicine or the originating malady for which we were told to take that antidote.

What can we do with our discouragement when we are trying so hard to get better but keep running into obstacles, new problems that arise when we're obeying doctors' orders? Is it the LORD who has pushed us so that we fall? Does God not want us to be well?

Putting the Lead-off Verses into Context

In all this book's chapters the various finds that we discover can be applied to more than the loss that is the focus of a specific chapter. That is especially true in this one because I want to deal with an element in theology that will enable us to read the Bible more encouragingly.

For that reason, I took the verses that introduce this chapter out of context to raise the question of whether our troubles originate with God. This was too large an issue to include in chapter 6 with its other examples of bad theology.

To begin our exploration, let us put the two half-verses at this chapter's head back into context.

> *I was pushed hard, so that I was falling,*
>   *but the LORD helped me.*
> *The LORD is my strength and my might;*
>   *he has become my salvation.*
> *There are glad songs of victory in the tents of the righteous;*
> *"The right hand of the LORD does valiantly;*
>   *the right hand of the LORD is exalted;*
>   *he right hand of the LORD does valiantly."*
> *I shall not die, but I shall live,*
>   *and recount the deeds of the LORD.*
> *The LORD has punished me severely,*
>   *but he did not give me over to death.*

Psalm 118:13-18

Notice all the emphases on the LORD's character as our strength and might and on the LORD's deeds; in response the covenant people sing jubilantly that His right hand has created victory. No wonder this psalm was a favorite for Martin Luther!

This psalm is the last of a series that is called the Egyptian Hallel. This set of psalms (113–118) was sung in connection with the Feasts of Passover, Weeks, Tabernacles, and

Hanukkah. Since the first two of the set were sung before the meal at the Passover, we can guess that Psalm 118 might have been one of the hymns Jesus sang with His disciples after the Last Supper. Imagine what the verses above must have meant to Jesus before He went to His wrestling in the Garden of Gethsemane and to the arrest, trial, scourging, and crucifixion that awaited Him.

Most scholars think that this psalm was originally an individual's hymn of thanksgiving, but it has been combined with other materials to create a community litany that seems to have been used for a worship processional. You might want to read the entire psalm at this point to see how the individual's praise and thanks (vv. 5-21, encompassing the verses above) is enfolded into the larger festivities at the sanctuary.

Note that the psalm begins and ends with a repeated statement (found in many psalms) of God's character, that His "steadfast love endures forever." The Hebrew word for what persists unceasingly is *chesedh*, which is sometimes translated "loving kindness" or, in the King James, "mercy." *Chesedh* is a capacious word, stressing the fully-faithful, never-ending, all-encompassing greatness of God's extraordinary, yet tender love. Surely the poet's confident assertion contradicts our feelings sometimes that God is punishing us.

Why, then, in between the declarations of God's steadfast love does the poet think that God is punishing him?

On the surface, the problem is merely a case of over-translating the Hebrew and making it tougher than it really is. The Hebrew verb *yasar*, even in its Piel or intensified form as in the case in Psalm 118:18, is more often rendered as "disciplined... severely" (in the NASB) or "chastened... severely" (NIV). Such discipline, even if it is severe, comes out of love and is meant for the purpose of correction, not punishment.

But the point that we need to make in this chapter is larger than a mere case of too heavy of a translation. We will be immensely helped for reading other texts if we learn that they should be read in their complete context and that there is a progression in the First Testament as the Israelites became more aware of the character of their LORD.

A Defense of Monotheism

In the earliest literature of the people of Israel, there is a strong concentration on monotheism—that *YHWH* is the only God and is sovereign over all. This was necessary because the nations around Israel had several gods and various figures to represent them. The children of Abraham emphasized then—and still do today, as we see in Islam, Judaica, and Christianity—that there is only one God and that all other gods are not truly gods, but merely idols.

To accentuate the LORD's sovereignty, the writers of the Hebrew Bible would say such things as this:

> *I am the LORD, and there is no other.*
> *I form light and create darkness;*
> *I make weal and create woe;*
> *I the LORD do all these things.*

> Isaiah 45:6-7

Because the writers wanted to underscore the LORD's supremacy over everything, passages in most of the First Testament attribute all things to God.

This all changed when the people of Israel were taken into the Babylonian Captivity. There they encountered Zoroastrianism, the religion of the Persians before they converted to Islam. This almost dualistic religion held that there were two basic forces in the world, a spirit of good (Spenta Mainyu) and a spirit of evil (Angra Mainyu), and that these two were perpetually in conflict. Zoroaster, though, avoided dualism and the consequent worry over which spirit would eventually triumph by positing the existence of a supreme god, Ahura Mazda, who made his will known through Spenta Mainyu.

The people of Israel were able, thus, to understand that they could posit a principal force of evil (now called by the proper name *Satan* with a capital *S*), without weakening their emphasis on the preeminent supremacy of God.

We can see what a difference this nuance makes when we compare 2 Samuel 24:1 and 1 Chronicles 21:1. The former passage records, "Again the anger of the LORD was kindled against Israel, and he incited David against them, saying, 'Go, count the people of Israel and Judah.'" The latter text asserts instead, "Satan stood up against Israel, and incited David to count the people of Israel."

What is the difference between the two verses? Six hundred years! The first, written before the Babylonian Captivity, stresses the sovereignty of God and notes that the LORD is in control of the census. The second text, written after the captivity, can name Satan as the direct cause of the census. This is one of the few places where the word *Satan* is actually a proper noun in the First Testament. In most places, including the book of Job, the Hebrew is *ha-satan*, or "the accuser" and is not a proper name.

I am definitely not saying that the passages which assert that God sends evil are wrong, for indeed God is sovereign over everything and nothing happens without His care. But as the New Testament makes very clear, God is not the source or direct cause of evil. So Samuel and Chronicles are both right. Satan was the immediate cause of the census, but the counting of the people was not out of God's control.

To recognize this progression in the First Testament helps us immensely so that we are not confused by passages that seem to turn God against us. Just as our faith matures over time and we can nuance things more precisely, so the people of God were able over the course of several thousand years to be able to state more plainly the origin of evil and to make clear that it will not succeed in the end. We know that hope most assuredly in the Resurrection of Christ, who thereby triumphed over all the evil powers, including the last enemy, Death.

The Character of Our God

Thus, when we encounter renewed suffering—and especially when we are afflicted in spite of how hard we are trying to take care of ourselves—we can trust that God is not "punishing" us. Our adversities are caused by evil forces, by the nature of this broken world, sometimes by our own sinfulness, occasionally by the sinfulness of others, by all other sources of infirmities in this world. But they are not "sent" by God to teach us a lesson, though the LORD in His sovereignty can bring good lessons out of them.

When I am tempted to think that God does not love me and therefore that I suffer the side effects of medicines (or any of the other losses recorded in this book), I try to keep in mind these nuances:

1. God is not the source of evil. Evil is a corruption of all the good that comes from God.

2. Other forces cause evil. There are many such forces, but the Bible names Satan (or the Devil or Lucifer) as their head.

3. Even though the powers of evil are strong and wreak all sorts of havoc, they are not out of the control of our omnipotently sovereign God, who will work all things together for good "for those who love God, who are called according to his purpose" (Rom. 8:28).

Thus, when we encounter passages in the Scriptures that seem to imply that God has caused evil, we can remember these nuances and that earlier writers of the Bible did not know them—not that God changed or that the text is not inspired by the Holy Spirit, but that the people grew in their ability to articulate the sources of good and evil and the nature of God's sovereignly gracious and loving character.

I am not denying God's wrath either with this explanation of the progression in Israel's comprehension. But wrath (which is too large a topic to address here+) must also be understood as a subset of God's love, because the LORD wields it for the sake of life and His covenant with Israel and out of His own grief.

Besides, those who are afflicted with various kinds of infirmity do not need to conceive of God's wrath as the source of their troubles. In fact, it causes us great problems when we do think that way. When we imagine that we are being punished or that God has turned against us, we get more depressed or feel guilty, and neither of those responses contributes to our being well. Instead, let us focus on the often-repeated line of Psalm 118, the good news that "the steadfast love [of the LORD] endures forever."

Knowing That God Is For Us

We New Testament people know for sure that God is for us because we can see it in Jesus, who showed us how much the Triune God loves us by taking divine wrath against sin and evil into Himself so that we might be saved. As 1 John 4:9-10 makes very clear, God's love is manifested toward us in all that Jesus did so that we might live through Him.

This gives us the courage to keep pushing on, even though we encounter such troubles as serious side effects from medicines. When I had cancer and lost all my hair (and I was a severely ugly bald person), God's love freed me to be creative with turbans and scarves. I figured that any wild combination I came up with couldn't be as bad as what the funny shape of my head looked like without any covering. The nurses at the clinic where I went for chemotherapy treatments would vote for their favorite combinations of colors. One man at one of my speaking engagements commented when he saw me with hair several years later that he had even thought that such head decorations were my "signature"; he'd had no idea that they were a necessity!

I can laugh about it now, but of course it is terribly embarrassing for a woman to lose her hair—and now with my immuno-suppressants I've lost enough to make my hair terribly thin and not enough to wear colorful turbans. We can endure such awkward things much more easily if we keep remembering that God is for us—and, as Paul says to the Romans, "If God is for us, who is against us?" (8:31b). The original Greek of that sentence has neither verb *is*, so the statement is even more strongly accentuated. Nothing can stand against us because God is for us. As the chapter goes on to say, nothing can separate us from "the love of God in Christ Jesus our Lord" (Rom. 8:39).

The fullness of triune love can free us to keep working at being as well in body as we are in spirit. But sometimes we get so discouraged that we need not only an assurance of love, but perhaps also a little push. Maybe sometimes we require a rebuke.

Strengthening What Remains

It seems funny to say that a certain biblical rebuke is my favorite, but one in the book of Revelation actually is, because it gives me a phrase to hold on to for motivation. Perhaps it can be helpful for you, too.

Among the seven letters to the seven churches in Revelation 2 and 3 appears this admonition,

I know your works; you have a name of being alive, but you are dead. Wake up, and strengthen what remains and is on the point of death, for I have not found your works perfect in the sight of my God.

Revelation 3:1b-2

We have to remember that these words were written to a church that needed to be stirred to wake up and become God's people as He designed them to be. But ever since the onset of my handicaps I have loved the phrase *strengthen what remains*.

That phrase encourages me that the situation with infirmities is never unalterable and totally bleak. There is always something we can do to make our circumstances more bright—even if that be simply to light a candle so that we can be cheered by its flame.

For me, however, the phrase has been a strong incentive to do what I can to remain as healthy as I can, throughout many struggles. When people ask how I am in spite of my disabilities, I like to answer, "For the mediocre shape I'm in, I'm doing great!" That has been hard to say since my small stroke two weeks ago, but by forcing myself to "strengthen what remains" I am slowly starting to see some improvement.

To concentrate on strengthening what remains inspires us to look in other directions. Rather than highlighting our troubles, we hunt for areas in our lives that enable us to work for improvement. Instead of fixating on the side effects that come along with our medical treatments, we can investigate our options for maintaining the best health possible under the circumstances. Most of all, the change in direction of our thoughts enables us to be well in spite of our infirmities.

One great example of strengthening what remains was a good friend of mine who was dying of metastasized breast cancer. In her last months she became a spokesperson for the anti-euthanasia movement. Though she needed oxygen to help her breathe, still she spoke strongly in favor of life and made the most of her last days to deepen her family relationships.

Diet and Exercise

Doing what we can to strengthen what remains makes us an ally of our own body and its own resources for healing, rather than at war with it (which is what happens when we look at our infirmity as our enemy). Two areas that especially deserve our concentration are what we eat and how we exercise.

No doubt your own doctor has already addressed the subject of your diet with you so there is no need for me to say much here. With so much literature available on the benefits of a diet packed with fresh fruits and vegetables, we all know the great benefits of eating the gifts of God's good creation, especially with gratitude.

In addition, we have the motivation of wanting to do our best to care for the "temple of the Holy Spirit" (1 Cor. 6:19). The apostle Paul uses that phrase to urge the Corinthians and us to be chaste in our sexual behavior, but it is also a good reminder to keep us wholesome in our eating habits.

We also want the temple to be as fit as possible. Ever since my childhood as a sports-aholic, the discipline of exercise has been so ingrained in my brain that even in the busiest days it is usually not forgotten, nor even questioned. Ever since I first started working in churches, a period for exercise has been on my calendar, as are all other appointments. Doing that kept me from filling the time with other activities; to go for a workout was as important as meetings and counseling sessions.

The value of this emphasis on exercise was made surprising clear when I underwent tests to evaluate my candidacy for a kidney transplant. Various medical personnel doing the tests commented on the relative clarity of my blood vessels, the strength of my heart and lungs, and the good level of my cholesterol. All of this seemed to be the result of regular workouts.

God be praised for His gracious sustaining and for my husband and other friends who support me in bodily disciplines that strengthen what remains.

I need say no more except to urge you to engage as much as you are physically able in those activities that keep you as well as possible. Larger than my encouragement, of course, is the rebuke of the Lord to strengthen what remains and the motivation of caring for the temple of the Holy Spirit.

The Peace of God

Side effects of medications are indeed troublesome, and many times we get discouraged that we can't make progress in caring for our bodies. How important it is, then, that above all we pray for God's peace—to do what we can as well as we can, all the time knowing that our lives are in God's hands and that ultimately our well-being is His gift to give.

No matter our struggles and losses, the steadfast love [of the Lord] endures forever! Into His care, we entrust our spirits, souls, and bodies.

 The Lord be with you. [And also with you.] Let us pray:

In the tumult and trouble of our lives, O God, grant us thy peace; that we may be greater of soul for all that befalls us, and better fitted by our very sorrows for the uses of thy love. Through Jesus Christ, our Lord. Amen.[1]

15. Wrong Perceptions and Expectations — Truth-Telling

Be merciful to me, O God, be merciful to me,
*   for in you my soul takes refuge;*
in the shadow of your wings I will take refuge,
*   until the destroying storms pass by.*
I cry to God Most High,
*   to God who fulfills his purpose for me.*
He will send from heaven and save me,
*   he will put to shame those who trample on me.*
*   Selah*

God will send forth his steadfast love and his
faithfulness.

Psalm 57:1-3

The canonical tradition ascribes this psalm to David, and the poem's title (which is verse 1 in the Hebrew text) names the circumstance that gave rise to his writing it—"when he fled from Saul, in the cave," a situation described for us in 1 Samuel 24. David had a chance to kill King Saul in that cave, but he would not raise his hand against the LORD's anointed. However, he did speak truth to the king and told him that he had had the opportunity to kill him, but did not to prove that he was not treasonous and did not intend to harm Saul, even though the latter was hunting him to take his life. Truth-telling was David's response to Saul's hostile misunderstanding.

In this chapter we're not dealing with such a violent situation as David's, but occasionally we do encounter misguided people who cause harm to our soul, oftentimes without their realizing it. Depending on the setting, various phrases in the psalm section above teach us good responses so that we can be well in the occasions when people have wrong perceptions or expectations of us and our afflictions. We might need to plead with God (and perhaps the other person) for mercy, take refuge under the shadow of God's wings "until the destroying storms pass by," let out a good "cry to God Most High" (see chapter 5 on laments), or find someone whom God will "send from heaven" to save us from those who trample on us. There is also a positive place for constructive shaming if that is necessary to change mistaken perceptions.

In all these actions, the key is truth-telling. And in all of them we can count on God to "send forth his steadfast love and his faithfulness" so that we might be well.

Truth-telling to Prevent Harm

I first thought of the importance of this more specifically practical chapter because of an encounter many years ago with an eye specialist. The doctor wasn't known for a very good bedside manner. At one appointment, he was grousing about my traveling for speaking engagements, and I was getting frightened that it might be necessary to quit accepting them for the sake of my sight.

Eventually I asked him whether flying on airplanes actually hurt my retinas. He admitted that it didn't. Why, then, did it matter if that was my work? He replied that what bothered him was that my seeing eye would hemorrhage while I was somewhere across the country. (I would have heard his concern in that remark if he had said it a wee bit less gruffly!)

I asked if there was anything he could do immediately if the eye did bleed, and he acknowledged that there was nothing. What was the point, then, of staying home waiting for a calamity to happen?

Finally, I said, "Doctor, you have to get one thing straight. I am a not a blind person. I am a theologian with bad eyes."

It was startling how much that comment changed his attitude toward me. Thereafter he treated me with respect and a kinder voice. At future appointments he always asked where my next speaking engagements might take me. (And my seeing eye is doing very well!)

When I have told this story in conversations with other people with chronic conditions, they have given me many examples of truth-telling for the sake of avoiding much more serious harm than the minor incident of my account—to keep one's dignity, to avoid dangerous misdiagnoses, to help one's children cope with their parent's serious illness, to let the medical system know the seriousness of one's complications, and so forth.

We need to have the courage to speak the truth whenever someone else's treatment of us or attitude toward us causes us to feel less good about ourselves or to forget that we are God's beloved. I'm not talking about times, for example, when a doctor needs to reprimand us for not taking proper care of ourselves, but rather about such times as those when medical personnel treat us as an illness rather than a human being. Remember also chapter 6 in which we discussed the bad theologies (or anti-theologies) with which other people might harm us verbally.

Doctors' truthful rapport with their patients is also crucial for their well-being. Norman Cousins, whose work on the body's natural healing responses we considered in chapter 10, emphasizes the importance of trust in the relationship of patient and doctor. Discussing "a study of 176 cases of cancer that remitted without surgery, X-rays, or chemotherapy," Cousins reports that Dr. Jerome D. Frank of the Johns Hopkins University School of Medicine said in a commencement speech that "the question raised by these episodes was whether a powerful factor in those remissions may have been the deep belief by the patients that they were going to recover and their equally deep conviction that their doctors also believed they were going to recover."[1]

This chapter has more personal examples than I would prefer, but I can't remember enough particulars of the stories on this subject that others have told me to illustrate the kind of truth-telling that might be helpful to readers of this book. Please keep remembering that I use these specific accounts not only to encourage you that I share your limitations and concerns, but also to stimulate your own reflections on your unique conditions and context.

The goal of being well isn't helped if we experience a loss of respect for our doctors or family or caregivers. My aim is that by using the phrases of the psalm section above we can each find better ways to engage in the truth-telling that is necessary for us to be well. Thinking about these possibilities in light of God's steadfast love and faithfulness can give us clearer insight into how to proceed and greater courage for the actual undertaking.

Pleading for Mercy

When we bring our cries for mercy to God, we gain more clarity and insight concerning what pleas for compassion we should bring to other people. Sometimes we discover that the appeal for kindness changes our own attitude so that we need tell the truth to no one else except ourselves. Otherwise we might find the right words to ask for tenderness or forbearance from someone else. Perhaps we even learn that we need to become more merciful toward ourselves!

Moreover, becoming more lenient toward ourselves can also free us to ask for understanding and compassion from others. This is especially true for those who have multiple handicaps that take an inordinate amount of time for care.

As a minor example, one of my physical handicaps takes about an hour a day to attend to it, but the physician asked me to add another procedure. At consecutive appointments he reiterated his expectation. I tried to add the procedure, but in the midst of everything else I have to do for all my other limitations I felt unable to attend to my studying and writing. At speaking engagements, I had less time to be available to the people present at the conference because of one more physical requirement.

I know that this example is minor, but that, I discovered, was exactly the point. The benefits gained by the routine were far outweighed by the stress it added to my life to take even more time for my personal care. It was my own perfectionism that made me assume that I had an obligation to comply with the doctor's request.

Before my next appointment I typed up a list of all the physical procedures that I do during a day—and it totaled more than 60. When the doctor repeated his request, I asked for mercy and showed him the list.

Please don't get this wrong—this was not an urgently needed procedure. The physician has since determined that my handicap is being suitably cared for without it. The problem that kept me from being well was my own obsession to get everything right. I needed to show myself more mercy and thereby have the courage to ask the specialist for mercy.

Sometimes the need for mercy is on a large scale. One of my friends who had metastasized cancer asked her specialist at every appointment to help her weigh her options. At every stage of the cancer's progression she balanced the time to be gained by a new procedure against how much it would cost her in disruption to her family life, in suffering, in monetary expense, in interference to her capacity to pray and commune with God.

When the cost to her ability to function far outweighed the meager and miserable length of life she would gain by the new treatment, she chose not to pursue it. The doctor mercifully commended her decision, and she spent her last days fully aware and able to prepare herself and her family for her death.

In what areas of your life might you need more compassion from someone? In what areas are you too hard on yourself? How have you seen God's mercy shown toward you recently?

Some people have to ask their families for more kindness to help them deal with their afflictions. One of the reasons that I stress so much the importance of the Christian community (see chapter 9) is that members of the Body of God's Beloved could be the best people from whom we could ask for additional forbearance and care. That call for mercy is especially important when our families have become too overburdened by our requirements.

Another kind of need that persons conversing with me have raised is to ask for courtesy from medical personnel or even family members who do not share our faith. Some people have told me that doctors have been derogatory about their trust in God to care for them. Then it is almost an obligation for us to request that they respect our beliefs, even as we will respect their lack of them for the sake of a better working relationship so that we can be well.

Taking Refuge in God

The phrases "for in you my soul takes refuge" and "in the shadow of your wings I will take refuge, until the destroying storms pass by" occur after the request for mercy in Psalm 57; otherwise I might have addressed this topic first. But there is a great advantage to considering it now, for sometimes our appeals for mercy go unheeded or aren't answerable in the ways we would prefer.

When we need to flee for refuge, probably all the spiritual practices in this book will enable us to find the sheltering wings of God in order to be well. As you can see throughout this book, the discipline of praying the Psalms has been an important one for me to enter God's shadow. Once I was engaged in Psalm 31 while waiting for the brace maker to come back to his consulting room with a new orthotic that would not rub on my protruding bones. I had read these verses just before he returned:

> *Have mercy on me, O LORD, for I am in trouble;*
>   *my eye is consumed with sorrow . . .*
> *For my life is wasted with grief,*
> *and my years with sighing;*
>   *my strength fails me because of affliction,*
>   *and my bones are consumed.*
>
>   Psalm 31:9-10[2]

I read the passage aloud to him, and we both had a good laugh. The humor dispelled my anxiety, and I felt a wee bit more enfolded in God's protection for my crippled leg.

Another important practice to find sanctuary is participating in worship and resting in the community that has faith on our behalf. God often provides refuge in the sanctuary. (There is good reason for that name.)

The person with cancer described above chose to contemplate God's everlasting refuge when there were no more procedures to gain quality time with her family. By concentrating on God's eternal haven she was extremely well in the midst of terminal illness.

When we are in public situations, such as a doctor's office, to take refuge in God might utilize a simple device, such as imagining God saying that you are His beloved when someone treats you harshly. One person told me that when the "destroying storms" of another person's words passed by she kept telling herself that those words came out of that individual's own pain and not because of her afflictions. We could take that insight one step further and pray at the moment for that person to find God's refuge, too. We will be especially well when we can use our own pain to call us to care for another's well-being.

Lamenting

We don't need to spend much time discussing lamenting (see chapter 5 instead), but the portion of Psalm 57 printed above adds a new dimension with verse 2, "I cry to God Most High, to God who fulfills his purpose for me." Our lamenting takes a fresh turn when we start looking in our weeping for how God might fulfill His purposes through the very situation of another's false expectation or cruel perception that causes us grief. An example is given at the end of the previous paragraph.

We have to realize that medical personnel are severely stressed by the principalities and powers of hospital systems, insurance companies, drug producers, and lawyers who are only too eager to find patients wanting to sue. Some of the harsh perceptions and wrong expectations that lead to words that harm us might come from our doctors' and nurses' own fears. God's purpose might include our becoming more sensitive to their battles, so that we can uplift them or love them with the Trinity's perfect love that casts out all fears.

Once one of my doctors was razzing me rather callously while I was being prepped for surgery. During my silent lamenting, the Holy Spirit gave the insight that the doctor was feeling inferior to his co-surgeon from a prestigious institute. It seemed to me at the time that my words of response to his razzing were also from the Holy Spirit to encourage him to trust his own gifts. And then it suddenly occurred to me that fear of being second-rate might account for other times when his treatment of his patients seemed uncaring.

Another group of people who especially need our lamenting with a view to what God's purposes might be are members of our family or those who most closely attend us. They carry a heavy burden with nursing us. Perhaps we could invite them to lament with us so that they could understand us more thoroughly and so that we could deepen our emotional and spiritual bonds with them.

It is also necessary that we encourage them to lament with us so that God can use us to bring balm to their overburdened bodies and spirits. Such communal lament might also give us further insight into how our afflictions might be part of God's larger purposes for their lives and how we might support them in discovering those designs.

Finding Someone to Save Us

Sometimes it is urgent that we take decisive action to offset someone's false perception of our sufferings. Once when I had been badly burned by a floor heating vent when my leg brace was off, I was an (im)patient in the hospital to receive intravenous antibiotics. The podiatrist also prescribed whirlpool treatments to debride the wound.

The doctor wrote that in his orders, but the attending nurse didn't seem to get around to scheduling the daily procedure. After waiting an entire day and getting no response the next day from the nurse when I asked at what time I would be taken for debridement, I called the treatment room on the telephone. When the person answering my call asked if I were a doctor, I quickly told her about the doctor's orders not getting through, that my body wasn't fighting the infection very well, and that the whirlpool treatment would probably help if I could just get there.

God sent her from heaven to save me!

She immediately came with a wheelchair to get me and promised that she would make sure I got an appointment every day. Her manner was gentle as she gave me the treatment, and that day of the whirlpool was the turning point after which my foot began to heal.

Perhaps I am too pushy, but maybe you also have experienced times when you had to take an unusual course to find what you needed to be well. In their extreme busyness medical personnel sometimes don't rightly perceive the urgency of various aspects of our care.

The key for us again is to cry to God first, so that we are not exaggerating the urgency or making undue demands on overworked medical workers. Let us ask God to "send from heaven and save" us by showing us whatever way is best to nurse our afflictions.

Constructive Reproach

At first I was bothered by the second line in Psalm 57:3 that God would "put to shame" those who trample on us—especially because the line is followed by the word *selah* which, most scholars think, invites us to reflect upon what has just been said. When I checked the Hebrew words, however, they seemed to suggest that we could better translate the phrase in terms of God "reproaching" those whose behavior harms us.

Of course, we would never do this in public. We are not intending to shame a doctor, for example, in a way that humiliates him or her in front of other people. What we desire to do instead is to call the person to account, to urge the individual to take proper responsibility.

This happened with the nurse in the incident described in the previous section. I apologized to her that I had had to go around her by calling the treatment room for the sake of the urgently needed debridement. As far as I could discover she didn't suffer any consequences for my action. But I do pray that she would pay more attention to her patients' concerns in the future.

Of course, we always need constructive reproach ourselves. That takes us back to the two keys mentioned before we began this more practical discussion. Before taking any actions such as those suggested in this chapter, let us cry to God for wisdom so that what we do is truthful. And in our crying, let us never forget that above all "God will send forth his steadfast love and his faithfulness" (Ps. 57:3c). We can entrust our lives and afflictions to the Trinity's grace and goodness.

Two Prayers

Because this chapter is unusual and requires careful application on your part, I'm concluding it with two prayers, one for you and one for the medical personnel and family members who care for you in your afflictions. May the result of these considerations be good truth-telling on all of our parts, and may these reflections also give all of us who suffer a deeper sense of the steadfast love and faithfulness of the Triune God.

Here's my prayer for you from Hebrews 13:20-21:

Now may the God of peace, who brought back from the dead our Lord Jesus, the great shepherd of the sheep, by the blood of the eternal covenant, make you complete in everything good so that you may do his will, working among us that which is pleasing in his sight, through Jesus Christ, to whom be the glory forever and ever. [Amen.]

May you find peace, in spite of others' false expectations of you or their harmful perceptions. May your laments lead to God's purposes being fulfilled in and through you. May the LORD always be your refuge in every situation.

Now let us pray together for those who attend us:

Sanctify, O Lord, those whom you have called to the study and practice of the arts of healing, and to the prevention of disease and pain. Strengthen them by your life-giving Spirit, that by their ministries the health of the community may be promoted and your creation glorified; through Jesus Christ our Lord. Amen.[3]

16. Regrets—
Forgiveness

Out of the depths I cry to you, O LORD.
Lord, hear my voice!
Let your ears be attentive
to the voice of my supplication!
If you, O LORD, should mark iniquities,
Lord, who could stand?
But there is forgiveness with you,
so that you may be revered.

Psalm 130:1-4

One of the hardest elements to deal with in our chronic illnesses and disabilities is the remorse we feel for anything we might have done to contribute to our infirmities. I am not writing here about false guilt—we will deal with that in the following chapter. In this one, we will focus on genuine fault, our sins which have contributed to our present plight.

The psalmist models the way we should handle our penitence. Out of the depths of our remorse, we are encouraged to cry to our covenant LORD. Our sovereign Lord will certainly hear our voice, for God's ears are always attentive to our petitions and supplications. We realize that by ourselves we couldn't stand before the LORD in the fullness of our iniquities, for they are too many and too grievous. But the Scriptures thoroughly assure us of the Triune God's forgiveness. The Holy Spirit has worked in our hearts and minds to bring us the guarantee that in Christ Jesus all our sins have been forgiven. We have been reconciled to the Father through His complete work of redemption on our behalf, so we may come into God's presence with reverent adoration and thanksgiving.

At least, this is the goal: that our confession will bring us the comfort of complete forgiveness. But sometimes we ourselves obstruct God's healing pardon and release. Then our fears and regrets get in the way of the spiritual wellness that God's total exoneration could create.

Depending on how we were raised, we might see God as an unforgiving God and think that our continued suffering is a sign of His disfavor. As a result, we get caught in a downward spiral of feeling regret, which causes us to do more poorly than we might, which leads us to assume that God is even less pleased with us—which prompts us to feel even more remorse and thereby increases our sufferings.

Distinguishing Between God's Disfavor and Sin's Consequences

For those of us with any afflictions for which we bear some of the blame, it is crucial that we make careful distinctions for the sake of our emotional and spiritual well-being. First and foremost, let us think through specifically what mistakes or neglects were our fault, so that we can confess them clearly.

Perhaps that process isn't necessary for you, but I have a tendency (and maybe you do, too) to lump everything together and feel falsely guilty about the whole mess. When I try to be more specific, I realize that many of my handicaps came through no fault of my own. I had done nothing to cause my cancer or arthritis or the intussusception when my intestine caught on a polyp. The misdiagnosis and corrective surgery that led to my crippled leg were done by medical personnel, and I had simply been obedient to a doctor's orders to walk extensively on a foot that turned out to have been broken.

But I do know my genuine sin in taking for granted the supremely healthy body that I had as a youth and not taking seriously the changes in lifestyle that were necessitated by my becoming a diabetic. I did not take care of myself as I should have during some really rough years.

This distinguishing between our true errors and our false guilts enables us, then, to be very clear about another essential distinction. Concerning those mistakes that we have confessed, we can be sure of God's forgiveness. Our continuing problems are not signs of God's displeasure, but merely sin working out its own consequences. God is not punishing us for our failures.

How can we make that point strong enough? Too many people whom I have encountered have continued to think that their infirmities are God's ongoing punishment for their past sins, instead of receiving God's thorough forgiveness, which increases our courage to bear the consequences of our sins.

It is essential for us to know that God is drawing near to us, rather than moving away in disgust. Through the reconciliation made possible by Jesus Christ, we are brought near to God and given access to the thoroughness of triune grace and forgiveness (see Rom. 5:1-2). The release from anguish that comes with confidence in the Trinity's grace enables us to work courageously against the lingering effects of our mistakes. We are freed to participate in God's larger story instead of dwelling on our regrets.

The Biblical Dialectic of Repentance and Forgiveness

The more thoroughly we confess our sins, the more rich forgiveness is and the more we banish the negative regrets that clutter up our thoughts and emotions. Since we are working to clean the house of our lives, we want to get rid of every spot. James invites us into such a comprehensive purging with this hope-ending sequence of instructions for our penitence:

*Draw near to God, and he will draw near to you. Cleanse
your hands, you sinners, and purify your hearts, you double-
minded. Lament and mourn and weep. Let your laughter be
turned into mourning and your joy into dejection. Humble
yourselves before the Lord, and he will exalt you.*

James 4:8-10

How grace-filled it is that this progression ends in exaltation! We do not humble ourselves harshly to the point of
knowing ourselves only as sinners, for by the Trinity's forgiveness we are also saints at the same time. Our laughter is
turned into lamenting and our delight into dejection solely
for the purpose of thorough repentance (and to share God's
mourning heart for the world), but the Scriptures repeatedly
promise us that God does not leave us in our grieving and
weeping.

The dialectic of repentance and forgiveness must be kept
in tension; otherwise, we can fall off on either pole into theological confusion. If we concentrate only on repentance, then
we drown in our self-blame and let it overpower the good
news of God's reprieve in Christ. If we only delight in pardon,
then we start to take grace for granted and forget how much
we need it.

This is the biblical dialectic that lies behind Martin
Luther's emphasis in his Small Catechism's explanations to
all the commandments. They begin, "We should so fear and
love God." We fear God because we deserve His displeasure
because of our sins, but the Triune God's entire involvement
in humankind has been to rescue us from what we deserve.
As a result, we can't help but respond to the greatness of the
Lord's grace with love.

Fear is necessary so that we don't take God's love for
granted, as if we earned it, deserved it, or could pay it back.
Love is necessary to keep our fear from turning into terror. If

the dialectical tension between fear and love, repentance and forgiveness, is held well, our love is increased because we are so grateful for God's magnificent grace.

That is why I love the ritual of confession and absolution in the Sunday morning worship service. We completely repent so that we can get rid of all the gunk, all that is contrary to God. Our lives are exhaustively scrubbed so that we can utterly rejoice in the purity of forgiven lives.

Repentance

We are all equally sinners; everyone sins. To join together in the practice of corporate confession enables us to realize that we are not alone in our mistakes and carelessnesses, our transgressions and rebellions against God. Knowing that we all need God's forgiveness empowers us to join the community in crying for it. And we are especially freed to confess if we have unshakable hope for that forgiveness.

In my earliest childhood I felt welcomed to confess because of the loving invitation that the pastor gave and the assuring litany that preceded our corporate confession. The pastor attracted our confession with this reminder:

> Beloved in the Lord! Let us draw near with a true heart and confess our sins unto God, our Father, beseeching Him in the name of our Lord Jesus Christ to grant us forgiveness.
> [after this statement we could kneel, and the pastor continued,]
> *Our help is in the name of the Lord.*[1]

The latter assertion from Psalm 124:8 acknowledged that we could not even confess without the covenant LORD's gracious empowering. We were glad to respond by singing the second half of the psalm verse, "who made heaven and earth." By this recognition of the Trinity's cosmic might, we realized that it would not be enough to be God's beloved if God weren't also strong to rescue us.

The final exchange between the pastor and congregation before confession was Psalm 32:5. The clergyperson recited, "I said, 'I will confess my transgressions to the LORD,'" and we all sang, "and Thou forgavest the iniquity of my sin." This acclamation of God's pardon in the past freed us to come again with our wrongdoings and to trust that the Trinity's consistent character would reply to our plea for grace with the same warm reprieve.

Another such compassionate invitation could be a text like 1 John 1:8-9: "If we say that we have no sin, we deceive ourselves, and the truth is not in us. If we confess our sins, he who is faithful and just will forgive us our sins and cleanse us from all unrighteousness." This passage presents clearly the dialectic of fear and love. It convinces us of our sin and our tendency to deceive ourselves about it, but we are equally persuaded that God is ready to accept us and purify us.

The new *Evangelical Lutheran Worship* includes the following superb invitation:

> God of all mercy and consolation, come to the help of your people, turning us from our sin to live for you alone. Give us the power of your Holy Spirit that we may confess our sin, receive your forgiveness, and grow into the fullness of Jesus Christ, our Savior and Lord. Amen.[2]

This petition offers several elements that encourage us to renounce our sin—a declaration of the character of the God who receives our penitence, a reminder that we are not capable of true repentance without the Holy Spirit's empowerment, an assurance that we will indeed be showered with the pardon that we crave, and the hope that the Triune God will work in us to form us into the image of Christ our Lord.

No matter what form a congregation uses, it is compelling if we are convincingly welcomed into confession by the assurance that God will receive us and relieve us. Then we all gladly get rid of our burdens.

From all the worship services in which I have participated across the denominational spectrum and around the world through my work, I have come to love best those confessions that are really thorough and don't let any of us escape. Often during the years after *Lutheran Book of Worship* was introduced, I would offer its confession as a model to conferences for other denominations, and participants would find it very fruitful. That happened most recently at a Mennonite conference in Canada. Let us look closely at that confession and analyze why it appeals to so many.

> **Pastor [P]**: Most merciful God,
>
> **Congregation [C]**: we confess that we are in bondage to sin and cannot free ourselves. We have sinned against you in thought, word, and deed, by what we have done and by what we have left undone. We have not loved you with our whole heart; we have not loved our neighbors as ourselves. For the sake of your Son, Jesus Christ, have mercy on us. Forgive us, renew us, and lead us, so that we may delight in your will and walk in your ways, to the glory of your holy name. Amen.[3]

The first reason why so many have found this confession appealing is that it acknowledges how impossible it is for us to fix ourselves. To recognize that we are in bondage to sin (or "captive" as the new *Evangelical Lutheran Worship* expresses it) delivers us from all our attempts to liberate or reconstruct ourselves. The phrase emancipates us not to "try harder," but to rest in the gift of confession and absolution.

Secondly, this confession covers every imaginable way in which we sin. What we don't do or say wrongfully, we often think. We not only make mistakes, but we also fail sometimes by not doing anything (perhaps for fear that we'll err!). It is not only God whom we have not loved with our whole being; we've flagged in our concern for those around us. Nobody can escape this confession, thank God. It encompasses us each and all, and, as a result, we can rid ourselves of all our loads of sin.

Third, this confession relies on the Triune God for mercy because Christ has achieved total redemption for us. The result will be not only forgiveness, but also renewal, guidance, and eternal Joy as we become by God's grace and for His glory the people that He has designed us to be.

My aim in offering these samples from worship liturgies is so that each of us, if we are bogged down by regrets, can experience God's wooing us to lay down our burdens, can enunciate our repentance, and thereby can be open to the fullness of God's comprehensive exoneration.

Forgiveness

It is hard to forgive ourselves. Usually we can talk ourselves out of it. Often we don't *feel* forgiven so we doubt whether acquittal is real and unlimited.

We need someone else to tell us we're forgiven. And the good news is made more tangible when someone marks our forehead with the sign of the cross. Such a ritual can enable us to find new wholeness and hope if we are suffering from remorse for whatever we might have done to contribute to our infirmities.

For years it has been a colossal Joy to me to hear every Sunday morning this assurance of pardon from *LBW*:

> Almighty God, in his mercy, has given his Son to die for us and, for his sake, forgives us all our sins. As a called and ordained minister of the Church of Christ, and by his

authority, I therefore declare to you the entire forgiveness
of all your sins, in the name of the Father, and of the Son,
and of the Holy Spirit. Amen.[4]

This absolution contains all that our spirits require to *know* a
new freedom. We hear that God is both powerful and merciful to forgive. We know why our sins are forgiven. We receive
that pardon from a leader who represents the whole Church
whose great mission throughout the ages has been to announce
this very good news that God abundantly discharges our fail-
ings, remedies our wrongdoings, and releases us from our captivities. That leader has been authorized by Christ Himself,
whose purpose together with the Father and the Holy Spirit
has eternally been to bring us back to God.

Our world is crying for such forgiveness. We run into
situations that require it in daily life. Once a flight attendant
spilled hot water on me and kept coming back to apologize. I
finally realized what was going on and pronounced simply her
forgiveness. She didn't need to worry that I was going to sue
her or complain about her. All she required was pardon, and
that was easy to give.

How often we need to tell others that they are forgiven,
and how often we need to hear it ourselves! I pray that this
chapter will encourage you to engage in rituals of confession
and absolution (whether that be in public worship services
or in the privacy of your own home) so that you might know
freedom from remorse, so that you might "taste and see" how
good the LORD is, how ardent to absolve us.

We began this chapter acknowledging our sin with the
opening verses of Psalm 130. At this point, let's remember
that same psalm's later assurance of God's reconciling love:

> O Israel, hope in the LORD!
>   For with the LORD there is steadfast love,
>   and with him is great power to redeem.

It is he who will redeem Israel
    from all its iniquities.

Psalm 130:7-8

One of my favorite elements of Rite One in the Episcopal liturgy is that the absolution is followed by a recitation of several passages from the Scriptures that confirm the unsurpassed grace of our restored union with God. These texts (though in an older version in the prayer book) offer immense solace:

Come to me, all you that are weary and are carrying heavy burdens, and I will give you rest. (Matt. 11:28)

For God so loved the world that he gave his only Son, so that everyone who believes in him may not perish but may have eternal life. (John 3:16)

The saying is sure and worthy of full acceptance, that Christ Jesus came into the world to save sinners. (1 Tim. 1:15)

But if anyone does sin, we have an advocate with the Father, Jesus Christ the righteous; and he is the atoning sacrifice for our sins, and not for ours only but also for the sins of the whole world. (1 John 2:1b-2)

The first time I heard this recital of promises affirming God's readiness to absolve us I wept. May its listing here console your heart and bring you wellness if you are struggling with regrets for past mistakes.

Fleeing for Refuge

Whenever our consciences plague us with regrets from the past, we can flee again to our God of abundant mercy. One remarkably beautiful alto aria from J. S. Bach's *St. Matthew Passion* invites us to return to Christ as little chicks run for refuge to the safety of their mother's wings. The location of solace is underscored in the aria by the answer to the chorus's repeated question, "Where?" This is aria #60 for alto solo with chorus:

> See! Jesus has His hand
> outstretched to embrace us.
> Come!—Where?—in Jesus' arms
> seek release, take compassion.
> Seek!—Where?—in Jesus' arms
> live, die, rest here,
> you desolate little chicks.
> Remain here!—Where?—in Jesus' arms.

This piece occurs in the *Passion* just after Jesus is cruci-fied, so the invitation to come into His outstretched arms is overwhelmingly vivid, for those arms are extended on the cross so that we might seek redemption. We are also welcomed to find release in Christ's arms by a threefold repetition of the alto call, "Come," and the chorus's reply, "Where?" These make us ready to hear the answer, "In Jesus' arms." There, we can be sure, we will be wholly embraced.

Learning the Fullness of Forgiveness

We can come again and again, and our reception will always be the same. The Triune God never gets tired of us coming to Him for forgiveness.

We sometimes make God's work of reconciliation much too small. Hebrew literature is much more tangible. One Hebrew noun that is usually translated "salvation" (the word *yeshuah* from which we get the name *Jesus*) derives from a verb root that accentuates breadth or openness. The Triune God's liberation endows us with abundant room—freedom from remorse and regret, extrication from our confining captivities and hampering imprisonments. Furthermore, the LORD is always ready to release us from our snares and entanglements. Are we open to receive the immensity of His forgiveness and the fullness of His salvation—not only in the future, but now in our present griefs?

Psalm 103 is perhaps one of the strongest passages in the Scriptures to assure us that God does not treat us according to our sins. Next time you are feeling overwhelmed with shame for your failures, reread this section of the psalm to hear the faithfulness and thoroughness of the Trinity's pardon:

> *The LORD is merciful and gracious,*
>   *slow to anger and abounding in steadfast love.*
> *He will not always accuse,*
>   *nor will he keep his anger forever.*
> *He does not deal with us according to our sins,*
>   *nor repay us according to our iniquities.*
> *For as the heavens are high above the earth,*
>   *so great is his steadfast love toward those who fear him;*
> *as far as the east is from the west,*
>   *so far he removes our transgressions from us.*
> *As a father has compassion for his children,*
>   *so the LORD has compassion for those who fear him.*
> *For he knows how we were made;*
>   *he remembers that we are dust.*
>
>   Psalm 103:8-14

Because we know that we are dust and unable to rise above it, we are astonished at the fullness of God's grace and mercy, the faithfulness of His loving kindness and patience. I especially love this passage because of its two powerful cosmological images for God's *chesedh*—that steadfast love is as enormous as the span between the stars and earth and that forgiveness is so comprehensive that our sins are separated from us as distantly as the east is from the west. The latter is especially significant since we can eventually meet south if we go north, but we can't ever reach the west by going east because we will continually circle the globe.

J. S. Bach set this point to music in Chorale #40 of the *St. Matthew Passion*. Though the first word should probably be rendered "although," I have translated it with the word *scarcely* to urge us to hurry to God with our repentance, for His compassion is stupendously larger than our faults, His redemption so extraordinarily encompassing to cancel all our sins.

> Scarcely have I strayed from you
> Than I have again come back,
> For Your Son has redeemed us
> Through His dread and mortal suffering.
> I do not deny my fault;
> But your mercy and grace
> are much greater than the sin
> which I always find within me.

Bearing the Consequences by Grace

I have stressed forgiveness so much in this chapter because our failure to receive it so often impedes our wellness. We get so bogged down in our sins that we are prevented from dealing with their consequences.

To the contrary, when we know that we are God's beloved and are assured of His grace and pardon, then we have confidence to deal with any repercussions from our mistakes. We might not be able to change sin's effects on our infirmities, but we will have the hope of present and eternal Joy to sustain us in them.

The desperation of our situation without forgiveness as recorded in the first verse at the beginning of this chapter led Martin Luther to pen his famous hymn, "Aus tiefer Not," or "out of the deepest need." This hymn, in its rendering by famous 19th-century translator Catherine Winkworth, is a fitting closing for this chapter because it underscores the proper kind of fear that we should have in realizing how desperately we need God's pardon and also the overflowing love that we have in discovering the fullness of the Lord's compassionate care for us.

Let us sing this hymn together:

From depths of woe I cry to Thee,
Lord, hear me, I implore Thee.
Bend down Thy gracious ear to me,
My prayer let come before Thee.
If Thou rememb'rest each misdeed,
If each should have its rightful meed,
Who may abide Thy presence?

Thy love and grace alone avail
To blot out my transgression;
The best and holiest deeds must fail
To break sin's dread oppression.
Before Thee none can boasting stand,
But all must fear Thy strict demand
And live alone by mercy.

Therefore my hope is in the Lord
And not in mine own merit;
It rests upon His faithful Word
To them of contrite spirit
That He is merciful and just;
This is my comfort and my trust.
His help I wait with patience. Amen[5]

The LORD be with you. [And also with you.] Let us pray:

O God, where is there another like you? You forgive sin
and forgive the iniquity of the lowest of your people. You
do not stay angry forever, for you are merciful and you
pardon our transgressions and cast all our sins into the
deep sea. Do continue forever to be merciful, so that we
may walk in the light of your word and escape every trap
of Satan and of the world, through Jesus Christ, your Son,
our Redeemer. Amen.[6]

17. False Guilt—
Medicine Is a Stochastic Art

I am utterly bowed down and prostrate;
all day long I go around mourning.
For my loins are filled with burning,
and there is no soundness in my flesh.
I am utterly spent and crushed;
I groan because of the tumult of my heart.

Psalm 38:6-8

In the previous chapter we learned that to keep battering ourselves for our past sins does not contribute to our wellness. How extraordinarily much better it is to confess those sins and to receive God's forgiveness—as we assuredly are always given it—so that we can have the courage to deal with whatever consequences from our mistakes we face. In this chapter we recognize that oftentimes we blame ourselves for ill effects that are not our fault. We don't require forgiveness for anything that has given rise to this false guilt; we ache for freedom from it. We need healing to stop blaming ourselves.

Psalm 38 is a mixed poem. At some points David confesses his sins, but in other verses he speaks of his enemies and foes. We who have chronic illnesses and disabilities possess such a mixture. Of course, we sin; everyone does—and in our repentance we can indeed cry to God for mercy.

But some of our problems are due to enemies beyond ourselves. We carry a false guilt if we blame ourselves for those troubles that are caused by the forces of evil that bring infirmities. For example, it was certainly not my fault that there was a measles epidemic in my high school, nor that the measles virus attacked my systems and caused me to become a diabetic. If you are suffering from afflictions, no doubt you can name many adversaries that have caused you suffering.

Because of this jumble of woes with which we deal, we can join David in bewailing our adversities and the lack of health that results from attacks by diverse antagonists. We lament these things, but always remember that they have not been caused by God. Because of forces outside of our control we are "bowed down and prostrate"; we grieve and are crushed; we groan with confusion and "the tumult of [our] heart[s]."

Clearing Up Our Theology

When we are plagued by false guilt, let us first make sure that we are not dealing still with some leftover doctrine of retribution (see chapter 6). Might we be feeling unconsciously that because we are not well physically we must have done something wrong? Let us remember that retribution is not a biblical doctrine and that the world is founded on grace, rather than on any sort of notion that God punishes or seeks vengeance.

Our deepest problem when we struggle with false guilt is that we accentuate it by continuing to look at ourselves instead of at the Triune God, who embraces us and claims us as His beloved.

Our expectations often cause us to bear a false guilt. We keep forgetting that we are human. We expect ourselves to be perfect, and when we're not—largely through processes of illness that are out of our control—we feel guilty for our frailty. Or we expect ourselves to be as strong as we were when we were younger. We feel blameworthy when we can't do what we once did.

Oftentimes our erroneous burdens arise because we-perhaps unconsciously—compare ourselves with others (and usually with those who do not have the physical problems that we have). For example, if I watched others in the swimming pool when I worked out by doing laps, I would always feel bad that I couldn't keep up (not consciously remembering that the others weren't dealing with any of the impairments that kept me slower), and then I would feel that dull ache of false guilt that I wasn't as strong as I *should* be. Why did I put that unreal culpability upon myself?

I use that example because I encounter many with infirmities who are kept from wholeness by their false guilts. God does not demand that we keep up with anyone else. God only asks us to be faithful with who we are—with all our limitations.

One theological gift that we will find exceptionally helpful is the fact that *ha-satan* is Hebrew for "the accuser." If we are accusing ourselves, we are outside of God's will for us, for our Comforter wants us instead to find hope and wellness through grace. Whenever we are made to feel guilty about matters that are unrelated to our actual sinfulness, we know that this sense of blame does not come from God, but from the temptations of the accuser.

A Stern Rebuke

When we wallow in false guilts, we need a friend, pastor, or relative to give us a stern rebuke, to give us a cold shower of truth to snap us out of our doldrums. We can hardly convince ourselves that our feeling of responsibility is untrue. Usually we have harbored it and nurtured it for too long to be easily dissuaded.

Several weeks ago my devotion book included as the fourth reading for the day a letter to a woman harassed by self-accusation. The message was sent to her by the German Lutheran pastor J. K. Wilhelm Loehe (1808–1872), who established churches in three midwestern states. Pastor Loehe admitted that he was not her pastor, but that he felt compelled to write to her because of her mistaken notions. Then he admonished her quite strongly:

> All your torment, your doubt, your terrors, your fears, your fancies, your reminiscence on the sins of your youth, your affirmation to be inhabited by the sin against the Holy Spirit—all these things are partly illness, partly temptation, and like most temptations are pure lie and deceit. The truth is that God in Jesus Christ is merciful unto you.

After these words Loehe urged her to find her hope entirely through grace and to stop thinking about herself. He closed, "This is written to you with the heart-felt sympathy of your fellow pilgrim and fellow combatant."[1]

Often our very illness leads us to accept false guilts. This is complicated by the temptations that accompany our discouragements. We need to hear again and again the truth of God's love in Christ. We need to be bolstered to resist the accuser with a clear cognizance of his deceptions.

Think of someone who could shake you out of your mistaken notions. Do you have friends who remind you of the hope that is unquestionably ours in Jesus Christ? If not, I pray that this chapter is strong enough to divest you of your false guilts. Or perhaps your caregiver could read this chapter and be the spokesperson that you need to dismantle your insidiously erroneous blamings.

Medicine Is a Stochastic Art

One find that helps me overcome false guilt about medical problems I discovered in a magazine for diabetics and tracked down through the grace of our local library's research assistants. Katerine Ierodiakonou and Jan P. Vandenbroucke wrote an article called "Medicine as a stochastic art" primarily to warn doctors against misusing one patient's statistics or case history as a general rule to expect certain outcomes in other patients.

However, the article is helpful for us here because it outlines the ancient Greeks' proposal "that the aim of medicine should not be seen as the achievement of the desired end, but as doing everything possible to achieve this end."[2] The authors suggest that medicine is somewhat like Chaos theory, which asserts that "the behaviour of whole systems can become unpredictable, even if their components behave in a simple way."[3] Perhaps you have heard the example that a butterfly flapping its wings on one side of the globe could result in a hurricane on the other.

What this means for our infirmities is that we might do everything we are supposed to do, we might have perfectly followed the doctors orders, and yet the outcome is not what we expected. Rather than blame ourselves, we should simply recognize that medicine is a stochastic art—that is, that it is not as precise as a science, but instead involves probability and random occurrences.

Too many factors intervene. For example, a diabetic might eat the exact same number of calories and give the same precise amount of insulin, but stress or discouragement or false guilt might interfere with the normal processes and cause the blood glucose level to go higher nonetheless.

So many chance factors can make it difficult to control our chronic illnesses. This is not because we are being lazy or disobedient or imprecise or inattentive. It is simply because we don't know how to figure in other factors within ourselves and even in the outside environment.

We can find great well-being if we acknowledge those other elements and stop blaming ourselves when medicines don't work perfectly as we expected them to. (I especially need to hear this good news myself: since my kidney transplant two years ago I have run into numerous instances of not getting the results I'd anticipated with various medications, and I tend to hold myself responsible instead of accepting the stochastic nature of pharmaceutical treatments.)

Doing the Best We Can

The truth about the nature of medicine does not excuse any carelessness. It does not exempt us from obedience to our doctors' orders. Instead, it invites us to do the best we can and leave the results up to God, who judges us for our faithfulness rather than for our accomplishments.

That is the significant distinction that enables us to handle our infirmities without falling to false guilt when all does not go as well as we expected. We try to judge ourselves not by whether or not we achieved our desired end, but by whether or not we did everything possible to move in the right direction.

I have to keep that distinction in mind these days as I wait to recover from what seems three weeks ago to have been a stroke of a small blood vessel caused by low blood pressure. I am faithfully doing the assigned exercises designed to stimulate and improve small motor functioning in my hands, but I don't see much progress. I continue to go to the exercise club for bicycling on a machine that also conditions the arms with bars to push and pull in tune with my pedaling, but I'm not as fast as I was before the stroke. If I measured myself by the ultimate goal of fitness, that would stir up a hornet's nest of personal accusations.

Self-blame is out of place. My low blood pressure is being treated by medications, which haven't been working very well lately. We never thought that I was in danger of a stroke because my heart is healthy and my blood vessels more clear than usual for someone my age and with my disabilities (according to the doctors).

You perhaps have a somewhat similar situation—chronic illnesses or disabilities that came to you unpredicted and out of your control. What we each are called to do is the best we can with all that we've got, both strengths and weaknesses.

God does not demand the impossible. He asks us only that we be true to our own situation and responsibilities in light of our capabilities.

Remember in the parable of the talents in Matthew 25:14-30 that the head of the household said, "Well done, good and faithful slave; you were faithful with a few things, I will put you in charge of many things; enter into the joy of your master" (Matt. 25:21 and 23 NASB) to both the servant who had gained an additional five talents and the one who had gained two. The master was displeased only with the slave who misunderstood his character and thought that he was a hard man.

Even so, let us keep in mind the goodness of God's character and, in response, apply ourselves faithfully to whatever we can do to take care of our infirmities. Then we will know the wholeness of freedom from false guilt and the hope of all the Trinity's promises to us.

God's Deliverance

God's character has been shown throughout the Scriptures to be gracious and full of steadfast love. His desire is to deliver us for the sake of His glory. Sometimes we might be released from our physical afflictions, but even more important is that we be liberated into wellness of soul and spirit as we place our hope in the Trinity.

Oftentimes we discover that God delivers us one step at a time. We don't know how we will manage because we look too far ahead and then feel falsely guilty because we haven't made more progress toward the ultimate (or our illusory or unreal) goal. On the contrary, if we entrust ourselves to the LORD, we find our enemies defeated or exposed as friends instead. We detect the path that we can take with our limitations, and we learn what pleases God.

Because these ideas are in Psalm 143, it has become one of my favorites. Pray a portion of this psalm with me and notice how it both extricates us from false guilt by acknowledging the adversaries that afflict us from outside of ourselves and also releases us to do our best:

> *Let me hear of your loving-kindness in the morning,*
> *for I put my trust in you.*
> > *show me the road that I must walk,*
> > *for I lift up my soul to you.*
> *Deliver me from my enemies, O LORD,*
> > *for I flee to you for refuge.*
> *Teach me to do what pleases you, for you are my God;*
> > *let your good Spirit lead me on level ground.*
> *Revive me, O LORD, for your Name's sake;*
> > *for your righteousness' sake, bring me out of trouble.*
> *Of your goodness, destroy my enemies*
> *and bring all my foes to naught,*
> > *for truly I am your servant.*
>
> Psalm 143:8-12[4]

 The LORD be with you. [And also with you.] Let us pray:

O LORD, look down from heaven, behold, visit and relieve thy servants, for whom we offer our supplications; look upon them with the eyes of thy mercy; give them comfort and sure confidence in thee; defend them from the danger of the enemy and keep them in perpetual peace and safety; through Jesus Christ, thy Son, our Lord. Amen.[5]

18. Depression—
Medical Gifts

"I loathe my life;
I will give free utterance to my complaint;
I will speak in the bitterness of my soul.
I will say to God, Do not condemn me."

Job 10:1-2a

There are times when our coping skills simply run out. We get tired of dealing with all the medicines that we have to take so many times in the day, the little things that go wrong one after the other after another, the pile of stressors that constantly afflict us. We dread what might hit us next. We cry out with Job, "I loathe my life!" Our souls shrivel under the onslaught of unremitting physical troubles.

What happened yesterday provides a minor example. I've been busy going to my family doctor, a neurologist, and an occupational therapist to figure out whether I really had a small vessel stroke three weeks ago and what to do about it. In addition, I'm spending three or four periods a day doing finger exercises to try to clean up my handwriting and improve my small motor coordination after that mysterious event. Then suddenly yesterday I had an allergic reaction to some cantaloupe and my whole face puffed up. I've already lost so much time and energy for working on this book that I surely didn't need to be scared by something new that required (to offset the reaction) an antihistamine, which put me to sleep for the rest of the day. "Lord," I complained, "I don't need something else to worry about." Frightened, I protested, "God, why does everything bad have to happen to me?"

Perhaps you, too, have been frazzled by an endless stream of deteriorations or even of little harassments. Maybe you have been repeatedly frightened by new difficulties or surprising reactions, unknown complications, or worsening symptoms. As the inconveniences or distresses pile up, we struggle not to get depressed.

Depression Is NOT a Moral Failure

Depression has been grossly misunderstood by society and, even today, by Christians. Too often believers think that their depression is a failure of not trusting God enough, and so they feel guilty about it. Since gratitude is a good antidote for whatever ails us, Christians feel even more guilt if they cannot be thankful. This leads to a downward spiral, for guilt intensifies the depression, which makes one feel more at fault, and so the despair increasingly snowballs.

Kathryn Greene-McCreight stresses this confusion about guilt and depression in her book, *Darkness Is My Only Companion*, which she wrote out of her own experience with bi-polar disorder. Because she deals from a theologically sound base and from personal familiarity with the travails of severe depression, I will not duplicate her work and explore Christian responses to mental illnesses in this chapter, but will refer you instead to her book.[1] Here we have space and competence only to consider how, when we suffer from mild depression, we can be well.

As a beginning step, it is crucial that we not blame ourselves for being depressed. Physicians explain that any one of us at any time in our lives may suffer from a little depression. Depression may occur due to any stress, such as a job change, the death of a loved one, sudden onset of an illness, chronic disease, or the like. It is right for us to feel sadness at such times, and our griefs or strains will undoubtedly cause us to be "down."

Certain factors, however, aggravate the symptoms and increase our need for care. God created our brains equipped with a chemical, serotonin, to help us cope with the normal stresses and struggles of life, but over time the amount of serotonin gets depleted. When this occurs, contending with our problems becomes much more difficult because our body's chemistry has become unbalanced.

How much it frees us to work actively to treat our depression if we understand that it is due to a chemical imbalance, rather than to a lack of faith or some sort of moral failure on our part! It is important that we or our friends who cherish us recognize when sadness has moved into depression that requires particular care.

Signs of Depression

Your doctor, clinician, or healthcare provider can give you a checklist of the symptoms of depression. This list can help you determine whether or not you are suffering from depression. (Let me encourage you to seek professional advice if you are.) Here is a list of symptoms gathered from various sources. Medical personnel suggest that if we evidence three or four of the following traits we should consider taking positive steps to address the depression symptoms. Active measures include going for a walk, beginning a daily exercise routine, attending to hobbies or a garden, or engaging in other pleasurable activities. If we exhibit five or more of the following symptoms nearly every day for more than two weeks, we should seek medical help:

- we don't have the will to go on—or even to get up in the morning; we feel helpless
- we have an "empty" feeling, continuing sadness, anxiety, or hopelessness
- we lose interest or do not take pleasure in our usual activities

- we are excessively tired, have low energy
- we have trouble falling asleep or staying asleep, or we sleep too much
- we have an increase or decrease in appetite or find ourselves suddenly gaining or losing weight
- we cry too often or too much
- we have aches and pains that do not respond to treatment
- we feel restless or fidgety or, the opposite, we move or speak more slowly than usual and others notice it
- we are unable to concentrate, stay focused, remember, or make decisions
- we feel guilty, worthless, that we have failed ourselves or our family

If we have any thoughts that we would be better off dead or of harming ourselves in any way, then we should seek immediate help. Remember that these are symptoms of an illness, not a weakness in faith, and should be treated medically as any other malady.

In the process of becoming depressed we may experience loss of self; we may feel that we have become a different person. The great poet John Donne might have experienced depression along with his illness, for he wrote, "Of all the miseries that people experience, sickness is greater than any of them.... In poverty I lack things and in banishment I lack the company of other people, but in sickness I lack myself."[2] The good news is that, when we can't find our selves, our God is still the same and desires our healing.

Though gratitude is a gift for healing, one distress of a depressed person is that he or she has trouble feeling or expressing thankfulness. This, too, might cause guilt feelings, for we think our ingratitude is due to hardness of heart, rather than to the affliction in our mind.

All these symptoms make us crave the gracious embrace of a loving God, but when we are depressed we have trouble knowing that He really cares about us. We need reminders of the faithfulness of the Trinity's compassion, but we also need medical advice or attention to ease our illness so that our depression symptoms don't prevent us from hearing the very consoling Word that we require.

"There Is Now No Condemnation . . ."

Paul insists in Romans 8 that there is absolutely no condemnation ever for those who are in Christ Jesus (v. 1), that nothing—including our depression—can ever separate us from the love of God (vv. 38-39), and that throughout our worst illnesses the Holy Spirit intercedes for us when we cannot even begin to pray (vv. 26-27). All this is because "the law of the Spirit of life in Christ Jesus has set [us] free from the law of sin and of death" (v. 2).

We ourselves or any of our friends or relatives who may be depressed need to hear this assurance again and again. Science has demonstrated clearly the effects of depression on our brain, and we now know that depression is a medical condition just like any other disease. Since depression is not a lapse in faith, therefore, we can affirm these truths repeatedly for those who suffer:

- God has not abandoned you. Though you do not feel His presence, He has promised to be with you always, and He has *never* broken His promises.

- Your depression is not sin, but illness. You do not need ever to feel guilty. For any past, actual sins that you have committed and for which you have repented, you do not need to feel guilty anymore, for God has forgiven them.

- You need not feel shame that you are unable to give thanks to God or others. Shame is a symptom of your illness and not your fault.

- You are not worthless or hopeless. You are the beloved of God, and, by God's grace and healing mercies, this illness can be treated.

- To receive treatment for depression is not a sign of your weakness, but of your wisdom (see below).

That is just a sample list of the kinds of assurances people with depression continually need to hear. All the biblical truths in this book might be appropriate words to offer those whom we want to console.

Kathryn Greene-McCreight offers us two important teachings out of her experience with profound depression that we can add to our arsenal of consoling truths. The first is that even our despair is not contrary to faith. She writes:

> Despair is a reaction to evil, evil as the forces that work against God's good creation and providence. Despair may even be involuntary, caused by a brain disorder; it may be voluntary, caused by giving up. But it is always a reaction to some form of evil, some deprivation of the good, and therefore understandable as such. This is an exceedingly important lesson: *despair can live with Christian faith*. Indeed, having despair while knowing in your heart that God has conquered even that is a great form of faith, for it is tried by fire.[3]

That is really good news for all of us, for at various points in our lives we all fall into despair over the state of things, perhaps over the situation the world is in. To be in despair because there is so much violence and injustice in the world is right and healthy because it is a reaction to sin and evil in the cosmos. But let us remind each other also that such despair is coupled with believing in God's victory over all the forces of evil at the cross and empty tomb. Someday all oppression and inequity will cease; at that time all sorrow and illness will be gone. Because this is our hope in Christ, we can endure through our times of despair and depression.

The other gift that Greene-McCreight offers for us here is her insight into the loss of our self that many, even with mild depression, experience. She startles us with this reversal of perceptions:

> The personality dissolves. Tastes, desires, dispositions that formerly marked our personality vanish with mental illness. Will I ever be me again, and if so, what will me be on the other side of this madness? So what does this mean? What does this mean *coram Deo*, before God, that the personality should dissolve? I suppose it means that the personality is relatively unimportant vis-à-vis God. In God's eyes we are not how we feel, we are not what we think, we are not even what we do. We are what God does with us, and what God does with us is to save us from our best yet perverse efforts to separate ourselves from his presence, from his fellowship, communion, sharing.[4]

Again, what great news this is: even when we think we are losing our self, our true self is held by God, who is saving us. By becoming incarnate to rescue us, Jesus Christ revealed that God desires our relationship with Himself much more than we do. I remember many years ago crying to a pastor, "I can't hold on any longer." He consolingly answered, "Don't forget: God is always holding on to you, and He will not let you go."

The Gifts of Medicine

One great find for me when I struggle with depression (because of such things as the effects of medicine and low blood pressure and the situation of not feeling better after my kidney transplant) is that the personnel in my HMO's "depression management program" are so caring and instructive. God certainly has blessed us with scientists who have intensively studied the brain and the causes and effects of depression, with those who have developed many kinds of medicines and therapies to treat it, and with those who render care.

My case manager explained to me the effects of the proliferation of my handicaps on my brain's serotonin level. No wonder I was struggling with depression; I'd been hit with a constant barrage of new physical problems for the last two decades. She instructed me in the pleasurable activities that can offset depression, many of which, such as exercise, I participate in assiduously. She gave me several questionnaires to determine my level of depression so that we could find the best treatment plan.

Treatment of depression can involve many different types of antidotes. Recently, for the purposes of this chapter, my case manager sent me a list of "Pleasant Activities" that can counter the progression of depression. The list includes such things as reading novels or spiritual literature, watching videos, learning a new hobby, participating in sports or other activities outdoors, church and social events, playing musical instruments or singing, or visiting people who are sick or shut-in. Altogether the list contained 70 entries which could be gifts for the one depressed as well as for others. Such a compendium guides us because, when we are depressed, it is hard to think of what to do that might lift us from our emptiness.

Treatment for depression varies with the individual. Some find their best resource to be support groups that enable them to discuss with others their frustrations and fears and to gain new insights. Support groups can be especially beneficial for those who contend with chronic illnesses and disabilities. Our infirmities seem more manageable when we discuss them with others who have the same struggles.

Talk therapies assist us in reframing our perceptions and attitudes. Church groups can be especially constructive in enabling us to articulate and grow in our trust and hope in the Triune God.

Antidepressant drugs can improve our moods, our sleeping and eating habits, and our concentration. We are blessed to have so many different types of drugs available to us, because each person finds different prescriptions more or less suitable. For example, many medications are not effective for me because they lower the blood pressure and thus increase the fatigue. My exhaustion level is already too high because of extremely low pressure.

Treating depression takes longer than does management for simple illnesses, so let me encourage you to be patient with the process. Our depression is likely the result of a large accumulation of stresses, so we may presume that its reversal will also take more than a few weeks.

Also, Greene-McCreight urges us not to shun hospitalization, if our illness necessitates this. She calls it "God's castle to keep us safe."[5] Let us keep remembering that all the things mentioned above—scientists and researchers, doctors and clinicians and other case management personnel, medicines and therapies—are God's gifts to bring us wellness.

Changing Habits

We probably all have habits that could be modified to protect us from, or to treat, depression. One gift of therapy might be to transform our negative thought patterns into positive recollections of blessings. If, for example, we dislike ourselves because we feel that we have failed, we can learn to concentrate instead on the gifts that God has brought to us and, through us, to others.

Other aspects of our thought patterns that might be modified include our attitudes about getting help. We all need to learn more humbly to receive grace, so discovering how to accept anyone's assistance will always benefit us and free us from both pride and our fear of weakness.

Another gift might be to change our physical habits. The more we can be physically engaged, the more our body will produce endorphins and other chemicals that deal with our pains and our ability to cope. I realize that many of you reading this book might be limited by your infirmities, but with the assistance of experts we can all learn new ways to use those parts of our body that are still functioning. I think of a close friend with quadriplegia, who, for as long as it was workable, insisted on using a push wheelchair so that he could maintain as much strength in his arms as possible. I watched him turn corners by bashing his arm against the doorframe, and his courage and zeal astounded me. He was taking action. He was doing the best he could with his physical limitations.

One way of taking action may be to develop habits of service to others. Several of the items on the "Pleasant Activities" list from my HMO involved engagement with others, like writing to or calling friends, making crafts for others, or doing volunteer work. We know that bringing love to others increases our sense of well-being. We often know God's love for us best as it passes through us to others.

Prayer, Prayer, and More Prayer

One of our most important habits to cling to, or to develop, in our times of depression is the practice of prayer. We recognize, however, that to pray is exceedingly difficult when we are depressed. One of the signs of our situation might be that we have trouble focusing on anything, but prayer requires great concentration. Furthermore, we have already noted above that sometimes depression makes it hard to be grateful. Kathryn Greene-McCreight observes that with these obstacles, "one has to try all the harder, or maybe not at all: to let the Holy Spirit pray through you is a form of prayerful surrender."[6] What a great relief that is! When we cannot pray, the Scriptures assure us not only that the Holy Spirit intercedes for us as we noted before (Rom. 8:26-27), but also that Jesus lives eternally at the Father's right hand to make intercession for us (Heb. 7:25).

We also find extremely helpful the prayers of others. That is why each chapter in this book concludes with a prayer or hymn from the saints of the Church. Greene-McCreight writes,

> I strapped myself to the prayers and praises of Israel, the scripture, and relied on others' prayers from ancient Israel to my present-day parish and family. . . . But I learned that we must always pray, even and especially when we don't feel it or it feels compulsory and rote and dry.[7]

Hymnbooks, devotion books of all sorts+, prayer books, and lectionaries can all assist us in continuing to pray even when we don't feel like it.

Above all, Jesus inspires us to pray because of His own prayer "Why have you forsaken me?" (Matt. 27:46) during His time on the cross. As psychologist John White stresses, we do better to cry "Why?" than to refrain from crying.[8]

Notice that when Jesus wailed in His desolation, He still addressed His Father as "My God, my God." The question "Why?" implies that someone will listen to us.

As has been emphasized in other places in this book, it is good to cry out our confusions to God. The Scriptures frequently show us that the Trinity certainly listens and answers with exceedingly compassionate care. No matter how difficult it is to pray or how feeble our prayers are, no matter how far we feel from God, the LORD is our covenant God who has promised never to leave us.

We know that with certainty because of what Jesus has done for us; because He bore the Father's abandonment for us (which meant suffering for the whole Trinity!), we can trust that we will never be forsaken. John White summarizes beautifully what we can learn from the cross for our depression:

> But the most important point to grasp is that you will not be the first to tread so dark a valley, to feel so alone, so alienated from God. There is someone who has trodden it before you. And the valley will end. Calvary was followed by a tearing aside of all that hid God, by a bursting from the tomb and by ascension to glory. The glory that is to be revealed in you will shine the brighter against the blackness from which you will emerge.[9]

Of course, when we are in the midst of depression, we have trouble believing that we will truly emerge from the blackness, but that is why this chapter has emphasized both the consolations of God and His gifts of medical technology and expertise and therapies. Just as for other illnesses, the right treatment is available to us if we seek it.

As for the darkness that we feel when we are depressed, it is exceedingly comforting that the Scriptures repeatedly picture the LORD as a God of light and that, when we are knit to Him, we shall be in the light, too. For example, in Psalm 139, which so beautifully describes God's intricate care in our creation, we read this excerpt:

> *If I say, "Surely the darkness shall cover me,*
> *and the light around me become night,"*
> *even the darkness is not dark to you;*

the night is as bright as the day,
for darkness is as light to you.

Psalm 139:11-12

Similarly, the First Letter of John emphasizes that "God is light and in him there is no darkness at all" (1 John 1:5).

Not only *is* God light, but in Christ He has defeated the darkness for all time. John's Gospel underscores this:

In the beginning was the Word, and the Word was with God, and the Word was God. . . . What has come into being in him was life, and the life was the light of all people. The light shines in the darkness, and the darkness did not overcome it.

John 1:1, 3-5

The darkness did not overcome it, cannot overcome it, will never be able to overcome it! What great exultation fills us when we learn to trust in the one true Light! Darkness can never win in our life—it has been defeated for all time and eternity.

 The LORD be with you. [And also with you.] Let us pray:

Lord Jesus, hanging on the cross and left alone by your disciples, you called on your Father with a mighty cry as you gave up your spirit. Deliver us from the prison of affliction, and be yourself our inheritance in the land of the living, where with the Father and the Holy Spirit you are blessed now and forever.[10]

Amen.

19. Dying —
Dying Daily and Well

In my despair I said,
"In the noonday of my life I must depart;
> *my unspent years are summoned to the portals*
> *of death."*
And I said,
"No more shall I see the LORD in the land of the
living,
> *never more look on my kind among dwellers*
> *on earth.*
My house is pulled down and I am uncovered,
> *as when a shepherd strikes his tent.*
My life is rolled up like a bolt of cloth,
> *the threads cut off from the loom.*
Between sunrise and sunset my life is brought to
an end;
> *I cower and hope for the dawn. . . ."*

Isaiah 38:10-13a[1]

As Isaiah 38:1 tells us, the prayer of Hezekiah recorded above was written after he had recovered from his seemingly terminal illness. He speaks to us about how he felt at the edge of death. It is the way many of us feel at times if we are suffering from chronic infirmities. Perhaps we, too, have an affliction that will eventually be fatal. What we don't know—as nobody knows—is how soon or long it will be until we depart this life.

The striking images in Hezekiah's prayer enable us to articulate graphically what we feel. Of course, we think that our life is cut off too soon; we've been waylaid by tribulations and grieve that we haven't been able to spend our years as we would have wished.

As when bedouins strike their tents to move on, so we feel that our exterior shell is being torn apart, leaving our souls exposed. We have been cut off from normal activities like cloth is cut from the loom. Each anguished night we wonder if we will live till sunrise.

All of Life Is Dying

Certainly we all know that we begin dying the moment we are born. We have been taught that every seven years our total body undergoes an entire rebuilding. If you are 70 years old, by now your anatomy has been completely reconstructed 10 times.

That is not much comfort, however, to those of us whose bodies are breaking down, but not being mended. We are dying faster than we are being repaired. If we possessed any visions for our future, our imminent or impending death has now crushed them. We are left instead with questions about how to die well.

What do we do with the immense disappointment? Three responses strike me immediately. One is to recognize that the situation is not as meaningless as it might seem (see chapter 4). Second, we must deal with depression (see previous chapter) if our frustration drops into despair. Third and most important, our faith in the Triune God gives us magnificent resources both for the disappointment of our unspent years and for dying well.

Dying Has Already Been Conquered

The entire meta-narrative of faith in the Triune God places Jesus Christ at its center as the turning point of all of history.

Too often we think about the work of Jesus for the sake of eternal life or for the fact that He sent His Spirit to guide us in the present, but do we realize what gifts He offers us for the sake of facing our death and dying well?

The Letter to the Hebrews startles us with this perspective on the treasures we can find in Christ:

> *Since, therefore, the children share flesh and blood, he himself likewise shared the same things, so that through death he might destroy the one who has the power of death, that is, the devil, and free those who all their lives were held in slavery by the fear of death. . . . Because he himself was tested by what he suffered, he is able to help those who are being tested.*
>
> Hebrews 2:14-15, 18

First, Jesus gives us unfailing hope that He has conquered not only death, but also the one who had the power of death. Because Christ has passed through death and come out the other side, we need not fear the dark unknown. Because He meanwhile overthrew Satan and all the powers of evil, we need not fear the way into the murky future.

Jesus has turned death from a scary, unknown cessation of life into, instead, a door through the last barrier (our earthly existence) that keeps us from eternal life and the radiant gladness of knowing our Creator face to face. We rejoice that we will no longer be separated from the Trinity, but will enter into the infinite Joy of God's glorious and voluminously loving presence.

Because we no longer have to fear death, we do not need unnecessarily to prolong life. We can prepare advanced directives to make sure no extraordinary measures are taken to extend our lives when our brains are dead. Certainly we can make use of technological advances to maintain our lives when we are truly still alive. Of course, we do not want to rush death if God still seems to have reason for us to be living. But when our normal processes have ceased, we will certainly be ready to "go home" into eternal life with the Triune God.

Nevertheless, many human beings throughout life have been enslaved to the fear of death. Making our lives worthwhile somehow haunts us—that is why we seek meaning or accomplishments so much or want to pass on the best of ourselves to our children. We want somehow to make sure that our lives were not lived in vain.

We know that Jesus understands us and our longings, for as Hebrew 2:16-17 stresses, He did not become incarnate for the sake of the angels, but for our sake. Therefore, He became exactly like us—His very own brothers and sisters—to every extent imaginable. He even shared our fears in the face of death and three times begged His Father that the cup of suffering and death might be removed from Him.

Yet He serves as a gracious and trustworthy high priest for us because He willingly entered into that process of death and completed the sacrifice of atonement in order that our sins might be forgiven. Too often, however, we restrict His priesthood to that sacrifice itself (as supremely important as it is) and do not envision what it also means for accompanying us through the whole process that leads to death.

Hebrews 4:15 stresses that our high priest Jesus was tested in every way that we are tried. Consequently, we know that He understands all our agonies and bears them with us. Hebrew 2:18, cited above, underscores His ability to assist us throughout our testings through His own experience of suffering. We all know that those who encourage us the most in our afflictions are usually people who have gone through trials themselves. Imagine that multiplied to infinity to catch a vision of the inconceivable compassion with which Jesus accompanies us in our infirmities.

Isn't this astounding, almost beyond belief? The God of the cosmos, Lord of the universe, became as one of us so that He could pass through the process of dying and through death itself in order that He might comprehend all our sufferings and be our companion in the midst of them and to the other side of them.

As a result, we no longer have to be frightened by either death or even the manner in which we move toward it. God's love for us is all encompassing; He will not leave us to ourselves, no matter what is happening in our life—or death.

Looking at Our Resurrection

Because we suffer infirmities—whether or not we can see death on the horizon—our Christian faith offers us unfathomed encouragement in the sure hope of the resurrection. Knowing that this life is only a mere fragment of our eternal existence, we can always put our afflictions in perspective.

I love the colossal turns that the biblical writers make with such adversative words as *but* or *yet*. One of the best is this move from desolation to exaltation in the apostle Paul's sublime chapter on the resurrection:

> *If for this life only we have hoped in Christ, we are of all people most to be pitied.*
> *But in fact Christ has been raised from the dead, the first fruits of those who have died. For since death came through a human being, the resurrection of the dead has also come through a human being; for as all die in Adam, so all will be made alive in Christ.*
>
> 1 Corinthians 15:19-22

What great liveliness we will have after our resurrection has been demonstrated by the One who was the first example of what immortal existence can be.

How do you imagine it? I sometimes think of the things I cannot do now and try to envision instead what it will be like when we are endowed with inconceivable powers, agility, and vitality. I've always wanted to be able to play the cello, the oboe, the flute, and the French horn. Fantasize with me what music we will be able to make on instruments no one has yet even invented. That is just a small example of the immense bliss and rapture in which we will someday partake in our new mode of the eternal life that we already enjoy in part.

What are your happiest memories from this life? Dream with me of multiplying that elation to the highest possible degree, and we have only just begun to envision the Joy of knowing the Trinity personally, of abiding in God's everlasting love and grace.

John Chrysostom (344–407), who was known as a great preacher and who served as the bishop of Constantinople, delivered a sermon once using two vivid images to heighten our hope in our resurrection renewal. His creativity inspires us to bear bravely the breakdown of our bodies along the way to death and rebirth.

One figure that Chrysostom offered in his sermon was of a statue decayed by rust and age and mutilated in some of its parts. Rather than merely patching it, the sculptor breaks it up, throws it into the furnace to be melted, and then casts it into a different, more beautiful form. As the statue is thus completely remodeled, so the death of our bodies is not destruction, but renovation.

In the other image Chrysostom pictured people living in an old, tottering house. How glad those residents would be when the owner temporarily sends them out of the house so that he can thoroughly rebuild it! They watch as he tears down the old structure, but far more greatly they rejoice because they know that to do so is necessary so that he can construct a more splendid edifice. In the same way, Chrysostom suggested, God removes our soul from our decaying house so that He may build it a new home with greater glory.[2]

Chrysostom probably derived his idea from this section of Paul's second letter to the Corinthians:

> *So we do not lose heart. Even though our outer nature is wasting away, our inner nature is being renewed day by day. For this slight momentary affliction is preparing us for an eternal weight of glory beyond all measure, because we look not at what can be seen but at what cannot be seen; for what can be seen is temporary, but what cannot be seen is eternal.*
>
> *For we know that if the earthly tent we live in is destroyed, we have a building from God, a house not made with hands, eternal in the heavens. For in this tent we groan, longing to be clothed with our heavenly dwelling. . . . For while we are still in this tent, we groan under our burden, because we wish not to be unclothed but to be further clothed, so that what is mortal may be swallowed up by life. He who has prepared us for this very thing is God, who has given us the Spirit as a guarantee.*
>
> 2 Corinthians 4:16—5:5

Many of us, however, become too attached to this mere tent and its surroundings, the accoutrements of this life, and we forget the glories of our heavenly dwelling. Or, on the other hand, perhaps we become so despairing of our present body and its afflictions that we forget that God, who is preparing us for a much more magnificent life, has given the Holy Spirit as a down payment on its fullness, so that we do not lose heart (see also Eph. 1:13-14).

Let us, then, concentrate not on the manner in which our diminished bodies are breaking down, but on the splendors of the limitless life that we shall enjoy eternally.

This image from the apostle Paul encourages us during the process of our dying to focus our attention on God's renovation of our souls and spirits, our inner nature, even as God continues the process of refurbishing our bodies. We want to be transformed more and more into the likeness of Christ by the power of the Holy Spirit (2 Cor. 3:18).

Then we perceive that our temporary afflictions are cultivating us as one nurtures the soil so that we can receive the "eternal weight of glory beyond all measure," the gift of God's brilliance past our wildest imaginings. That is why we can keep from losing heart, even in the tribulations of dying.

Nostalgia for What Has Been

One of my biggest problems in dealing with the breakdown of my body is that I keep looking in the wrong direction. I look to the past and the capabilities I once had, instead of looking to the future and what I will someday become in the presence and by the grace of God. Perhaps that is the strongest temptation for you, too. Our culture reinforces that mistake by its refusal to talk about heaven, as if it were an old-fashioned and outdated notion. We also intensify the problem by craving present health (as limited as it can be) more than we desire God.

A friend once said to me, "This is so hard getting old—there are so many things we can't do any more. I guess the Lord wants to teach us something." Indeed, our bodies will never be what they previously were, and we find that difficult because we miss our former activities. But God wants to teach us to hunger for Him, our greatest treasure. Instead of rejecting the notion of heaven, we genuinely ache in our deepest self to fill that concept with a larger landscape of the Joy of basking in God's presence.

Grief for Our Unspent Years

There is a place for lament that we are robbed by our infirmities of the years we might have spent serving God and others.

Several considerations modify that lament, however, We have to admit that it is often our pride that causes us to think we could have fulfilled some service better than someone else.

Besides, who creates our good works that we might walk in them? Ephesians 2:9-10 insists that all is grace, rather than our works, but that God created us as His very own craftsmanship so that we might accomplish what He has planned for us. Who are we to think we have more to do than we have days in which to do it?

I often joke that I have several books to write yet before I die or numerous speaking engagements that must be fulfilled first—but, if the books are God's and if the teaching opportunities serve to glorify God, then they can certainly be done by others (and probably better!). Our lamenting for our unspent years must always be coupled with the humility of remembering to whose glory we live in the first place. Perhaps God will be better glorified by our dying and death than by our life.

That leads to a second consideration that affects our laments for unspent years. Instead of focusing on what could perhaps be, we spend our time more profitably if we concentrate on how we could use the time that is now given to us in the best achievable way. Sometimes we miss opportunities for ministry that are present to us at the moment because we are preoccupied instead with potential options in a vague future.

Dying Daily to Our Self

As it turns out, then, our actual process of moving toward our physical death is much like all of life—daily we learn to die to ourselves so that we might live for God and His glory and for the sake of the world.

We are freed to do this because of our eschatology. That term comes from the Greek word *eschaton*, which means the "last" things. As believers in the Triune God, we know that the work of Jesus brought the new aeon into the present, that God's culmination of His design for the universe has already been begun in Christ, that the Kingdom has already come, though it has not come fully.

Our eschatology, consequently, is twofold. For the future, we look for the return of Christ (or our death, whichever happens sooner) when our lives will be perfected in Him. In the present, we already live in the Kingdom and pray for its perfect attainment.

It is not that someday we die and then we go to heaven, but that we experience heaven (or God's presence) all along, yet only in part. Someday there will be no sorrow or affliction mixed in with the fullness of the Kingdom Joy.

That is why our hope never disappoints us (Rom. 5:5), for we already have foretastes of heavenly Joy now, and the resurrection of Christ proves that the Kingdom will be brought to its completion in God's perfect timing. In that hope, furthermore, we are more than willing to die daily to our desires and petty plans so that we might participate more fully in God's purposes to recapitulate the cosmos (see chapter 2).

Getting Ready for a Good Death

One bad mistake that I made in ministry stands at the forefront of my mind so that I never make it again. I was young and inexperienced, though I participated in our church staff's rotation of weekly hospital visitations. One day I went with a senior pastor to visit a woman who had terminal cancer and whom I had visited frequently.

She said to us, "What is it like to die?" and the pastor responded, "Now we don't need to talk about that." I felt uneasy at the time and wished that we could let her talk, but unsure of my notion and not knowing how to contradict a senior colleague graciously, I remained silent at the time. Our friend died that night. I prayed that someone else came during that day to assist her with talking through the actual experience of dying.

Those of us with chronic disabilities and illnesses have an advantage over other people because we have already faced the realities of our death so much. Let me encourage you, if you have not done so, to talk through your fears and hopes about dying with those whom you love. I'm not referring only to such things as funeral plans, though they are a great gift that you can give to your loved ones, but I'm praying that we can all be bold witnesses about our sure hope in the resurrection for the sake of others' faith and God's glory.

Usually we who are impaired are also more able to face death alongside of others because, having worked through the process for ourselves, we are more willing to talk honestly about what comes after death. We have probably prayed Psalm 71 with its request to God to "not cast me off in the time of old age" many times and can guide others to pray it with us.

Psychologist John White instructs us in following Jesus so that we learn to die a Christian death. He assures us that if we are always living for God, then we do not have to fear an "untimely death." God will certainly hold us in His care until our call is fulfilled.

He proposes that the problem in our posture toward death is that we usually ponder what might happen to us rather than planning what we should do. Our fears mount because our thoughts are fixed on the wrong thing. "We look at what we cannot control rather than at what we can."

White gives the example of how as a boy during World War II he knew exactly what he had to do to get into the air raid shelter, and how that equipped him to face the terrors of the times. His knowing precisely how to conduct himself reduced his fear considerably. Instead of being an impotent, passive casualty, he could participate energetically in the proper procedure.

In the same way, White insists, knowing what to do makes an immeasurable difference. If we form a plan and equip ourselves to behave in a certain way, we transform our perspective altogether. "Panic and fear are the companions of passivity."[3] He urges us as Christians to have Christ's active attitude toward death, so that we do not recoil before it as victims.

Jesus prayed a confident "declaration of firm trust." Even more so, when he prayed "Father, into your hands I commend my spirit" (Luke 23:46), He was committing Himself to God, not fancifully wishing that He might ultimately wind up in the Father's care.

We will certainly not be able to choose the moment of our death, but we can plan beforehand how we will conduct ourselves when it is time. "We may choose for instance whether we bear witness with joy to our faith in God or whether we are dragged off-stage."

White concludes by suggesting that throughout our lives we are like actors in a drama. Both human beings and the angelic forces of heaven are watching. We want to be sure that we close the scene appropriately. Christ not only gave us the final line, but also demonstrated how it should be exclaimed, for when we say "Father, into your hands I commend my spirit" we are making a ringing proclamation of our steadfast eternal hope.

During our processes of dying we can rehearse our line and know it well, "so that the curtains fall on a note of triumph."[4] Perhaps we can practice our line every night as we lie down to sleep so that we are ready whenever Christ comes to take us home.

Living and Dying with Hope

We can be well even when we are dying because we continually live in the hope of the resurrection. That hope frees us from our slavery to death and its fears. Hope enables us to sing, "It is well with my soul," no matter how much our infirmities hasten our death. All the sooner that hope will be changed to sight in the fullness of our participation in God's Kingdom.

 The LORD be with you. [And also with you.] Let us pray:

Watch, O Lord, with those who wake, or watch, or weep tonight, and give Your angels and saints charge over those who sleep. Tend Your sick ones, O Lord Christ. Rest Your weary ones. Bless Your dying ones. Soothe Your suffering ones. Pity Your afflicted ones. Shield Your joyous ones. And all for Your love's sake.[5]

Amen.

20. Loss of Certainty —
Redemptive Suffering, Eschatology

O God, why have you utterly cast us off?[1]
Why does your anger smoke against the sheep
of your pasture?

Psalm 74:1

After the exultant proclamation of the previous chapter, I
have come back in this one to our questioning because,
if we are typical human beings, our faith—no matter how
strong—wavers at times, and we start a new round of wondering. Sometimes we doubt whether God really cares about us
at all, and at other times we simply need to put our lives back
into an eternal perspective to regain our hope. We ask other
kinds of questions about the Bible and whether we can trust
it. Most of our perplexities concern our struggles and what
they mean for our relationship with God.

The verse cited above (in two strong renderings to show
the hyperbole) is the beginning of a poem that alternates
between historical remembrance and pleas to God to do
something about the situation. The poet recalls that horrific
event when enemies came to destroy the Temple, yet he also
praises the LORD for His magnificent work in the creation.
If God can control the days and seasons and all the forces of
earth, then certainly He could support the people whom He
had redeemed to be His own. Therefore, the poet challenges
God to recollect His covenant and to rise up to uphold His
people.

We are not burdened by so appalling an event as the
devastation of the Temple, but its result was the same as that
which we experience because of infirmities. We wonder where
to find God, and if He has hurled us away altogether. Why

does He seem so angry with us that we suffer as we do? We thought that we were His sheep, and that our Good Shepherd would always tend us.

The Larger Picture

Asaph (a man who lived later than the Asaph of David's day), the poet of Psalm 74, finds somewhat of an answer to his question by looking at the larger picture and noting that God his King has always been working salvation in the world (v. 12). Then he records several examples of God's mighty acts—dividing the seas and drying up ever-flowing streams so that the children of Israel could pass through the Red Sea and the Jordan (vv. 13a and 15b); creating the luminaries and the sun, summer and winter (vv. 16b and 17b). The poet even uses language from the myths of other gods in this section (a Babylonian story of creation and a Canaanite story of Baal) to show the falsity of these myths, but that the LORD's power had been triumphant in history as God had saved His people and even fed them in the wilderness.

The poet's final plea is a mixture of asking God to take care of His "dove," the covenant people, and a challenge to God not to let His enemies scoff at Him (vv. 18-23). Surely, the LORD wouldn't want to be put to shame Himself, as well as His people! The poet thereby emphasizes that God's reputation was at stake in the protection of His own people. Without doubt He would act against those who blasphemed Him.

That is a bold way to pray, and I include it here as a reminder that God does not reject our questions, our pleas, even our challenges to Him to answer us for the sake of the honor of His name.

Moses had prayed in a similar way in Exodus 32 (see also Num. 14:13-19). When the LORD threatened to consume Israel for building a golden calf and worshiping it, Moses protested, "Why should the Egyptians say, 'It was with evil intent that he brought them out to kill them in the mountains, and to consume them from the face of the earth'?" (v. 12). After all, the Lord had delivered them from Egypt mightily. If He would remember His covenant with Abraham, Isaac, and Israel, then certainly He wouldn't turn from His promises now.

Such prayer is astonishing! Asaph and Moses were so close to God that they knew they could hold Him to His character and His promises. Similarly today we can pray equally vigorously against the injustices in the world; certainly the Lord doesn't want the poor and needy to be oppressed.

Both of these biblical instances concerned intercession on behalf of the covenant nation. The third illustration involves a matter of prayer totally in line with God's will for righteousness. Can we be so audacious in praying for ourselves?

I don't know the answer to that question because it still seems to me to be somewhat selfish to demand God's answers for us personally for the sake of His reputation. But I raise the issue here because we are looking in this chapter for more courage when we start to question our faith. These First Testament prayer warriors model both a humility and an audacity in God's presence that invites our imitation. Above all, we need never fear to bring to God whatever is on our minds, whether that be questions, challenges, or protests. We can be sure that the Lord will listen to our cries and answer with the gift of Himself.

The Reliability of the Scriptures

Sometimes we slip from our confident faith in the eternal Trinity into skepticism or mistrust because we doubt the Scriptures on which our beliefs are based. How do we know that they are reliable?

I'm not referring here to minor questions about problematic incidents in the Bible. There are many passages that I don't understand, especially those for which the significance depends on historical situations that we cannot recover. When people ask me about such texts, I usually respond that I have a whole list of questions to ask God when we get to heaven, but the smashing truth about such a list is that when we get there—namely, in His presence—we won't need to ask them. Or else we'll have a great discussion, as did the disciples on the way to Emmaus, who exclaimed afterward, "Were not our hearts burning within us while he was talking to us on the road, while he was opening the scriptures to us?" (Luke 24:32).

I'm concerned here for the larger question of whether we can trust the Scriptures in general. What differentiates the Bible from the myths of cultures that surrounded Israel? In this contemporary postmodern age in which even scientists, especially physicists, claim that we can't be absolute about any knowledge because future discoveries will continually change what we can claim with confidence, can we rely on the Bible?

There is not space in this book for an entire exposition of the doctrine of the Scriptures, but for our purposes of finding trust in the face of our questions let us note the following reasons why we can place our hope in what we learn and know from the Bible:

1. We belong to a community of faith that goes all the way back in time to Abraham and Sarah and that stretches throughout the globe. That community has recorded its witness to who God is and what God has done and does, and we trust their testimony because they had no cause to make it up. In fact, they often gave their witness in spite of opposition or misunderstanding or ridicule.

2. The Bible's testimony to who God is is consistent throughout both Testaments. The Scriptures stress what the Trinity has done to care for His people, most clearly in Jesus of Nazareth.

3. We can trust the process of transmission of the Bible because God has worked triunely to oversee its dissemination. The Holy Spirit inspired not only the original writing, but also the Church which decided on the books that were most authoritative. Textual critics are amazed at how few scribal errors occur in the early manuscripts, and those that do exist do not pertain to any of the major doctrines of the Church.

4. No major archaeological or anthropological discovery has ever disproved the orthodox, catholic faith that has been derived from the Scriptures. The Bible is intellectually credible and so is the faith that it records.

5. Over time we have gotten new insights from archaeology, linguistics, and other theology-related fields to help us interpret specific passages in the Bible. For that reason, throughout the Church's history there have been many channels through which the heritage of faith has flowed. But always there have been basic elements of that multifaceted legacy that stream through the common faith of Christians throughout space and time.

6. The work of biblical interpretation is not the territory only of detached professionals in the field, but is the struggle, in community, of the whole Church, especially its lay people, whose faith is sometimes vulnerable to devaluation by some specialists. We

each explore the truth of the Scriptures in our own experience, and many times we gain more from those whose faith has been severely tested than from theological "experts."

7. The basic tradition of Christian faith passed on by our forebears in the Scriptures is a fountain of genuinely meaningful life, of verifiably devoted mission, of immeasurably profound elation and ardor.

For these reasons and many others, we can rely on the Scriptures and what they tell us about God's grace and love, even when our infirmities cause us to question that mercy. As we emphasized in chapter 3, we can trust what we know from the Bible more than we can depend on our feelings.

Let us cease our reflections for a minute and sing or speak a hymn that reassures us of the power of the Scriptures.

Father of mercies, in thy word What endless glory shines!
For ever be thy Name adored For these celestial lines.

Here the Redeemer's welcome voice Spreads heavenly
    peace around,
And life and everlasting joys Attend the blissful sound.

O may these heavenly pages be My ever dear delight,
And still new beauties may I see And still increasing
    light.

Divine Instructor, gracious Lord, Be thou for ever near;
Teach me to love thy sacred word And view my Saviour
    there. Amen.[2]

May we always cling to the Scriptures that guide and inspire us, that console and unite us, that hold us when we mistrust and fear.

Eschatology

We doubt and wrestle with questions because we are caught in the meanwhile times. That is what I call the period between Christ's defeat of the principalities and powers, including death, at the cross and empty tomb and God's final recapitulation of the cosmos. As we learned in the previous chapter, our eschatology (or doctrine about the "last" times) teaches us that we live in the Kingdom of God already, but we don't abide in it fully yet. There is still quite a bit of hell mixed in with the heaven that is our present possession.

When we experience the bitter struggles of our infirmities, we are less able to remember that our eternal life has already begun. It is hard to envision God's Kingdom when all the kingdoms of this world are so strong, including the reign of suffering.

We can find help in remembering our eternal present and future by discovering that in the meanwhile times our actual suffering is part of God's purposes to defeat the powers and to bring the world to Himself. Every time we trust God in the face of affliction we are defeating the evil force of despair. Every time someone is wooed into a deeper relationship with God by our courage in the face of tribulation, our suffering becomes redemptive.

We become more willing to endure adversity when we know that it is truly redemptive and that we thereby are following Jesus, whose saving suffering on our behalf was mysteriously much more thorough than we can ever imagine. The Bible uses numerous concepts to describe Christ's work of atonement. The more we study these, the more readily we can embrace our own part in suffering that completes Christ's work for the sake of the Church (Col. 1:24).

I'm not saying that our understanding of eschatology and of the place of redemptive suffering in the meanwhile times frees us from questions and doubts forever. But such comprehension is one tool that we find can help us deal with them when they arise.

An Even Larger Picture

Our questions and doubts arise also because our dreams, perhaps fostered by excellent or even superior health in our childhoods, have been drowned by the whole barrage of chronic problems that have developed in our systems. Or maybe our dreams were built on significant visions of what we could do with our training and gifts, but now we are not able to fulfill them.

We need a bigger and brighter vision than simply dreams for our own earthly life. We can find such an infinite outlook when we grasp a proper perspective on our desires and goals. The psalmist comprehends this comparison when he records this prayer:

> LORD, *let me know my end,*
>> *and what is the measure of my days;*
>> *let me know how fleeting my life is.*
> *You have made my days a few handbreadths,*
>> *and my lifetime is as nothing in your sight.*
> *Surely everyone stands as a mere breath.* Selah
>> *Surely everyone goes about like a shadow.*
> *Surely for nothing they are in turmoil;*
>> *they heap up, and do not know who will gather.*
> *And now, O Lord, what do I wait for?*
>> *My hope is in you.*

Psalm 39:4-7

If we recognize how small our dreams are in comparison with eternity, then we more willingly place our hope not in the fulfillment of our inconsequential longings, but in the Lord and His purposes.

If we always keep in mind the ephemerality of our lives, but also establish them inside the largest story, the grand meta-narrative of the faith that we discussed in chapter 2, then we learn continually to plant our hope in the only eternal One, our Triune God. Notice that it is the Lord, our faithful covenant God, whom we ask to enable us to know our end. This emphasizes that even though our lives are fleeting, they still are part of the story of salvation, and therefore we need not fear their transience.

Because every single person shares in the brevity of life, we all should be aware of the silliness of our accumulations and the fears that go along with them. As the psalmist asserts, the turmoils that often drive our lives as human beings are all for naught because we don't know who will gather what we leave. As we all should comprehend, the death rate is the same—one per person—so we are encouraged (as everyone is invited) to place our hope in the Lord.

Why does it console us to think about the fleeting nature of our lives? For me, the answer is fourfold. First, throughout my adulthood I have known that my life would be shorter than that of most people because of my handicaps, and that realization has urged me to live as well as I could for whatever time I had. We live well when we devote our lives to God and His glory, when we spend our energies serving others, when we don't concentrate on our impairments.

Second, to contemplate our life's ephemerality actually puts us in the same boat as all other human beings. Though our particular lives with infirmities might be shorter than others' and that might make us feel isolated, what is anyone's life-span in relation to eternity? While pondering God's infinity, another psalmist wrote, "So teach us to count our days / that we may gain a wise heart" (Ps. 90:12). We join with all other impermanent human beings in trying to acquire wisdom; our infirmities don't separate us from the rest of humanity, but perhaps they equip us to teach others what we have learned from our heightened awareness of life's quickness.

For example, we who have chronic illnesses and disabilities have an advantage over other people because we usually have daily or regular reminders of our transience and so are less likely to heap up earthly possessions, rather than depositing our treasures into enduring coffers by being generous for the sake of the poor and needy.

Third, though our lifetimes are as nothing in God's sight, as the poet says in the psalm section above, yet our *lives* matter enormously to the Trinity. Even though we have just a brief span of time in this world, God uses that time to call us to Himself and to fit us for His presence. Have we answered His call and placed all our hope in Him?

Fourth, the passing nature of our lives goads us to share the gospel with all those we encounter. What seed might we plant in another's life that could bear eternal fruit? Who might need assurance of God's love? We usually find that in giving away the truths of our faith, our confidence in them is deepened.

Of course, there are other reasons why it is good to locate our lifespans within the framework of eternity, such as that it awakens us to the gravity of spending more time in spiritual disciplines or the importance of loving our friends and family as deeply as we can. I listed the considerations above because they help me in times of doubts and questionings by reminding me of the supremacy of our gracious God and by inviting me to entrust myself and my existence into His merciful and compassionate hands.

Once Again, Hope

Because David, the poet of Psalm 16, kept the LORD always before him (v. 8), he could speak of true life forever long before there was much of an idea of heaven. In general, the First Testament doesn't deal with eternal hopes, which is why, by the time of Jesus and Paul, there was a major fight between the Pharisees and the Sadducees concerning the resurrection from the dead (see Acts 23:6-8). Consequently, the following words are much more reassuring to us in our questionings and doubts because they deal with life and inspire us to think beyond life:

> *Therefore my heart is glad, and my soul rejoices;*
> *my body also rests secure.*
> *For you do not give me up to Sheol,*
> *or let your faithful one see the Pit.*
> *You show me the path of life.*
> *In your presence there is fullness of joy;*
> *in your right hand are pleasures forevermore.*

Psalm 16:9-11

When you are fearful or full of confusion, Psalm 16 will serve you well because it brims over with exuberant trust. David has experienced the LORD's counsel and instruction; he knows the fullness of blessings that God has heaped upon him, even though the first two verses of the psalm hint at previous troubles. He has realized that *YHWH* is the true God and so he will not choose any other god. Because the LORD always stayed at his right hand, he believed that he would not be pulled away.

That is why he could affirm the verses given above. He lists three parts of his organism—heart, soul, and body—to underscore that his whole being reveled in the LORD's nearness. Because David mentions that his body remains secure, some scholars think that this psalm records David's experience of not being killed in battle, and that the last two verses speak only of his confidence for this life. Other scholars suggest that David was at the forefront in starting to contemplate the forevermore of eternity.

I believe that David by the inspiration of the Holy Spirit did not stop with pondering just his earthly life. By that same Holy Spirit we can be renewed by this psalm in our confidence for eternal hope fulfilled, especially because the New Testament frequently highlights that hope.

One special scene that affirms our heavenly hopes occurs in Revelation 7, when the seer John sees a countless multitude dressed in white and standing before the Lamb. By the rhetorical device of an elder asking who they were and from whence they had come and the seer answering that the elder himself knew, the scene accentuates the reply that they have come through the great tribulation and that they had cleansed their robes and whitened them in the Lamb's blood. That leads to this poem from the elder:

> *For this reason they are before the throne of God,*
> *and worship him day and night within his temple,*
> *and the one who is seated on the throne will shelter them.*
> *They will hunger no more, and thirst no more;*
> *the sun will not strike them,*
> *nor any scorching heat;*
> *for the Lamb at the center of the throne will be their shepherd,*
> *and he will guide them to springs of the water of life*
> *and God will wipe away every tear from their eyes.*
>
> Revelation 7:15-17

That song employs images from several places in the First Testament—Leviticus 26:11; Ezekiel 37:27; Isaiah 49:10; Psalm 121:5-6; Psalm 23:1-2; and Isaiah 25:8—so we see that David wasn't alone in having intimations of God's future grace and care. The New Testament adds many other sketches of heaven, but again only hints at its beauty and splendor. It is a good thing that we don't really know too much of the Joy of heaven or else we'd be so eager to get there that we wouldn't be much good in this life.

Those pictures that we do have are enough to assure us and woo us. They assist in freeing us from our fears and doubts, for we do know from them with certainty that the greatest blessing of eternal life is that God Himself will tabernacle among us and be our God (Rev. 21:3, a verse which is again followed by the promise that God will wipe away the tears from everyone's eyes).

Our postmodern age insists that we can't be certain about anything. I agree that our knowledge and understanding are limited, but one thing I am confident about—that God is. Furthermore, the Scriptures reveal that the Trinity loves us and will care for us forevermore. Whenever we are assailed by doubts, we can come back to the basics and entrust ourselves into God's hands for whatever may befall us.

 The LORD be with you! [And also with you!] Let us pray:

Lord Jesus Christ, you are for me medicine when I am sick;
you are my strength when I need help;
you are life itself when I fear death;
you are the way when I long for heaven;
you are light when all is dark;
you are my food when I need nourishment.[3]

21. Infirmity and the Trinity's Larger Story

O LORD, my heart is not proud, or my eyes haughty;

> *Nor do I involve myself in great matters,*
> *Or in things too difficult for me.*
> *Surely I have composed and quieted my soul,*
> *Like a weaned child rests against its mother;*
> *My soul is like a weaned child within me.*

Psalm 131:1-2 NASB

Instead of beginning with a lament over our losses, this chapter starts with a vision of being well, of resting our whole being serenely in the LORD's embrace. Notice that such rest and wholeness is possible only if we do not proudly insist on our own way.

The NRSV translates the end of the first line with the idea of our eyes being "raised too high," which might imply having too lofty of ambitions. Certainly the goals toward which we aspire, perhaps unreachable because of our health limitations, are another source of our uneasiness and disquietude or irritation, as we have seen in other chapters.

We also are troubled if we try to figure everything out, if we attempt to understand exactly how our infirmities fit into God's grand meta-narrative. The Hebrew word rendered "difficult" above could be translated "wondrous" or "marvelous" (as in the NRSV) to emphasize that what is too demanding for us also fills us with amazement and awe. If we respond with wonder instead of protest at the things we cannot comprehend, then we are much more able to find tranquility.

The image the poet uses for his peace strikes us with its vivid appropriateness. As a weaned child no longer fusses to get his mother's milk but is content to rest in her presence, so we become composed when we no longer fret to get certain blessings from God, but instead find the comfort of His gracious presence completely sufficient.

All the chapters of this book have pointed in this direction, but here let us state the matter clearly: We are most well when we entrust ourselves to our gracious God. We find our wholeness in the sure hope of God's eternal love for us.

Infirmity and the Desert Saints

In his book on different traditions of spirituality, Gerald Sittser, professor at Whitworth College in Spokane, Washington, introduces the desert saints, those men and women who retreated to the wilderness in the fourth and fifth centuries because Christianity was becoming too comfortable in the culture after Emperor Constantine made it the official religion of the Roman Empire. The desert saints believed that struggle, a word that we often use to describe our life with infirmities, is common and essential for the spiritual life. They chose struggle willingly to improve their spiritual health.[1]

Can we learn to be grateful for the troubles of our chronic illnesses and disabilities because they develop our spiritual well-being? Can we recognize our suffering as a gift because it creates for us a desert in which we can both battle our temptations to pride and self-pity and, more important, draw closer to God?

Sittser does not necessarily write for those with infirmities, but in general he compares Christians to the desert saints in this way:

> Our place of engagement will be different. It will be in our homes and schools and places of work. But the struggles we face are the same. We too must battle against the

world, the flesh and the devil. We too must confront the
darkness within, our persistent egoism. The desert saints
challenge us to dare to face these struggles squarely by
entering some kind of desert where, stripped of security,
distraction and comfort, we will confront the devil and
meet the living God, just as Jesus did. . . . The darkness of
the human soul is the real and ultimate enemy.[2]

Martin Luther once said that all sin was due to unbelief—
that we don't trust God enough to enable us to resist temptation. Ever since I learned that in college I have discovered
again and again how right Luther was. It seems that Sittser
means the same thing with his choice of the phrase *persistent
egoism*. We believe in our own strength and ability to with-
stand the forces that come against us from the culture around
us, from the powers of evil, and from our own sinful tenden-
cies. When we presume that we can handle life and the devil,
the world, and our flesh (Luther's trilogy, too) by ourselves,
we do not believe that we yearn for and require God and that
God will hear our cries and empower us to cling to Him for
all our needs.

We who have chronic health problems have an advantage in that our very tribulations have already put us in a desert where we have been stripped of all that makes life seem
secure, of the comfort most people feel in their bodily health.
But we are endlessly distracted by the necessities of caring for
our afflictions. Our desert trial, then, is to turn those distur-
bances into vehicles for growth in our intimacy with God and
in the maturity of our character. Often, too, we will thereby be
enabled out of these spiritual resources to serve others in the
world.

One significant method by which we can serve others
is by exposing the emptiness of what the society around us
thinks is important. As Sittser comments,

The desert will also enable us to see how unfriendly modern culture is to the spiritual life. It seduces us into being too busy, too ambitious, and too self-indulgent. We never seem to be satisfied; we always seem to want more.[3]

The solitude and pain of our chronic infirmities can keep us from getting swept up into the bustling schedules, aspirations, and self-coddling of our culture so that we have time and a hunger for spiritual growth. Our wellness arises from finding our satisfaction in God.

This calls us to be extremely countercultural. While others judge their wellness by their activities and successes, we discern that "The frenzied pace of our lives poses a threat to our spiritual health." We are called daily by the fragility of our lives to choose gratitude and prayer and obedience and other spiritual practices instead of the busyness of our culture. But let us also remember, as Sittser proclaims, that "Heroic feats are not as useful as the subtle and deliberate choices we make every day to submit ourselves to God."[4]

Of course, I am writing about the ideal—which I am far from living—but the truth about God, as we learn from the biblical meta-narrative, is that, through the merits of Christ, the Father has declared us to be saints. Moreover, by the power of the Holy Spirit at work within us, we are constantly being transformed into the saints that we are. In the Trinity's gracious and wholistic gift we find our wellness.

Always Praise and Gratitude

Two spiritual practices that many of these chapters have emphasized and which enable us more thoroughly to rest in God's gifts to us are the habits of praise and thanksgiving. Frequently we lump those two words together as if they signified the same thing, but it will equip us better here if we distinguish the two practices.

Thanksgiving is given to God because of what He has done for us. We thank the Trinity when something goes right for a change with our infirmities. For example, I've been extremely grateful today that my blood glucose tests have given me excellent numbers. On some days stresses or discouragements, too much activity, or who knows what throws my sugar levels off. (Remember that medicine is a stochastic art, as we learned in chapter 17.)

But why can't I be grateful on all days—at least for my testing machine (which didn't exist back in the early days of my diabetes) or for insulin, which keeps me alive? One thing I've learned in writing this book is that I need to concentrate more on all the things for which I am thankful.

What about you? Would more space in your life help you to improve the habit of gratitude? Wouldn't we find more wholeness if we focused on reasons for appreciation, rather than on the struggles of our infirmities?

Praise is larger than gratitude, for praise is directed to God solely on the basis of who He is. Especially in times of disappointment, we can still praise the LORD for His character. We know that the Trinity is faithful, even when our prayers are not answered the way we would like. Praise arises from our trust that God is good, that His character of grace is unsurpassable.

I know that I do not praise often and deeply enough, so I need training to cultivate the discipline. What about you? Shall we covenant together to increase praise in our lives?

The Psalms teach us good habits of praise and thanksgiving, for even the laments usually break into adoration and gratitude by the end. Let us study a psalm section specifically to expand our practices of acclamation and appreciation.

All your works shall give thanks to you, O LORD,
and all your faithful shall bless you.

They shall speak of the glory of your kingdom,
       and tell of your power,
to make known to all people your mighty deeds,
       and the glorious splendor of your kingdom.
Your kingdom is an everlasting kingdom,
       and your dominion endures throughout all generations.
The L*ORD* *is faithful in all his words,*
       and gracious in all his deeds.
The L*ORD* *upholds all who are falling,*
       and raises up all who are bowed down.

                    Psalm 145:10-14

We notice immediately that praise and thanksgiving are often mixed in together. Our only reason for distinguishing them here was so that we could develop both practices in our lives. Perhaps you would be helped to go through this psalm section to decide which of the two each line demonstrates.

The word translated "bless" in the second line above comes from the Hebrew root *barach* and emphasizes that our honoring of God actually blesses Him as He blesses us (of course, not in equal proportion!). Indeed, it does motivate our praise to discover that God is delighted by it.

From this same Hebrew root comes the noun *b'rakha* or "a blessing." Its plural form is the word *b'rakhot*, which is important for this chapter because of the Jewish practice of trying to say at least 100 *b'rakhot* a day. You might have heard similar words if you have ever participated in a Seder and heard the host chant "*Baruch atah Adonai Elohenu melek ha-olam,*" which means "Blessed are you, O L*ORD* our God, King of the universe." Though the covenant name *YHWH* would be in the original Hebrew text, the Jews would substitute the term *Adonai* because they would not say the former word out of reverence for the holy Name. We translate *Adonai* as "Lord," with only the *L* capitalized to mean "Sovereign One."

The Jewish practice is to say 100 of these sentences in a day to find Joy in each and every dimension of life since God is present in them all. Imagine what it would be like instead of being frustrated by all the pills we have to take if we said, "Blessed are you, O LORD our God, King of the universe, that you have created chemists and doctors who have discovered these medicines so that I might be as well as possible." Or perhaps we might say, "Blessed are you, O LORD our God, King of the universe that your Kingdom is filled with glorious splendor." How might this change our attitudes to bless the Trinity with such words of thanksgiving and praise?

When we aim for 100 *b'rakhot* a day, we grow in our appreciation for how God is the source of all that is good. We continually remember that the Trinity is King of the universe after all, so nothing happens outside of the Lord's control.

When upsetting things occur in the course of our infirmities, what would happen if we responded to them not with worry and fear, but with a *b'rakha* instead? How might it change our perspectives on the troubles of our lives if we said something like this: "Blessed are you, O LORD our God, King of the universe, that you have always been faithful to us, that you have undergirded us in all our life's hardships, that you have sent your Holy Spirit to strengthen our trust in you" and so forth?

The psalm section recorded above praises and thanks the LORD for all sorts of things—the glory and splendor of His kingdom, His power and mighty acts, the perpetuity of His dominion, His faithfulness and graciousness in both word and deed. Especially those of us with chronic afflictions can be grateful for the line that "the LORD upholds all who are falling" and its parallel completion "and raises up all who are bowed down." Certainly that can be the substance of one of our 100 *b'rakhot* each day, for we constantly experience, though we think we will fall out of God's care, that He is ever faithful to hold us fast and lift us to Himself (if we don't block Him or refuse to let our spirits turn to Him).

The Trinity's larger story gives us a multitude of subjects for our *b'rakhot*. When we think of all that God has done and shown Himself to be throughout the entire biblical history, we are overwhelmed by all the thanksgivings and praises we can offer. Surely, we will know a new wholeness as we grow in our habits of gratitude and adoration.

Being Well When We're Ill

We learned in the previous chapter in the section on eschatology that, though we are participants in God's kingdom already, we are still stuck with this world and also our own sinful natures. That is why we engage in the spiritual disciplines we have studied to move toward wholeness.

However, this book or your own reflections and efforts have probably not brought you into perfect emotional tranquility. As we learned from Marko Ivan Rupnik in chapter 9, such serenity of soul should not be turned into an idol. What leads us to wholeness in spite of our infirmities is, in Rupnik's words, "discovering that our lives are gathered and hidden with Christ in God."[5] Again we are reminded that our wellness is purely God's gracious gift. Everything that we are and do is transfigured in Christ to the glory of the Father by the power of the Holy Spirit.

In the Trinity's eyes we are completely well. The more closely we draw near to God and share His perspective, the more spiritually well we are. It is the secret of submission to, and dependence on, God that we have been learning throughout this book.

All Things Shall Be Well

Someday, we know, we shall be totally well. In perhaps the most famous of her revelations, the great English mystic Julian of Norwich (1343–1413) heard God promise, "I may make all things well; I can make all things well, and I will make all things well, and I shall make all things well; and you shall see for yourself that all manner of things shall be well."[6]

Julian's vision underscores what we learn throughout the Scriptures. God promises to bring all things to completion at the end of the world. When the Trinity recapitulates the cosmos, all shall indeed be well. We will know God face to face, and all suffering will be cast away forever. This is the vision at the end of the Revelation:

> *And I heard a loud voice from the throne saying, "Behold, the tabernacle of God is among [mortals], and He shall dwell among them, and they shall be His peoples, and God Himself shall be among them,*
>
> *And He shall wipe away every tear from their eyes; and there shall no longer be any death; there shall no longer be any mourning, or crying, or pain: the first things have passed away."*
>
> *And He who sits on the throne said, "Behold, I am making all things new." And he said, "Write, for these words are faithful and true."*
>
> Revelation 21:3-5 NASB

This text, as most of Revelation, utilizes images from the First Testament, especially from Isaiah 25:8; 35:10; and 51:11. I chose the NASB translation because in it the voice's message begins with the word *Behold*, which is a grab-you-by-the-shirtcollar word to wake us up to the wonder of what is being recorded. Surely it is breathtaking that God Himself will dwell among us! Also, in the first line the NASB renders the word *tabernacle* accurately for the original Greek word and reminds us that once Christ became flesh and *taberna-cled* among His people (a literal translation of John 1:14). Just as God Incarnate once pitched His tent and walked among humankind, so in the future we shall know God's overshadowing presence fully.

All shall be well, for there will be no more suffering of any kind. We can trust this promise because the grand metanarrative will end with God making everything new again, and His promises are trustworthy and veritable. Behold how extensively all things will be remade! Believe these assurances, for God's covenants with us are always faithful!

We shall be well. And the certainty of that hope enables us to be well now.

The LORD be with you. [And also with you.] Let us pray:

Almighty God, who art ever present in the world without me, in my spirit within me, and in the unseen world above me, let me carry with me through this day's life a most real sense of Thy power and Thy glory.

O God without me, forbid that I should look to-day upon the work of Thy hands and give no thought to Thee the Maker. . . . Let every fleeting loveliness I see speak to me of a loveliness that does not fade. Let the beauty of earth be to me a sacrament of the beauty of holiness made manifest in Jesus Christ my Lord.

O God within me, give me grace to-day to recognize the stirrings of Thy Spirit within my soul and to listen most attentively to all that Thou hast to say to me. Let not the noises of the world ever so confuse me that I cannot hear Thee speak. Suffer me never to deceive myself as to the meaning of Thy commands; and so let me in all things obey Thy will, through the grace of Jesus Christ my Lord.

O God above me, God who dwellest in light unapproachable, teach me, I beseech Thee, that even my highest thoughts of Thee are but dim and distant shadowings of Thy transcendent glory. . . . Teach me that if Thou art in my heart, still more art Thou greater than my heart. Let my soul rejoice in Thy mysterious greatness. Let me take refuge in the thought that Thou art utterly beyond me, beyond the sweep of my imagination, beyond the comprehension of my mind, Thy judgements being unsearchable and Thy ways past finding out.

O Lord, hallowed be Thy name. Amen.[7]

Epilogue

Two important, but opposite, sets of events happened between my revisions of this book and the final polishing before I sent it to the publisher. First, my husband and I delighted in a wonderful 11-day teaching trip to South Korea. We met incredibly kind people and learned greatly and gratefully from them. At Hanyang University in Ansan, we were with young Christians from Hong Kong, Indonesia, Japan, Korea, Macao, Malaysia, Mongolia, the Philippines, Singapore, Taiwan, and Thailand. They showed us the vibrancy of the Church in East Asia. Next, at a seminary in Daejeon we were with Christian doctors and nurses from all over South Korea, and I could use some of the ideas from this book to talk about their patient care and their own rest. People from various churches attended the final series of several seminars held at a large church building in Seoul. Each of these engagements encouraged me immensely for ministry.

However, that elation was soon put on hold. Since the trip had been rather exhausting, we spent several days after our return resting. On the morning that I planned to come back to working on this book, my blood pressure was quite low, and the small vessel stroke from two months before might have contributed, but I fell in the dining area in our home—and broke my upper leg inside the hip.

A skilled surgeon rebuilt my leg with two long rods (called "nails"), and I will spend months recovering because my immuno-suppressants will slow down healing. When I did begin work on this book after a month, I found that I read it more for my benefit than for yours. Particularly the chapters on spiritual drought (3), meaninglessness (4), pain (10), and unproductivity (11) spoke strongly to me. In the same way, I pray that certain chapters are especially helpful for you right now, according to your needs.

Though this past month's pain has been more severe than any I've experienced for a while, I still believe that we can be well when we trust and rest in the Triune God. Our wholeness comes from our prayerful (and maybe passive) participation in God's grand meta-narrative, and our hope abides in the clear biblical assurance that the Trinity's saving purposes *shall* be fulfilled.

Nonetheless, sometimes we are too tired to do anything but cry,

O Thou, from whom all blessings flow,
I lift my heart to Thee;
In all my sorrows, conflicts, woes,
Dear Lord, remember me. Amen.

Another significant event occurred during the final processes of preparing this book for publication. Our good friend Duane Vahsholtz died more quickly than expected from cancer. He looked well and did extremely well during his last nine months, but his sudden turn for the worse led to a quick demise. Throughout his struggles with cancer, his various concerns and regimens were often on my mind as I wrote these pages.

Duane was a gentle inspiration. He loved everyone he met with gracious hospitality. He enjoyed life immensely with his wife and family while he lived with his disease. He was certainly one of the most well men that I've ever known while he was ill.

I love to think about him with the familiar refrains, Blessed are they who die in the Lord. May they rest in peace, and may light perpetual shine upon them. Duane lived, suffered, and died to the glory of God.

It was a profound Joy to us on Christmas Day (10 days after his funeral) to realize all the life made possible by the life, death, and resurrection of the Child in the manger—life in His way of justice and peace, life in close union with the Trinity, life in the midst of suffering, eternal life.

May you be well in the fullness of life granted by the Triune God, Father, Son, and Holy Spirit.

Appendix

Resources on Suffering, Evil, and Healing

Beker, J. Christiaan. *Suffering and Hope: The Biblical Vision and the Human Predicament*. Grand Rapids: Eerdmans, 1993.

Blamires, Harry. *A God Who Acts: Recognizing the Hand of God in Suffering and Failure*. Ann Arbor: Servant Books, 1957.

Blumhofer, Edith L. *Her Heart Can See: The Life and Hymns of Fanny J. Crosby*. Grand Rapids: Eerdmans, 2005.

Boyd, Gregory A. *Is God to Blame? Beyond Pat Answers to the Problem of Suffering*. Downers Grove: InterVarsity, 2003.

Calvin, John. *Suffering: Understanding the Love of God*. Ed. and annotated by Joseph Hill. Darlington, England: Evangelical Press, 2005.

Carson, D. A. *How Long, O Lord?: Reflections on Suffering and Evil*, 2nd ed. Grand Rapids: Baker Academic, 2006.

Cousins, Norman. *Anatomy of an Illness as Perceived by the Patient: Reflections on Healing and Regeneration*. New York: Norton, 1979.

Dawn, Marva J. *Joy in our Weakness: A Gift of Hope from the Book of Revelation*, rev. ed. Grand Rapids: Eerdman, 2002.

Dobson, James. *When God Doesn't Make Sense*. Wheaton: Tyndale House, 1993.

Fanestil, John. *Mrs. Hunter's Happy Death: Lessons on Living from People Preparing to Die*. New York: Doubleday, 2006.

Gariepy, Henry. *Songs in the Night: Inspiring Stories behind 100 Hymns Born in Trial and Suffering*. Grand Rapids: Eerdmans, 1997.

Greene-McCreight, Kathryn. *Darkness Is My Only Companion: A Christian Response to Mental Illness*. Grand Rapids: Brazos, 2006.

Hall, Douglas John. *God and Human Suffering*. Grand Rapids: Eerdmans, 1992.

Hart, David Bentley. *The Doors of the Sea: Where Was God in the Tsunami?* Grand Rapids: Eerdmans, 2005.

Hauerwas, Stanley. *God, Medicine, and Suffering*. Grand Rapids: Eerdmans, 1994.

Hunsinger, Deborah van Deusen. *Pray without Ceasing: Revitalizing Pastoral Care*. Grand Rapids: Eerdmans, 2006.

Hymns of Fanny Crosby, Paul Gerhardt, James Montgomery, others.

Kreeft, Peter. *Making Sense out of Suffering*. Ann Arbor: Servant Books, 1986.

Lawrence, Roy. *How to Pray When Life Hurts*. Downers Grove: InterVarsity, 1993.

Lewis, Michael E. *A Theology of Suffering and Difficulty: Corporate and Personal Aspects*. Eugene: Wipf & Stock, 2006.

Luebering, Carol. *A Retreat with Job & Julian of Norwich: Trusting That All Will Be Well*. Cincinnati: St. Anthony Messenger, 1995.

Nouwen, Henri. *Turn My Mourning into Dancing: Finding Hope in Hard Times*. Nashville: W Publishing, 2001.

Poetry of George Herbert, Christina Rosetti, others.

Remen, Rachel Naomi. *Kitchen Table Wisdom: Stories That Heal*. New York: Riverhead, 1996.

Sittser, Gerald. *A Grace Disguised: How the Soul Grows through Loss*. Grand Rapids, Zondervan, 1996.

Soelle, Dorothea. *Suffering*. Translated by Everett R. Kalin. Philadelphia: Fortress Press, 1975.

Terpstra, John. *The Boys: Or, Waiting for the Electrician's Daughter*. Kentville, Nova Scotia: Gaspereau, 2005.

Tournier, Paul. *Creative Suffering*. Translated by Edwin Hudson. San Francisco: Harper and Row, 1982.

Tsevat, Matitiahu. *The Meaning of the Book of Job and Other Biblical Studies: Essays on the Literature and Religion of the Hebrew Bible*. New York: KTAV, 1980, pp. 1–37.

Van Inwagen, Peter, ed. *Christian Faith and the Problem of Evil*. Grand Rapids: Eerdmans, 2004.

Wangerin, Walter Jr. *Mourning into Dancing*. Grand Rapids: Zondervan, 1992.

Wright, N. T. *Evil and the Justice of God*. Downers Grove: InterVarsity, 2006.

Yancey, Philip. *Where Is God When It Hurts?* Rev. ed. New York: HarperCollins, 1996.

Young, Frances M. *Brokenness and Blessing: Towards a Biblical Spirituality*. Grand Rapids: Baker Academic, 2007.

Other Works by Marva Dawn

Chapter 1

For further discussion on pronouns for God, see "He, His, Him, Himself" in Part I of *Talking the Walk: Letting Christian Language* Live *Again* (Grand Rapids: Brazos, 2005).

Tapes of the week-long course, "A Theology of Weakness: Thinking Biblically about Suffering," can be ordered from the Regent College Bookstore: (604) 228-1820.

Chapter 2

For a larger overview of the Christian meta-narrative from both the First Testament and the New, see chapter 5 of *Unfettered Hope: A Call to Faithful Living in an Affluent Society* (Louisville: Westminster John Knox, 2003).

Chapter 3

For a consideration of the reversed roles of technology and intimacy in our society, see *Sexual Character: Beyond Technique to Intimacy* (Grand Rapids: Eerdmans, 1993).

For extended discussion of God as the Subject and Object of worship, see *Reaching Out without Dumbing Down: A Theology of Worship for This Urgent Time* (Grand Rapids: Eerdmans, 1995); *A Royal "Waste" of Time: The Splendor of Worshiping God and Being Church for the World* (Grand Rapids: Eerdmans, 1999); and *How* Shall *We Worship? Biblical Guidelines for the Worship Wars* (Wheaton: Tyndale House, 2003).

This distinction between reality and truth has been expanded in a discussion about dealing with the principalities and powers in chapter 5 of *The Unnecessary Pastor: Rediscovering the Call* (co-written with Eugene H. Peterson) (Grand Rapids: Eerdmans, 1999).

Chapter 5

To understand this idea that Christians are neither pessimists nor optimists, but hopeful realists, see Marva J. Dawn, trans. and ed., *Sources and Trajectories: Eight Early Articles by Jacques Ellul that Set the Stage* (Eugene: Wipf & Stock, 2003).

For a much broader discussion of the principalities and powers and the weapons that we use to deal with them, see *Powers, Weakness, and the Tabernacling of God* (Grand Rapids: Eerdmans, 2001) and "The Concept of 'the Principalities and Powers' in the Works of Jacques Ellul," Ph.D. diss., The University of Notre Dame, 1992 (Ann Arbor: University Microfilms, #9220014).

Chapter 7

For elaboration on the trinitarian names of God, see *Talking the Walk*.

Chapter 8

For an examination of a theology of weakness in suffering, see *Joy in our Weakness: A Gift of Hope from the Book of Revelation*, rev. ed. (Grand Rapids: Eerdmans, 2002).

The biblical foundation for this translation, "My grace is sufficient for you, for your power is brought to its end in weakness," is explicated in chapter 2 of *Powers, Weakness, and the Tabernacling of God*.

Chapter 9

For specific helps from the Psalms for dealing with loneliness and for in-depth study of some of the texts in this book and other passages from the Psalms, see *My Soul Waits: Solace for the Lonely from the Psalms*, rev. ed. (InterVarsity, 2007; first published in 1983).

An in-depth Bible study with discussion questions to be used in building the Christian community can be found in *Truly the Community: Romans 12 and How to Be the Church* (Grand Rapids: Eerdmans, 1992; reissued 1997).

For suggestions on how the Christian community can help an individual with making decisions, see *Joy in Divine Wisdom: Practices of Discernment from Other Cultures and Christian Traditions* (San Francisco: Jossey-Bass, 2006).

Chapter 11

On learning to cease from busyness and the need to accomplish, see *Keeping the Sabbath Wholly: Ceasing, Resting, Embracing, Feasting* (Grand Rapids: Eerdmans, 1989) and *The Sense of the Call: A Sabbath Way of Life for Those Who Serve God, the Church, and the World* (Grand Rapids: Eerdmans, 2006).

Chapter 13

For extended discussion of the temptations of today's youth and ways in which the whole Church can contribute to their growth in faith, see *Is*

It a Lost Cause? Having the Heart of God for the Church's Children (Grand Rapids: Eerdmans, 1997).

Chapter 14

For a thorough explication of the LORD's wrath as a subset of God's love, see the section, "Historical and Prophetic Visions of God's Wrath" in chapter 5 of *Unfettered Hope.*

Chapter 18

Devotion books that might be prayerful for you include *To Walk and Not Faint: A Month of Meditations on Isaiah 40,* 2nd ed. (Grand Rapids: Eerdmans, 1997), and Karen Dismer, ed., *Morning by Morning: Daily Meditations from the Writings of Marva J. Dawn* (Grand Rapids: Eerdmans, 2001).

Notes

Chapter 1

1. Along with many other scholars and clergypersons, I prefer to call the first three-fourths of the Bible the "First Testament" or the "Hebrew Scriptures" to avoid our culture's negative connotations of the name *Old Testament* and to emphasize both the consistency of God's grace for all God's people and also the continuity of God's covenants in the Bible, first with Israel and then in addition with Christians.

2. On the practice of praying the Psalms, I highly recommend the following books, all by Eugene H. Peterson, the translator of *The Message*: *Answering God: The Psalms as Tools for Prayer* (San Francisco: HarperSanFrancisco, 1992); *Praying with the Psalms: A Year of Daily Prayers and Reflections on the Words of David* (San Francisco: HarperSanFrancisco, 1993); *Psalms: Prayers of the Heart* (Downers Grove: InterVarsity, 1987); and *Where Your Treasure Is: Psalms That Summon You from Self to Community*, 2nd ed. (Grand Rapids: Eerdmans, 1993).

3. These are wonderfully explicated by Eugene H. Peterson in *A Long Obedience in the Same Direction: Discipleship in an Instant Society* (Downers Grove: InterVarsity, 1980).

4. The word *Church* is capitalized when it refers to the universal Church—that is, the Church in its faithfulness throughout the centuries and around the globe. The uncapitalized word *church* designates a local body of believers.

5. A prayer "For Those in Affliction," from *Service Book and Hymnal* (printed by eight Lutheran church bodies, 1958), 223.

Chapter 2

1. John Wright, *Telling God's Story: Narrative Preaching for Christian Formation* (Downers Grove: InterVarsity, 2007).

2. Ernest Fremont Tittle, *A Book of Pastoral Prayers* (Nashville: Abingdon-Cokesbury, 1951), 64–65, as cited in *For All the Saints: A Prayer Book For and By the Church*, Vol. III: Year 2 Advent to the Day of Pentecost, comp. and ed. Frederick J. Schumacher with Dorothy A. Zelenko (Delhi: American Lutheran Publicity Bureau, 1995), 1060.

Chapter 3

1. See Shirley K. Morgenthaler, ed., *Exploring Children's Spiritual Formation: Foundational Issues* (River Forest: Pillars, 1999). Most

pertinent in this volume to the concern discussed here is Stanley N. Graven, "Things that Matter in the Lives of Children: Looking at Children's Spiritual Development from a Developmentalist Perspective," 39–68, and Shirley K. Morgenthaler, "Discussion," 69–76.

2. You can read part of St. John's "Advice on Disregarding Spiritual Sweetness" and other excerpts of his writings in *Lamps of Fire: Daily Readings with St. John of the Cross*, ed. Sister Elizabeth Ruth ODC (London: Darton, Longman, and Todd, 1985).

3. Jacques Ellul, *The Humiliation of the Word*, trans. Joyce Main Hanks (Grand Rapids: Eerdmans, 1985), xi.

4. See David Van Birma, "Her Agony," *Time* 170, 10 (September 3, 2007), 36–41 and Father Brian Kolodiejchuk, MC, *Mother Teresa: Come Be My Light: The Private Writings of the Saint of Calcutta* (New York: Doubleday, 2007).

5. Flannery O'Connor, *The Habit of Being: Letters of Flannery O'Connor*, sel. and ed. Sally Fitzgerald (New York: Farrar, Straus & Giroux, 1979), 353–354.

6. Kathryn Greene-McCreight, *Darkness Is My Only Companion: A Christian Response to Mental Illness* (Grand Rapids: Brazos, 2006), 89.

7. John Baillie, *A Diary of Private Prayer* (New York: Charles Scribner's Sons, 1949), 71. This book is a classic treasure. It contains morning and evening prayers for a month, plus two extra sets for Sundays.

8. Anonymous, as cited in *For All the Saints: A Prayer Book For and By the Church*, Vol. III: Year 2 Advent to the Day of Pentecost, comp. and ed. Frederick J. Schumacher with Dorothy A. Zelenko (Delhi: American Lutheran Publicity Bureau, 1995), 964.

Chapter 4

1. Koheleth is the Hebrew title for the book of Ecclesiastes; in the past the word has usually been rendered "the Preacher."

2. Marko Ivan Rupnik, *In the Fire of the Burning Bush: An Initiation to the Spiritual Life* (Grand Rapids: Eerdmans, 2004), 60.

3. Martin Luther (1483–1546), "A reflection on the cross," *The Darkness of Faith: Daily readings with Martin Luther*, ed. James Atkinson (Springfield: Templegate, 1988), as cited in *For All the Saints: A Prayer Book For and By the Church*, Vol. III: Year 2 Advent to the Day of Pentecost, comp. and ed. Frederick J. Schumacher with Dorothy A. Zelenko (Delhi: American Lutheran Publicity Bureau, 1995), 1011.

4. The canonical tradition of the Jews and earliest Christians passed on psalms naming David as their author and various New Testament

letters naming Paul as their author. Since the reflections in this book are not intended as biblical commentary, but as spiritual and pastoral helps, we don't have to debate the historical accuracy of these or any other canonical ascriptions. Rather, because there are deep narrative and descriptive benefits from identifying the emotions and situations of the letters or various psalms with a particular apostle or poet, we will, throughout this book, accept the titles and names associated with these writings and honor them canonically.

5. Rupnik, *In the Fire of the Burning Bush*, 52–53.

6. Chris Erdman, *Countdown to Sunday: A Daily Guide for Those Who Dare to Preach* (Grand Rapids: Brazos, 2007), 165.

7. John White, *Daring to Draw Near: People in Prayer* (Downers Grove: InterVarsity, 1977), 89.

8. *The Lutheran Prayerbook: A Collection of Prayers and Inspiration for Every Lutheran* (Woodbury, 1989), 53.

Chapter 5

1. These questions are taken from *The Book of Common Prayer* (New York: Seabury, 1979), 302. I used the *BCP* questions because they are a bit more thorough and explanatory, but the same three basic questions are found in *Evangelical Lutheran Worship* (Minneapolis: Augsburg Fortress, 2006), p. 229. In the *BCP* the three questions about renouncing evil in all its manifestations are followed by three questions that draw those answering into deeper acceptance, trust, and obedience to Christ in imitation of the pattern of Jesus asking Peter three times whether he loved Him and then commissioning him three times (see John 21:15-19).

2. Stanley Hauerwas, *Naming the Silences: God, Medicine, and the Problem of Suffering* (Grand Rapids: Eerdmans, 1990), 83.

3. For more information and faith-based resources, please contact Larry Goodwin at Bread for the World at 1-800-639-9400; lgoodwin@bread.org; or on the web at http://bread.org\ONE.

4. You can call the Capitol Switchboard at 202-224-3121 and the White House at 202-456-1111.

5. These two psalm conclusions are given in the version used in the four volumes of *For All the Saints: A Prayer Book For and By the Church*, comp. and ed. Frederick J. Schumacher with Dorothy A. Zelenko (Delhi: American Lutheran Publicity Bureau, 1994–1996) and in *The Book of Common Prayer*. The third text is taken from the NRSV.

6. Herbert F. Brokering, ed. and Charles E. Kistler, trans., *Luther's Prayers* (Minneapolis: Augsburg Publishing House, 1967), 102.

Chapter 6

1. See Matitiahu Tsevat, *The Meaning of the Book of Job and Other Biblical Studies: Essays on the Literature and Religion of the Hebrew Bible* (New York: Ktav, 1980).

2. This can be better understood through the arts sometimes rather than through philosophical and theological speculation. On God's will and human free will, see the movie *Bruce Almighty*.

3. Hymn by Isaac Watts, 1719, #617 in *Voices United: The Hymn and Worship Book of The United Church of Canada* (Etobicoke, Ontario, Canada: United Church Publishing House, 1996).

Chapter 7

1. John White, *Daring to Draw Near: People in Prayer* (Downers Grove: InterVarsity, 1977), 20.

2. This is the version of the psalm portion used in the four volumes of *For All the Saints: A Prayer Book For and By the Church*, comp. and ed. Frederick J. Schumacher with Dorothy A. Zelenko (Delhi: American Lutheran Publicity Bureau, 1994–1996) and in *The Book of Common Prayer*.

3. White, *Daring to Draw Near*, 92.

4. Helen Barrett Montgomery, "Like a Tree Planted," *And Blessed Is She: Sermons By Women*, ed. David Albert Farmer and Edwina Hunter (New York: Harper & Row, 1990), 46–47.

5. The numbers *11* and more than *170* are given in Robert L. Wilken, *Remembering the Christian Past* (Grand Rapids: Eerdmans, 1995), 89.

6. *My Prayer Book* (Saint Louis: Concordia, 1957), 214.

Chapter 8

1. Bass Aria #57 from Johann Sebastian Bach's *St. Matthew Passion*. The translations in this book of the original German libretto by C. F. Henrici (who went by the pseudonym Picander) are mine, with supportive help from my husband.

2. John White, *Daring to Draw Near: People in Prayer* (Downers Grove: InterVarsity, 1977), 34.

3. C. S. Lewis, *The Screwtape Letters* (New York: Macmillan, 1959), 38–39.

4. Chorale #25 from Johann Sebastian Bach's *St. Matthew Passion*.

5. Roland Seboldt, *The Joy of Living: In Health and Suffering, In Success and Failure, In Every Time of Life* (St. Louis: Concordia, 1965), 83.

Chapter 9

1. See Norman Cousins, *Anatomy of an Illness as Perceived by the Patient: Reflections on Healing and Regeneration* (New York: Norton, 1979), 153–154.

2. Arthur Paul Boers, *The Way Is Made by Walking: A Pilgrimage Along the Camino de Santiago* (Downers Grove: InterVarsity, 2007), 104.

3. Tapes or CDs of hymns and songs and hymnbooks can be obtained from your denomination's publisher. Lovely CDs of children singing hymns can be ordered also from St. Paul Lutheran Church, 1126 S. Barr St., Fort Wayne, IN 46802; telephone: 260-423-2496.

4. Marko Ivan Rupnik, *In the Fire of the Burning Bush: An Initiation to the Spiritual Life* (Grand Rapids: Eerdmans, 2004), 53.

5. Kathryn Greene-McCreight, *Darkness Is My Only Companion: A Christian Response to Mental Illness* (Grand Rapids: Brazos, 2006), 88.

6. Norman Wirzba, *Living the Sabbath: Discovering the Rhythms of Rest and Delight, The Christian Practice of Everyday Life,* ed. David S. Cunningham and William T. Cavanaugh (Grand Rapids, MI: Brazos Press, 2006), 86.

7. *The Book of Common Prayer* (New York: Seabury, 1979), 250.

Chapter 10

1. For more information, search www.painfoundation.org and its many links.

2. Jeffrey H. Boyd, *Being Sick Well: Joyful Living Despite Chronic Illness* (Grand Rapids: Baker, 2005), 39.

3. René Dubos, introduction to *Anatomy of an Illness as Perceived by the Patient: Reflections on Healing and Regeneration* by Norman Cousins (New York: Norton, 1979), 15.

4. Cousins, *Anatomy of an Illness as Perceived by the Patient,* 85.

5. Though a much older list, Norman Cousins suggests works by Bennett Cerf, Stephen Leacock, Ogden Nash, James Thurber, Ludwig Bemelmans, and Max Eastman's *Enjoyment of Laughter,* 1937 ed. (New York: Johnson Reprint Company, 1971) or E. B. and K. S. White, *Subtreasury of American Humor* (New York: Capricorn, 1962). See Cousins, *Anatomy of an Illness as Perceived by the Patient,* 144–149.

6. See Richard Hasler, *Surprises around the Bend: 50 Adventurous Walkers* (Minneapolis: Augsburg Publishers, 2008).

7. Arthur Paul Boers, *The Way Is Made by Walking: A Pilgrimage Along the Camino de Santiago* (Downers Grove: InterVarsity, 2007), 116.

8. Joan Bauer, *Hope Was Here* (New York: Penguin Group, 2000), 176.

9. *The Book of Common Prayer* (New York: Seabury, 1979), 461.

Chapter 11

1. From an interview with Nathan Bupp on Mihaly Csikszentmihalyi's *Flow: The Psychology of Optimal Experience* (Harper Perennial, 1990) as reported in *Free Inquiry*, October/November 2006, cited in Martin E. Marty's *Context* 39, no. 2 (Feb. 2007, Part A), 1.

2. John Milton, "When I Consider . . . ," *The Viking Book of Poetry of the English-Speaking World* vol. 1, rev., mid-century ed., ed. Richard Aldington (New York: Viking, 1958), 408.

3. John White, *Daring to Draw Near: People in Prayer* (Downers Grove: InterVarsity, 1977), 106.

4. Arthur Paul Boers, *The Way Is Made by Walking: A Pilgrimage Along the Camino de Santiago* (Downers Grove: InterVarsity Press, 2007), 67.

5. Elizabeth O'Connor, "Learning from an Illness," *Cry Pain, Cry Hope: Thresholds to Purpose* (Waco: Word, 1987), 114–129, especially 114.

6. *My Prayer Book* (Saint Louis: Concordia, 1957), 184–185.

Chapter 12

1. *My Prayer Book* (Saint Louis: Concordia, 1957), 215.

Chapter 13

1. Gerald L. Sittser, *Water from a Deep Well: Spirituality from Early Martyrs to Modern Missionaries* (Downers Grove: InterVarsity, 2007), 138.

2. Sittser, *Water from a Deep Well*, 172–173.

3. Arthur Paul Boers et al., eds., *Take Our Moments and Our Days: An Anabaptist Prayer Book* (Scottdale: Herald, 2007), 216.

4. Boers et al., eds., *Take Our Moments and Our Days*, 217.

Chapter 14

1. Opening Prayer for Wednesday of the Week of Epiphany 8, as cited in *For All the Saints: A Prayer Book For and By the Church*, Vol. III: Year 2 Advent to the Day of Pentecost, comp. and ed. Frederick J. Schumacher with Dorothy A. Zelenko (Delhi: American Lutheran Publicity Bureau, 1995), 487.

Chapter 15

1. Norman Cousins, *Anatomy of an Illness as Perceived by the Patient: Reflections on Healing and Regeneration* (New York: Norton, 1979), 134.

2. This is the version of the psalm used in the four volumes of *For All the Saints: A Prayer Book For and By the Church*, comp. and ed. Frederick J. Schumacher with Dorothy A. Zelenko (Delhi: American Lutheran Publicity Bureau, 1994–1996) and in *The Book of Common Prayer*.

3. *The Book of Common Prayer* (New York: Seabury, 1979), 460.

Chapter 16

1. *The Lutheran Hymnal* (St. Louis: Concordia, 1941), 5. Responses in the next two paragraphs are also from this page.

2. *Evangelical Lutheran Worship* (Minneapolis: Augsburg Fortress, 2006), 94.

3. *Lutheran Book of Worship* (Minneapolis: Augsburg Publishing House, 1978), 56.

4. *Lutheran Book of Worship*, 56.

5. The first three verses of Hymn 329 in *The Lutheran Hymnal*.

6. Herbert F. Brokering, ed. and Charles E. Kistler, trans, *Luther's Prayers* (Minneapolis: Augsburg Publishing House, 1967), 86-87.

Chapter 17

1. J. K. Wilhelm Loehe, a letter, cited in *For All the Saints: A Prayer Book For and By the Church*, Vol. III: Year 2 Advent to the Day of Pentecost, comp. and ed. Frederick J. Schumacher with Dorothy A. Zelenko (Delhi: American Lutheran Publicity Bureau, 1995), 1104–1105.

2. Katerine Ierodiakonou and Jan P. Vandenbroucke, "Medicine as a stochastic art," *The Lancet* 341, no. 8844 (Feb. 27, 1993): 542.

3. Ierodiakonou and Vandenbroucke, "Medicine as a stochastic art," 543.

4. This is the version of the psalm used in the four volumes of *For All the Saints: A Prayer Book For and By the Church*, comp. and ed. Frederick J. Schumacher with Dorothy A. Zelenko (Delhi: American Lutheran Publicity Bureau, 1994–1996) and in *The Book of Common Prayer*.

5. A prayer "For Those in Affliction," from *Service Book and Hymnal* (printed by eight Lutheran church bodies, 1958), 223.

Chapter 18

1. See Kathryn Greene-McCreight, *Darkness Is My Only Companion: A Christian Response to Mental Illness* (Grand Rapids: Brazos, 2006).

2. John Donne (1572–1631), cited in Greene-McCreight, *Darkness Is My Only Companion*, 87.

3. Greene-McCreight, *Darkness Is My Only Companion*, 160.

4. Greene-McCreight, *Darkness Is My Only Companion*, 89.

5. Greene-McCreight, *Darkness Is My Only Companion*, 81.

6. Greene-McCreight, *Darkness Is My Only Companion*, 159.

7. Greene-McCreight, *Darkness Is My Only Companion*, 159.

8. John White, *Daring to Draw Near: People in Prayer* (Downers Grove: InterVarsity Press, 1977), 154.

9. White, *Daring to Draw Near*, 156–157.

10. Prayer for Psalm 142, as cited in *For All the Saints: A Prayer Book For and By the Church*, Vol. IV: Year 2 The Season After Pentecost, comp. and ed. Frederick J. Schumacher with Dorothy A. Zelenko (Delhi: American Lutheran Publicity Bureau, 1996), 746–747.

Chapter 19

1. This was the version of Hezekiah's prayer used in the Tenebrae service at The Church of the Good Shepherd (Episcopal) on Tuesday of Holy Week (March 3), 2007.

2. John Chrysostom, a sermon, as cited in *For All the Saints: A Prayer Book For and By the Church*, Vol. III: Year 2 Advent to the Day of Pentecost, comp. and ed. Frederick J. Schumacher with Dorothy A. Zelenko (Delhi: American Lutheran Publicity Bureau, 1995), 1063–1064.

3. John White, *Daring to Draw Near: People in Prayer* (Downers Grove: InterVarsity, 1977), 158.

4. White, *Daring to Draw Near*, 159.

5. Attributed to St. Francis, and cited in Jan Karon, *Light from Heaven* (New York: Penguin, 2005), 334.

Chapter 20

1. This first line of Psalm 74 is in the version used in the four volumes of *For All the Saints: A Prayer Book For and By the Church*, comp. and ed. Frederick J. Schumacher with Dorothy A. Zelenko (Delhi: American Lutheran Publicity Bureau, 1994–1996) and in *The Book of Common Prayer*. The parallel poetic line is in the NRSV.

2. Anne Steele (1716–78), sung to the tune of St. Agnes by John Bacchus Dykes (1823–76), Hymn 256 in *Service Book and Hymnal* (printed by eight Lutheran church bodies, 1958).

3. Ambrose of Milan (340–397), cited in Kathryn Greene-McCreight, *Darkness Is My Only Companion: A Christian Response to Mental Illness* (Grand Rapids: Brazos, 2006), 69.

Chapter 21

1. Two excellent books on the Desert Saints are *The Sayings of the Desert Fathers: The Alphabetical Collection*, trans. Benedicta Ward, SLG (Kalamazoo: Cistercian, 1975) and Mary Forman, OSB, *Praying with the Desert Mothers* (Collegeville: Liturgical Press, 2005).

2. Gerald L. Sittser, *Water from a Deep Well: Spirituality from Early Martyrs to Modern Missionaries* (Downers Grove: InterVarsity, 2007), 93.

3. Sittser, *Water from a Deep Well*, 93–94.

4. Sittser, *Water from a Deep Well*, 94.

5. Marko Ivan Rupnik, *In the Fire of the Burning Bush: An Initiation to the Spiritual Life* (Grand Rapids: Eerdmans, 2004), 53.

6. Julian of Norwich, *Revelation of Love*, ed. and trans. John Skinner (New York: Image, 1996), 60.

7. John Baillie, *A Diary of Private Prayer* (New York: Charles Scribner's Sons, 1949), 73.